Vocabulary in language teaching

CAMBRIDGE LANGUAGE EDUCATION
Series Editor: Jack C. Richards

This series draws on the best available research, theory, and educational practice to help clarify issues and resolve problems in language teaching, language teacher education, and related areas. Books in the series focus on a wide range of issues and are written in a style that is accessible to classroom teachers, teachers-in-training, and teacher educators.

In this series:

Vocabulary in Language Teaching

Norbert Schmitt
University of Nottingham

CAMBRIDGE
UNIVERSITY PRESS

PUBLISHED BY THE PRESS SYNDICATE OF THE UNIVERSITY OF CAMBRIDGE
The Pitt Building, Trumpington Street, Cambridge, United Kingom

CAMBRIDGE UNIVERSITY PRESS
The Edinburgh Building, Cambridge CB2 2RU, United Kingdom   www.cup.ac.uk
40 West 20th Street, New York, NY 10011-4211, USA   www.cup.org
10 Stamford Road, Oakleigh, Melbourne 3166, Australia
Ruiz de Alarcón 13, 28014 Madrid, Spain

First published 2000

Printed in the United States of America.

Typeface Times Roman 10½/12 pt.   [AG]

Library of Congress Cataloging in Publication data

Schmitt, Norbert.
   Vocabulary in language teaching / Norbert Schmitt.
      p.   cm.
   Includes bibliographical references and index.
   ISBN 0-521-66048-3 (hb) – ISBN 0-521-66938-3 (pb)
   1. Language and languages – Study and teaching. 2. Vocabulary. I. Title.
   P53.9 .S37   2000
   418'.007–dc21   99-057110

*A catalogue record for this book is available from
the British Library*

ISBN 0 521 660483 hardback
ISBN 0 521 669383 paperback

To Ron Carter, Mike McCarthy, Paul Meara, and Paul Nation for taking me under their wings when I was just starting out.

Contents

Series editor's preface

There is a curious absence in the curriculum of many MA TESOL programs and similar courses for second and foreign language teachers. Although such courses typically include required courses on grammar, phonology, and discourse analysis, vocabulary is often dealt with only incidentally in the preparation of language teachers. Yet as the author demonstrates in this lucid and fascinating account of the role of vocabulary in second language learning and teaching, lexical knowledge is central to communicative competence and to the acquisition of a second language. Vocabulary and lexical units are at the core of learning and communication. No amount of grammatical or other type of linguistic knowledge can be employed in communication or discourse without the mediation of vocabulary. Indeed, vocabulary and lexical expressions can sustain a great deal of rudimentary communication without much support from other aspects of the language system. Understanding of the nature and significance of vocabulary knowledge in a second language therefore needs to play a much more central role in the knowledge base of language teachers. This book convincingly reasserts the significance of vocabulary within applied linguistics.

As the author illustrates, approaches to the study of the nature of vocabulary and lexical knowledge in a second language have had a long history, though the status of vocabulary in teaching has tended to reflect preoccupations elsewhere, at times almost disappearing from view as scholars and applied linguists turned their attention to other dimensions of language knowledge. Recently, however, vocabulary has assumed a more prominent status prompted by corpus studies and awareness of the role of lexical units in learning and communication. Norbert Schmitt is one of an active group of scholars whose research has put vocabulary at the forefront of contemporary applied linguistics. In this book he reports on the current status and findings of this extensive body of research. His presentation, however, is for an audience of teachers and others interested in the applications of such research to language teaching.

The book provides a comprehensive overview of the role of vocabulary in language use, language teaching, and language testing, and it offers an original and insightful analysis and survey of the subject. Vocabulary is shown to include much more than knowledge of single words. The nature of vocabulary knowledge and learning is revealed from the research of the author and many other scholars, as are the ways in which corpus studies are changing our understanding of how vocabulary is used in discourse and its relation to other dimensions of linguistic knowledge including phonology and grammar. Schmitt treats a complex subject with masterful clarity, highlighting the applications of research to classroom teaching, testing, and materials design. Teachers, researchers, graduate students, and others interested in issues related to vocabulary and language teaching will therefore find much to interest them in this book. The detailed examples and activities found in the discussion tasks and appendices provide practical exemplification of the issues discussed. In offering criteria by which to make judgments about issues in the teaching and testing of vocabulary, *Vocabulary in Language Teaching* prepares educators to respond more effectively to issues related to the teaching and learning of vocabulary by second language learners.

Jack C. Richards

Preface

This book is for language teachers and other people who would like to know more about the way vocabulary works. It attempts to provide the background knowledge necessary for practitioners to make informed choices about vocabulary teaching and testing. In most chapters, key ideas are first discussed, and then the pedagogical implications of those ideas are explicitly stated in an *Applications to Teaching* section. Thus, the overall theme of the book is making research and theory accessible enough to be of use in informing best classroom practice. As such, I have written this book to be much more than a "how-to-do-it" manual. By the time you finish it, you should be aware of the major issues in the field and should be equipped to read more advanced writings on them if you so wish. To encourage this, I have included a *Further Reading* section in each chapter that suggests appropriate follow-up readings. I have also included a relatively large bibliography to provide leads for further exploration of issues.

The structure of the book can be divided into three sections. Chapters 1 and 2 provide some linguistic and historical background. Chapters 3 to 7 are the "heart" of the book, describing the various kinds of knowledge a person can have about a word, how vocabulary behaves in context, and how it is acquired. Chapters 8 and 9 focus on pedagogy, enlarging on issues in teaching and testing vocabulary. At the end of each chapter are *Exercises for Expansion,* which are designed to help you consider some of the key issues in more depth. As their purpose is to help you formulate your own views stemming from an interaction of the information in this book and your own experience, there are generally no "right" or "wrong" answers, and thus only a few exercises have an answer key. The value of the exercises comes from developing answers that make sense for you.

I have tried not to assume any prior knowledge about lexical issues in this book, but do assume that you will have some general linguistic background. For example, I assume that you know what *nouns* and *affixes* are. Without this assumption, the book would become too cluttered with basic definitions to be coherent. Important terms concerning vocabulary are printed in italics and are defined or described in the surrounding text. At all times, I have tried to make the text as direct and accessible as possible.

Vocabulary is a big topic area, and a number of perspectives are possible. A point worth remembering when reading this book is that the material contained within is not totally unbiased, and that it reflects my personal experience and research. I have tried to present an account of the field that is as broad and balanced as is possible under length constraints, but accept responsibility if my perspective highlights issues other than those you would have chosen.

Norbert Schmitt

Acknowledgments

It is difficult to decide on whom to acknowledge in a book like this, for so many people have influenced my thinking about language and linguistics in general, and vocabulary in particular. I am grateful to the Derelicts for early and continuing inspiration. Bob Bini, Rick MacDonald, and Philomena Victorine led me to Japan, where my career in English language teaching began. Friends from Temple University, Japan, helped me think about what effective language teaching is really about. My students at the University of Nottingham have given me useful feedback on earlier versions of much of the material in this book. Special thanks go to friends who have taken time to comment on portions of this book: Ron Carter, Averil Coxhead, Mike McCarthy, Paul Meara, Rosamund Moon, Paul Nation, John Read, Diane Schmitt, John Sinclair, and Cheryl Zimmerman. Others who have helped shape this book by supplying material or inspiration include Mickey Bonin, Jim Coady, Andrew Cohen, Nick Ellis, Steven Gaies, Debbie Goldblatt, William Grabe, Birgit Henriksen, Margot Haynes, Tom Huckin, Jan Hulstijn, Ramesh Krishnamurthy, Batia Laufer, Bill Nagy, Sima Paribakht, Jack Richards, David Singleton, Rob Waring, Mari Wesche, Dave and Jane Willis, and many others too numerous to mention. As always, my wife Diane has helped me to discover what is important, both in life and in Applied Linguistics. Finally, thanks to the four men who have done the most to open my eyes to the magic of vocabulary. It gives me great pleasure to call them my friends, and it is to them that this book is gratefully dedicated.

1 Introduction

- What is a word?
- What does it mean to know a word?
- How many words are there in English?
- How many of these words do I know?

> The White Rabbit put on his spectacles. "Where shall I begin, please your Majesty?" he asked. "Begin at the beginning," the King said, very gravely, "and go on till you come to the end: then stop."
> – Lewis Carroll, *Alice's Adventures in Wonderland,* p. 106

The advice given in this quote from *Alice in Wonderland* seems to be appropriate for an introductory text, so to start at the beginning we must consider what we mean by vocabulary. The first idea that probably springs to mind is *words,* a formulation that is admirably adequate for the layperson. But for anyone interested in exploring the subtlety and magic of lexis, the term *word* is too general to encapsulate the various forms vocabulary takes. Consider the following items:

die
expire
pass away
bite the dust
kick the bucket
give up the ghost

The six examples are synonymous, with the meaning "to die." (*Synonyms* are words that have approximately the same meaning.) However, they are made up of from one to four words. *Die* and *expire* are single words, *pass away* could probably best be described as a phrasal verb, and the last three are idioms. (An *idiom* is a string of words which taken together has a different meaning than the individual component words. Similarly, a *phrasal verb* is made up of a verb plus one or more other words, which also has an idiosyncratic meaning compared to the component words.) Thus there is not necessarily a one-to-one correspondence between a meaning and a single word. Very often, in English at least, meanings are represented by multiple words. To handle these multiword units, the term *lexeme* (also *lexical unit* or *lexical item*) was coined. These three interchangeable terms are all defined as "an item that functions as a single meaning unit, regardless of the number of words it contains." Thus, all of the six examples above are lexemes with the same meaning.

In addition to the possible lack of correspondence between individual words and individual meanings, the term *word* also has difficulties with the various grammatical and morphological permutations of vocabulary. It is not all that clear whether *walk, walked, walking,* and *walks* should be counted as a single word or four. Likewise, are *stimulate, stimulative,* and *stimulation* the same word? In these examples, there is a *base, root,* or *stem* word that is the simplest form of that word. To this stem, affixes are added. If the purpose of the affixes is grammatical, then the resulting word is called an *inflection. Walked, walking,* and *walks* are inflections of the root word *walk.* However, if the affixes change the word class of a stem, the result is a *derivative.* Thus *stimulative* (adjective) and *stimulation* (noun) are derivatives of *stimulate* (verb). It is clear that although these words have different *orthographic* (written) shapes, they are closely related in meaning. Sets of words like these are referred to as *word families.* A word family is usually held to include the base word, all of its inflections, and its common derivatives. The term *lemma* is more restricted and includes only the base word and its inflections (Nation & Waring, 1997). This terminology allows us to get around the potential ambiguity of *word,* and to speak of vocabulary in more precise terms when necessary. Not only is this expedient, but there is evidence that the mind groups the members of a word family together, giving a psychological justification for using word families as a unit for counting and teaching (Nagy et al., 1989). (To enhance the accessibility of this book, I will use the term *word* unless more precise terminology is required to make a point.)

These distinctions may seem a bit trivial, but they are essential if we are to answer interesting questions such as "How many words are there in English?" and "How many words do native speakers know?" Scholars have produced widely varying answers to these questions, mainly because they used different definitions of what counted as a word. Let us look at these questions in a bit more depth, because the answers will determine to a large extent how we conceptualize and teach vocabulary.

Size of the English vocabulary

Reports of the size of the English language in the popular press have a very wide range: from 400,000 to 600,000 words (Claiborne, 1983, p. 5), from a half million to over 2 million (Crystal, 1988, p. 32), about 1 million (Nurnberg & Rosenblum, 1977, p. 11), and 200,000 words in common use, although adding technical and scientific terms would stretch the total into the millions (Bryson, 1990). This discrepancy is due largely to differing definitions of a word, and so a study attempted to produce a more reliable estimate by using word families instead of words as the unit of counting. Goulden, Nation, and Read (1990) counted the number of word families in *Webster's Third New International Dictionary* (1963), which is one of the largest nonhistorical dictionaries of English. Dictionaries such as this obviously cannot contain every current word family, but they are still the best resource available, and therefore estimates of the number of words in a language have usually been based on them. After excluding entries such as proper names and alternative spellings, Goulden et al. found that the dictionary contained about 54,000 word families. This is a huge number of items (remember that each word family contains several words), and so we as teachers must give up on the idea of ever teaching all of them to our students in a classroom situation. Only a fraction are likely to be acquired through formal study, leaving the pedagogical implication that any others will have to be acquired through simple exposure to the language or not acquired at all. This puts a premium on nonteaching activities that can bolster exposure to a language, with reading being an especially important source.

How many words do native speakers know?

Mastery of the complete lexicon of English (and probably any other language) is beyond not only second language learners but also native speakers. Still, the amount of vocabulary the average native speaker acquires is prodigious. This is shown by studies that have estimated that English native-speaking university graduates will have a vocabulary size of about 20,000 word families (Goulden et al., 1990; D'Anna, Zechmeister, & Hall, 1991). Nation and Waring (1997, p. 7) review vocabulary size studies and conclude that

the best conservative rule of thumb that we have is that up to a vocabulary size of around 20,000 word families, we should expect that [English] native speakers will add roughly 1,000 word families a year to their vocabulary size. This means that a [L1] five year old beginning school will have a vocabulary of around 4,000 to 5,000 word families.

This would be consistent with a 20-year-old university student having 20,000 word families. In contrast to the impossibility of learning every word in English, these figures indicate that building a native-sized vocabulary might be a feasible, although ambitious, undertaking for a second language learner.

Let us put the scope of this task into perspective. Imagine learning 15,000 to 20,000 telephone numbers. For each of these numbers you must remember the person and address connected with those numbers. This might be somewhat analogous to learning all of the various kinds of lexical knowledge attached to each word. Then, because these are word families and not single words, you would have to learn not only the single number, but also the home, work, and facsimile variants. Of course, vocabulary and phone numbers are not directly comparable, but the example does indicate the magnitude of achievement in learning a such a vocabulary.

Indeed, learning language is probably the most cognitively (mentally) challenging task a person goes through. But whereas the grammar of a language is largely in place by the time a child is 10 years old (Crystal, 1987, p. 243), vocabulary continues to be learned throughout one's lifetime. This is because the grammar of a language is made up of a limited set of rules, but a person is unlikely to ever run out of words to learn.

The complex nature of vocabulary

The mechanics of vocabulary learning are still something of a mystery, but one thing we can be sure of is that words are not instantaneously acquired, at least not for adult second language learners. Rather, they are gradually learned over a period of time from numerous exposures. This incremental nature of vocabulary acquisition manifests itself in a number of ways. We have all had the experience of being able to recognize and understand a word when we see it in a text or hear it in a conversation, but not being able to use it ourselves. This common situation shows that there are different degrees of knowing a word. Being able to understand a word is known as *receptive knowledge* and is normally connected with listening and reading. If we are able to produce a word of our own accord when speaking or writing, then that is considered *productive knowledge* (*passive/active* are alternative terms).

The assumption is that people learn words receptively first and later achieve productive knowledge. This generally seems to be the case, but in language learning there are usually exceptions. An example of knowing a word productively (at least in speaking mode) but not receptively in the written mode happened to me with a word connected with law. I had often heard and verbally used a word describing the formal charging of a criminal with a crime or offense. I never had the occasion to write this word, although I assumed from its pronunciation (ɪn ′daɪt) that the spelling was "indite." At the same time I had occasionally seen the word *indict.* I did not know what it meant, but assumed that it rhymed with *predict.* It was only later that I figured out that *indict* was the spelling for the word I had used for years to talk about law.

This anecdote shows that framing mastery of a word only in terms of receptive versus productive knowledge is far too crude. I had good productive mastery over the spoken form of *indict,* but not over its written form. This suggests that we also need to consider the various facets of knowing a word. Of course, everyone realizes that a word's meaning must be learned before that word can be of any use. In addition, there is the practical matter of mastering either the spoken or the written form of the word before it can be used in communication. A person who has not thought about the matter may believe that vocabulary knowledge consists of just these two facets – meaning and word form. But the potential knowledge that can be known about a word is rich and complex. Nation (1990, p. 31) proposes the following list of the different kinds of knowledge that a person must master in order to know a word.

- the meaning(s) of the word
- the written form of the word
- the spoken form of the word
- the grammatical behavior of the word
- the collocations of the word
- the register of the word
- the associations of the word
- the frequency of the word

These are known as types of *word knowledge,* and most or all of them are necessary to be able to use a word in the wide variety of language situations one comes across. The different types of word knowledge are not necessarily learned at the same time, however. As we have seen, being able to use a word in oral discourse does not necessarily entail being able to spell it. Similarly, a person will probably know at least one meaning for a word before knowing all of its derivative forms. Each of the word-knowledge types is likely to be learned in a gradual manner, but some may develop later than others and at different rates. From this perspective, vocabulary acquisition must be incremental, as it is clearly impossible to gain immediate mastery of all these word knowledges simultaneously. Thus, at any point in time, unless the word is completely unknown or fully acquired, the different word knowledges will exist at various degrees of mastery.

Nation's list is convenient in that it separates the components of lexical knowledge for us to consider. But we must remain aware that this is an expedient, and in reality the different kinds of word knowledge are almost certainly interrelated. For example, frequency is related to formality (part of register) in that more frequent words tend to be less formal, and less frequent words tend to be more formal. Thus, greater awareness of formality is likely to be somehow related to awareness of a word's frequency of occurrence, even if this awareness is unconscious. It would therefore be logical to suspect that increasing knowledge of one word-knowledge aspect could help improve knowledge of related aspects. At this point, however, it would still be speculation, as research into these connections is just beginning (e.g., Schmitt & Meara, 1997; Schmitt, 1998b). Therefore, although we can use a word-knowledge perspective to *describe* "what it means to know a word," we will have to wait and see whether it can be used to *explain* lexical acquisition and processing. My own opinion is that word knowledge is a useful framework to discuss vocabulary, and so I have used it as a scaffold in this book to ensure that all of the major vocabulary issues are addressed. Thus, in Chapters 3 to 5, all of the word-knowledge types will be discussed in more detail, hopefully giving you a broad understanding of lexical knowledge.

Summary

In this introduction, I defined several terms that are necessary to discuss vocabulary with precision. I also indicated that languages contain huge numbers of words, something that was probably already obvious from the thickness of your dictionary. Although nobody can learn all of these words, learning the amount of vocabulary a native speaker knows is still an amazing feat. Moreover, the learning process is not an all-or-nothing process in which a word is suddenly and completely available for use. Rather, our knowledge of individual words grows over time, both in our ability to use them receptively and productively and in the different kinds of word knowledge we come to master. With the background knowledge from this chapter in hand, we should be ready to explore the fascinating world of how vocabulary is learned and used. But first we start by considering how people have viewed vocabulary over the ages, and how this has led to our current thinking in the field.

Exercises for expansion

1. Take a text several pages long and choose a few relatively common words. Count how often they occur according to the "word" versus "lexeme" versus "word family" definitions. Is there a great deal of difference in the counts?
2. Make your own estimate of the number of words in a language. Take a dictionary and find the average number of words defined on a page. Then multiply this by the number of pages in the dictionary. From this total, scholars have typically eliminated classes of words such as proper names (Abraham Lincoln) and compound words (dishwasher). Do you agree with this, and should any other classes be disregarded? How does the size of the dictionary affect the total size estimate?
3. To estimate how many word families you know, take this test developed by Goulden et al. (1990).

You will find below a list of fifty words that is part of a sample of all the words in the language. The words are arranged more or less in order of frequency, starting with common words and going down to some very unusual ones.

Procedure

1. Read through the whole list. Put a check mark next to each word you know, that is, you have seen the word before and can express at least one meaning of it. Put a question mark next to each word that you think you know but are not sure about. (Do not mark the words you do not know.)
2. When you have been through the whole list of fifty words, go back and check the words with question marks to see whether you can change the question mark to a check mark.
3. Then find the last five words you checkmarked (i.e., the ones that are farther down the list). Show you know the meaning of each one by giving a synonym or definition or by using it in a sentence or drawing a diagram, if appropriate.
4. Check your explanations of the five words in a dictionary. If more than one of the explanations is not correct, you need to work back through the list, beginning with the sixth to last word you checkmarked. Write the meaning of this word and check it in the dictionary. Continue this process until you have a sequence of four checkmarked words (which may include some of the original five you checked) that you have explained correctly.
5. Calculate your score for the fifty-item test on the next page by multiplying the total number of known words by 500. Do not include the words with a question mark in your scoring.

1. bag	11. avalanche	21. bastinado
2. face	12. firmament	22. countermarch
3. entire	13. shrew	23. furbish
4. approve	14. atrophy	24. meerschaum
5. tap	15. broach	25. patroon
6. jersey	16. con	26. regatta
7. cavalry	17. halloo	27. asphyxiate
8. mortgage	18. marquise	28. curricle
9. homage	19. stationary	29. weta
10. colleague	20. woodsman	30. bioenvironmental

31. detente	41. gamp
32. draconic	42. paraprotein
33. glaucoma	43. heterophyllous
34. morph	44. squirearch
35. permutate	45. resorb
36. thingamabob	46. goldenhair
37. piss	47. axbreaker
38. brazenfaced	48. masonite
39. loquat	49. hematoid
40. anthelmintic	50. polybrid

(Adapted from Goulden et al.)*

Nation and Waring (1997) suggest that an average university-edu-cated English native speaker has a vocabulary of about 20,000 word families. How do you compare? Why do you think you are above or below the figure they mentioned? How accurate do you think this test is? See Chapter 9 for more on this and other vocabulary tests.

4. Consider your own level of knowledge of the words in your lexicon. Lis-ten for words in conversations and watch for words in texts that you understand well but never use yourself productively. Do there seem to be many words like this? Are there any examples of the opposite case where you use them easily when speaking, but have trouble spelling them? Words for which we have these partial states of knowledge are often the rarer ones. Considering that the majority of the words in a language are relatively rare, how would you evaluate the following statement?

The standard state of vocabulary knowledge, even for native speakers, is partial knowledge.

---

* From R. Goulden, P. Nation, & J. Read (1990). How large can a receptive vocabu-lary be? *Applied Linguistics 11,* 358–359. Reproduced by permission of Oxford University Press and the authors.

5. Choose two or three words. List everything you know about these words. Do the same after you have read Chapters 3, 4, and 5. Does the second list indicate a greater awareness of vocabulary knowledge? If so, recommend this book to a friend. If not, try to sell him or her your copy.

Further reading

For receptive versus productive vocabulary: Melka (1997), Meara (1997), Laufer and Paribakht (1998), and Waring (1998).

For the word-knowledge perspective of vocabulary: Richards (1976), Nation (1990), Schmitt (1995a), Schmitt and Meara (1997), Schmitt (1998b), and Nation (1999).

For two good places to begin researching vocabulary on the Internet:
http://www.swan.ac.uk/cals/calsres.html
http://www1.harenet.ne.jp/~waring/vocabindex.html

For bibliographies of vocabulary research: Meara (1983), Meara (1987), Meara (1992).

2 History of vocabulary in language learning

- What methodologies have been used to teach second languages through the ages?
- What has been the role of vocabulary in these methodologies?
- What was the "Vocabulary Control Movement"?
- What are some of the notable strands of vocabulary research?

People have attempted to learn second languages from at least the time of the Romans, and perhaps before. In this period of more than two thousand years, there have been numerous different approaches to language learning, each with a different perspective on vocabulary. At times, vocabulary has been given pride of place in teaching methodologies, and at other times neglected. In order to help you better understand the current state of vocabulary studies as discussed in subsequent chapters, this chapter will first briefly review some of the historical influences that have shaped the field as we know it today. (Instead of digressing to explain terminology in this historical overview, key terms are cross-referenced to the page in the book where they are discussed.)

Language teaching methodologies through the ages

Records of second language learning extend back at least to the second century B.C., where Roman children studied Greek. In early schools, students learned to read by first mastering the alphabet, then progressing through syllables, words, and connected discourse. Some of the texts gave students lexical help by providing vocabulary that was either alphabetized or grouped under various topic areas (Bowen, Madsen, & Hilferty, 1985). We can only assume that lexis was considered important at this point in time, as the art of rhetoric was highly prized, and would have been impossible without a highly developed vocabulary.

Later, in the medieval period, the study of grammar became predominant, as students studied Latin. Language instruction during the Renaissance continued to have a grammatical focus, although some reforming educators rebelled against the overemphasis on syntax. In 1611 William of Bath wrote a text that concentrated on vocabulary acquisition through contextualized presentation, presenting 1,200 proverbs that exemplified common Latin vocabulary and demonstrating homonyms in the context of sentences. John Amos Comenius created a textbook drawing on this idea of contextualized vocabulary. He suggested an *inductive* (page 85) approach to language learning, with a limited vocabulary of eight thousand common Latin words, which were grouped according to topics and illustrated with labeled pictures. The notion of a *limited* vocabulary was important and would be developed further in the early twentieth century as part of the "Vocabulary Control Movement." Scholars such as William and Comenius attempted to raise the status of vocabulary, while promoting translation as a means of directly using the target language, getting away from rote memorization, and avoiding such a strong grammar focus.

Unfortunately, the emphasis of language instruction remained firmly on *deductive* (page 112), rule-oriented treatments of Latin grammar. This preoccupation filtered over to English as well. The eighteenth and nineteenth centuries brought the Age of Reason where people believed that there were natural laws for all things and that these laws could be derived from logic. Language was no different. Latin was held up as the language least corrupted by human use, so many grammars were written with the intent of purifying English based on Latin models. It was a time of prescription, when authors of grammar books took it upon themselves to decide correct usage and to condemn what seemed to them to be improper. Usually they had no qualifications to do so, other than being important men in the world. Robert Lowth's *A Short Introduction to English Grammar* (1762) was one of the most influential of the prescriptive grammars, outlawing features in common use, such as double negatives (I *don't* want to study *no* more grammar rules!). These grammars received general acceptance, which helped prolong the domination of grammar over vocabulary.

Attempts were also made to standardize vocabulary, which resulted in dictionaries being produced. The first was Robert Cawdrey's *A Table Alphabetical* (1604). (Kelley [1969, p. 24] notes that the first *bilingual* lexicology dates from around 2500 B.C.) Many others followed until Samuel Johnson brought out his *Dictionary of the English Language* in 1755, which soon became the standard reference. With the exception of printing in general, his dictionary did more to fix standard spelling and lexical usage than any other single thing in the history of English. Johnson's genius lay in his utilization of contemporary pronunciation and usage to guide his spellings and definitions. Only in ambiguous cases did he resort to arbitrary decisions based on logic, analogy, or personal taste. The result was a dictionary that would remain unchallenged in influence until Noah Webster published an American version in the following century.

The main language teaching methodology from the beginning of the nineteenth century was *Grammar-Translation.* A lesson would typically have one or two new grammar rules, a list of vocabulary items, and some practice examples to translate from L1 (first language) into L2 (second language) or vice versa. The approach was originally reformist in nature, an attempt to make language learning easier through the use of example sentences instead of whole texts (Howatt, 1984, p. 136). However, the method grew into a very controlled system, with a heavy emphasis on accuracy and explicit grammar rules, many of which were quite obscure. The content focused on reading and writing literary materials, which highlighted the obsolete vocabulary of the classics. In fact, the main criterion for vocabulary selection was often its ability to illustrate a grammar rule (Zimmerman, 1997). Students were largely expected to learn the necessary vocabulary themselves through bilingual word lists, which made the bilingual dictionary an important reference tool.

As the method became increasingly pedantic, a new pedagogical direction was needed. One of the main problems with Grammar-Translation was that it focused on the ability to *analyze* language, and not the ability to *use* it. In addition, the emphasis on reading and writing did little to promote an ability to communicate orally in the target language. By the end of the nineteenth century, new use-based ideas had coalesced into what became known as the *Direct Method.* It emphasized exposure to oral language, with listening as the primary skill. Meaning was related directly to the target language without the step of translation, and explicit grammar teaching was downplayed. It imitated how a native language is naturally learned, with listening first, then speaking, and only later reading and writing. The focus was squarely on use of the second language, with some of the stronger proponents banishing any employment of the L1 in the classroom. It was thought that vocabulary would be acquired naturally through the interaction during lessons. Concrete vocabulary was explained with pictures or through physical demonstration, with initial vocabulary being kept simple and familiar, for example, objects in the classroom or clothing. Thus, vocabulary was connected with reality as much as possible. Only abstract words were presented in the traditional way of being grouped according to topic or association of ideas (Zimmerman, 1997).

Like all other approaches, the Direct Method had its problems. It required teachers to be proficient in the target language, which was not always the case. It mimicked L1 learning, but did not take into account the differences between L1 and L2 acquisition. One key difference is that L1 learners have abundant exposure to the language, whereas learners of a second language typically have little, usually only a few hours per week for a year or two. In the United States, the 1929 Coleman Report took this limited instruction time into account, and concluded that it was not sufficient to develop overall language proficiency. It decided to recommend a more limited goal: teaching secondary students how to read in a foreign language. This was considered the most useful skill that could be taken from schooling, particularly as relatively few people traveled internationally in the early twentieth century. At the same time, in Britain, Michael West was stressing the need to facilitate reading skills by improving vocabulary learning. The result was an approach called the *Reading Method,* and it held sway, along with Grammar-Translation and the Direct Method, until World War II.

During the war, the weaknesses of all of the above approaches became obvious, as the American military found itself short of people who were conversationally fluent in foreign languages. It needed a means to quickly train its soldiers in oral/aural skills. American structural linguists stepped into the gap and developed a program that borrowed from the Direct Method, especially its emphasis on listening and speaking. It drew its rationale from behaviorism, which essentially said that language learning was a result of habit formation. Thus the method included activities that were believed to reinforce "good" language habits, such as close attention to pronunciation, intensive oral drilling, a focus on sentence patterns, and memorization. In short, students were expected to learn through drills rather than through an analysis of the target language. The students who went through this "Army Method" were mostly mature and highly motivated, and their success was dramatic.

This success meant that the method naturally continued on after the war, and it came to be known as *Audiolingualism.* Because the emphasis in Audiolingualism was on teaching structural patterns, the vocabulary needed to be relatively easy, and so was selected according to its simplicity and familiarity (Zimmerman, 1997). New vocabulary was rationed, and only added when necessary to keep the drills viable. "It was assumed that good language habits, and exposure to the language itself, would eventually lead to an increased vocabulary" (Coady, 1993, p. 4), so no clear method of extending vocabulary later on was spelled out. A similar approach was current in Britain from the 1940s to the 1960s. It was called the *Situational Approach,* from its grouping of lexical and grammatical items according to what would be required in various situations (e.g., at the post office, at the store, at the dinner table) (Celce-Murcia, 1991). Consequently, the Situational Approach treated vocabulary in a more principled way than Audio-lingualism.

Noam Chomsky's attack on the behaviorist underpinnings of Audiolingualism in the late 1950s proved decisive, and it began to fall out of favor. Supplanting the behaviorist idea of habit formation, language was now seen as governed by cognitive factors, particularly a set of abstract rules that were assumed to be innate. In 1972, Hymes added the concept of *communicative competence,* which emphasized sociolinguistic and pragmatic factors (page 37). This helped to swing the focus from language "correctness" (accuracy) to how suitable language was for a particular context (appropriateness). The approach that developed from these notions emphasized using language for meaningful communication – *Communicative Language Teaching* (CLT). The focus was on the message and fluency rather than grammatical accuracy. It was taught through problem-solving activities, and tasks that required students to transact information, such as information gap exercises. In these, one student is given information the other does not have, with the two having to negotiate the exchange of that information.

In any meaning-based approach, one would expect vocabulary to be given a prominent place. Once again, however, vocabulary was given a secondary status, this time to issues of mastering functional language (e.g., how to make a request, how to make an apology) and how language connects together into larger discourse. CLT gives little guidance about how to handle vocabulary, other than as support vocabulary for the functional language use mentioned above. As in previous approaches, it was assumed that L2 vocabulary, like L1 vocabulary, would take care of itself (Coady, 1993). It has now been realized that mere exposure to language and practice with functional communication will not ensure the acquisition of an adequate vocabulary (or an adequate grammar, for that matter), so current best practice includes both a principled selection of vocabulary, often according to frequency lists, and an instruction methodology that encourages meaningful engagement with words over a number of recyclings.

One of the most important current lines of thought is the realization that grammar and vocabulary are fundamentally linked. Evidence from large *corpora* (language databases) shows that there is more lexical patterning than ever imagined, and that much of what was previously considered grammar is actually constrained by lexical choices. In effect, this makes it difficult to think of vocabulary and grammar as separate entities. Rather, one must conceptualize them as partners in synergy with no discrete boundary, sometimes referred to as *lexicogrammar* (page 58). Pursuing this idea should finally put to rest the notion that a second language can be acquired without both essential areas being addressed.

The Vocabulary Control Movement

This survey has shown that language teaching methodology has swung like a pendulum between language instruction as *language analysis* and as *language use*. Likewise, vocabulary has had differing fortunes in the various approaches. However, a recurring thread is that most approaches did not really know how to handle vocabulary, with most relying on bilingual word lists or hoping it would just be absorbed naturally. Systematic work on vocabulary did not begin in earnest until the twentieth century. One major strand of lexical research concerns the patterning of vocabulary in discourse, blooming from about the 1980s with the advent of computer analysis techniques. This research will be covered in detail in Chapters 5 and 6. The other high-profile strand of lexical research concerned efforts to systematize the selection of vocabulary. Because it also included an attempt to make vocabulary easier by limiting it to some degree, the research came to be collectively known as the Vocabulary Control Movement.

There were two competing approaches. The first attempted to limit English vocabulary to the minimum necessary for the clear statement of ideas. C. K. Ogden and I. A. Richards developed a vocabulary with only 850 words (known as *Basic English*) in the early 1930s, which they claimed could be quickly learned and could express any meaning that could be communicated in regular English. This was done by paraphrasing, for example, the words *ask* and *want* were not included in Basic English, but could be expressed as *put a question* and *have a desire for,* respectively (Carter, 1998, p. 25). Basic English consisted of 150 items representing Qualities (essentially adjectives), 600 Things (nouns), and 100 Operations (a mixture of word classes). However, the suffixes *-ed* and *-ing* could be attached to the Things, and so many could be used as verbs (*dust→dusted*).

For a number of reasons, however, it turned out that Basic English did not have much lasting impact. First, it was promoted as a replacement language for English itself, which was never going to happen. More important, perhaps, despite the small number of words, it was not necessarily that much easier to use. The same number of concepts existed in the world that needed to be addressed, but instead of learning many *words* to cover these concepts, Basic English merely shifted the learning burden to learning many *meaning senses*. In fact, it has been estimated that the 850 words of Basic English have 12,425 meanings (Nation, 1983, p. 11). Learning multiple meaning senses is not necessarily any easier than learning multiple words, so Basic English's apparent simplicity is largely an illusion. Two practical problems also counted against the adoption of Basic English. First, teachers would have had to be retrained to use this essentially "new" language.

Second, it was not very suitable for social interaction, as key items such as *Good-bye, Thank you, Mr.,* and *Mrs.* were not included, nor were very common words such as *big, never, sit,* or *want.* In the end, Basic English produced what seemed to be "unnatural" English, and many teachers felt that "if courses were offered which claimed to teach Basic English, they should in fact teach basic English" (Howatt, 1984, p. 254).

The second (more successful) approach in the Vocabulary Control Movement was to use systematic criteria to select the most useful words for language learning. This was partially in reaction to the Direct Method, which gave little guidance on the selection of either content or vocabulary. Several researchers had been working in this area during the first part of the twentieth century, and their efforts merged in what came to be referred to as the Carnegie Report (Palmer, West, & Faucett, 1936). The report recommended the development of a list of vocabulary that would be useful in the production of simple reading materials. Word frequency was an important criterion for the selection of words on this list, but it suffers from the fact that, apart from the most frequent words, the vocabulary required in any situation depends on the context it is used in. For example, *pencil, valve,* and *pint* may not be particularly frequent words in general English, but they are indispensable in classrooms, automobile repair garages, and British pubs, respectively. Thus, the eventual words on the list were selected through a wide-ranging list of criteria:

1. Word frequency
2. Structural value (all structural words included)
3. Universality (words likely to cause offence locally excluded)
4. Subject range (no specialist items)
5. Definition words (for dictionary making, etc.)
6. Word-building capacity
7. Style ("colloquial" or slang words excluded)

(Howatt, 1984, p. 256)

The list ended up having about two thousand words, and was finally published as the *General Service List of English Words* (GSL) (West, 1953) (page 84). The advantage of the GSL is that the different parts of speech and different meaning senses are listed, which makes the list much more useful than a simple frequency count. The GSL has been immensely influential, but, as it is based on very old word counts, it is being revised and should be available by the time this book comes out.

A major feature of this second approach to vocabulary control is the use of frequency information. The practice of counting words to see how frequently they occur has a long history, dating as far back as Hellenic times

(DeRocher, Miron, Patten, & Pratt, 1973). In 1864, Thomas Prendergast, objecting to the archaic word lists used in the Grammar-Translation Method, compiled a list of the most common English words by relying solely on his intuitions (which proved to be surprisingly accurate) (Zimmerman, 1997, p. 7). However, the first modern frequency list, compiled by counting a large number of words (11 million), was created by Kaeding in Prussia in the 1890s (Howatt, 1984, p. 257).

Michael West is probably the best-known scholar to harness the idea of frequency to second language learning. In addition to compiling the GSL, he was active in promoting reading skills through vocabulary management. To improve the readability of his *New Method Readers* texts, he substituted low-frequency "literary" words such as *isle, nought,* and *ere* with more frequent items such as *island, nothing,* and *before.* This followed the ideas of Harold Palmer, with whom he collaborated. A second step was to limit the number of new words occurring in the text. He increased the length of the overall texts compared to others current at the time, and also decreased the number of new words. This had the effect of dramatically reducing the percentage of new words that a reader would meet in a text. Whereas a reader would be introduced to a new word every 5–20 words in previous texts, in West's readers the reader would meet a new word every 44–56 words on average. This gave readers the chance to improve their reading fluency without constantly having to cope with new words in every sentence, and it also meant that previously met words would be recycled at a higher rate. The readers would presumably also be able to understand more of what they read.

Research into vocabulary acquisition and organization

Scholars operating within the "vocabulary control" paradigm worked to help students by lightening the learning load, mainly through controlling the type and amount of vocabulary learners were exposed to. But it would be misleading to imply that this was the only type of lexical research being pursued in modern times. In fact, there has also been a great deal of vocabulary research carried on from a psychological frame of reference. To give some sense of this, I will touch on three areas that are illustrative of this strand of vocabulary inquiry.

One of the first modern scholars to concern himself with L2 vocabulary acquisition was Ebbinghaus (1885, cited in Woodworth & Schlosberg, 1955). He ran a self-experiment in which he methodically tried to learn an

imitation language and carefully charted his progress. To measure his retention of the nonwords he studied (e.g., JEV, ZUD, VAM), he tested himself by means of a *paired-associates* procedure. He looked at the nonword
and if he could give the English equivalent, he considered it learned. This
experiment established how the amount of practice affected the amount
learned, and indicated that a number of shorter practice periods are more effective than one longer period. Through his careful design and implemen-
tation of the research, Ebbinghaus set a rigorous and scientific standard for
future study of L2 vocabulary acquisition.

A second line of research looked into how words were connected to one
another in the mind. The technique used to determine this was *word associations* (page 37). Subjects were given a prompt word (*red*) and were asked
to give the first word that came to mind (e.g., *white, blood, color*). Galton
(1879–1880) carried out the first experiment on word associations, using
himself as a subject. Soon after, Cattell and Bryant (1889) carried out the
first large-scale association study, collecting association responses from
about five hundred subjects. The new century saw a considerable amount of
interest in association research, with one of the most important studies aim-
ing to use associations as a measurement tool for mentally ill people (Kent
& Rosanoff, 1910). Their findings were similar to those of later research:
there is a great deal of consistency in the associations produced by a group,
suggesting that members have similar kinds of mental connections between
words. (See page 38 for a more detailed discussion.) The list of associations
from the Kent-Rosanoff study proved influential until they were finally su-
perseded by Russell and Jenkins's (1954) association norms compiled from
their University of Minnesota students.

Of course, not all research that informs about second language acquisition has to focus on L2 learning. A third strand of inquiry is the huge amount
of research done on L1 acquisition. Much can be gained by examining this
research for insights into L2 acquisition. In some cases, the L1 findings
seem to be fairly closely related to second language learning. For example,
children learning their L1 have a silent period where they listen to language
input before they begin to speak. When they do begin producing language,
much of it takes the form of *preformulated speech* (memorized strings of
language) (page 101). These findings suggest that teachers should give L2
learners at least some exposure to the L2 before requiring them to speak.
Likewise, we can expect that early L2 vocabulary production will have
some preformulated "chunks" in it. In my teaching experience, for example, beginning learners who could barely string two English words together
could all say *How do you do?*

On the other hand, L2 acquisition is clearly different from L1 acquisition in some ways. Second language learners have the experience of already acquiring a first language, and are typically older and more cognitively mature. Thus, they probably learn vocabulary in somewhat different ways than L1 children. Whereas L1 children must learn how things exist and operate in the real world at the same time that they are learning their vocabulary, second language learners are likely to already know these concepts, and so for them the process may be closer to relabeling the known concept with an L2 word. Still, even though some L1 research may not prove informative, it remains a remarkable resource. From the massive amount of L1 acquisition research available, it must be said that only a fraction has yet been examined from a second language perspective.

Historical overview of vocabulary testing

People are naturally interested in their progress when they are studying a foreign language. Teachers are likewise interested in their students' improvement. Because one of the key elements in learning a foreign language is mastering the L2's vocabulary, it is probably safe to assume that there has been interest in testing vocabulary from the earliest times in which foreign languages were formally studied.

As we have seen, one of the first modern researchers to concern himself with systematic vocabulary measurement was Ebbinghaus, who provides an early account of a self-assessment method of testing. Self-assessment may be fine for a careful researcher like Ebbinghaus, but there are obvious problems, especially the one of people overestimating the vocabulary they know. Institutionalized testing situations require measures that are more verifiable and this involves testees demonstrating their knowledge of words in some manner. Especially in the United States, this need led to an emphasis on objective testing, and the creation of a new field, psychometrics, which attempted to provide accurate measures of human behaviors, such as language learning. Spolsky (1995) believes that the first modern language tests were published by Daniel Starch in 1916. This was the time when psychometrics was beginning to establish itself. Vocabulary was one of the language elements commonly measured in these psychometric tests, and Starch's tests measured vocabulary by having testees match a list of foreign words to their English translations. This is similar to Ebbinghaus's method, except that Ebbinghaus required himself to give the answer (productive knowledge), whereas Starch's tests only required recognition of the correct answer (receptive knowledge).

Standardized objective tests became the norm in the United States in the 1930s, with vocabulary continuing to be one of the components commonly included. In 1964, this trend culminated in the creation of the *Test of English as a Foreign Language* (TOEFL), which, similar to other standardized tests of the time, included a separate vocabulary section.

Interest in vocabulary testing did not always stem solely from an interest in vocabulary itself. The relative ease of isolating words and testing them was also attractive. Vocabulary items set in a multiple-choice format tended to behave consistently and predictably, and they were considered relatively easy to write. Words were thus seen as a language unit particularly suited to objective testing, for technical as well as linguistic reasons.

Since the 1970s, the communicative approach to language pedagogy has influenced linguists' views, and this has in turn affected perceptions about how vocabulary should be tested. Many scholars now reject testing vocabulary in isolation, and believe it is better measured in context. Congruent with this thinking, in the most recent version of the TOEFL, implemented in 1998, vocabulary items are embedded into computerized reading passages (TOEFL, 1998a, 1998b). Parallel to this trend toward greater contextualization is a trend towards more integrated testing of language, with testing of discrete items, such as words, falling out of vogue. These trends will be discussed in Chapter 9.

Summary

In the more than two thousand years of second language instruction, there have been numerous methodologies. Recent ones have included Grammar-Translation (with explicit grammar teaching and translation as language practice), the Direct Method (emphasizing oral skills), the Reading Method (emphasizing reading and vocabulary control), Audiolingualism (building good language habits through drills), and Communicative Language Teaching (with a focus on fluency over accuracy). A common feature of these methodologies, with the exception of the Reading Method, is that they did not address vocabulary in any principled way.

During the first part of the twentieth century, several scholars were working on ways to lighten students' vocabulary learning load. Particularly as applied to reading, they developed principles of presenting common vocabulary first, and limiting the number of new words in any text.

This line of thinking eventually resulted in the General Service List. *Another approach was to create an extremely limited vocabulary that could be used to replace all other English words* (Basic English). *Taken together, these approaches were known as the "Vocabulary Control Movement."*

Along with this movement, there has been a great deal of other vocabulary research. Much of it has been psychological in nature, such as looking into the nature of memory and practice, word associations, and L1 acquisition. At the same time, other researchers have been trying to develop improved ways of measuring vocabulary knowledge from a testing standpoint.

Exercises for expansion

1. Think of a language teaching methodology you were taught with. With hindsight, was the vocabulary presented in a principled way? Were you as a student aware of why any particular vocabulary was presented? Was it presented in any particular order? Did it make any difference whether you were aware or not?
2. From the brief descriptions in this chapter, do any of the methodologies seem similar to the way you teach? If so, do you have a more systematic way of dealing with vocabulary than what I attribute to the methodologies? What are your ideas on the selection and presentation of vocabulary?
3. Principles coming out of the Vocabulary Control Movement were mainly targeted at reading. To what extent can they be applied to the other three skills (writing, listening, and speaking)?

Further reading

For a more detailed description of the history of language teaching: Kelly (1969), Howatt (1984), Bowen, Madsen, and Hilferty (1985), and Celce-Murcia (1991).

For a more detailed description of the history of vocabulary instruction: Zimmerman (1997).

For a detailed description of the various methodologies as they appear in the classroom: Larsen-Freeman (1986).

For a complete listing of Basic English, including commentary: Carter and McCarthy (1988).

For the historical development of vocabulary tests: Spolsky (1995), Read (1997), and Read (2000).

3 Aspects of knowing a word: Meaning and organization

- What does the meaning of a word entail?
- Are some parts of a meaning definition more important than others?
- People use different vocabulary depending on where they come from and whom they are talking to. How do we account for this?
- Are words organized in people's minds in any way? How can we tell?

An adequate answer to the single question "What does it mean to know a word?" would require a book much thicker than this one. An impressive amount of information must be known and seamlessly manipulated in order to use words fluently, and even finding a framework to explain this complexity is not an easy matter. One could frame the answer in terms of how words are used in context, how they are acquired, or how they move from receptive to productive states. For the present purposes, I have chosen Nation's (1990) components of word knowledge approach (discussed in Chapter 1) as the framework for the theoretical discussion of vocabulary. This allows the various aspects of knowing a word to be dealt with separately, and hopefully more clearly than if overall vocabulary knowledge were discussed as a whole. But it is important to remember that this is an expedient for discussion only; the different kinds of word knowledge are interrelated and affect each other in fundamental ways. In the mind's psycholinguistic reality, it is unlikely that they could be separated so easily. Because meaning is the most obvious kind of word knowledge, let us start there.

Word meaning

Most of us equate the meaning of words with definitions in dictionaries. However, when one studies meaning in more detail, a whole host of interesting issues appear. Philosophical and psychological discussion about meaning can become quite complex and obscure, but at the most basic level, meaning consists of the relationship between a word and its *referent* (the person, thing, action, condition, or case it refers to in the real or an imagined world). This relationship is not inherent; rather, it is arbitrary until formalized by the people using the word (Drum & Konopak, 1987, p. 73). The spotted animal with a very long neck in Africa could have been called a *golf,* a *glisten,* or a *glabnab;* only consensus within the English-speaking community that the label for this animal should be *giraffe* gives this particular word any meaning. However, there are exceptions where words clearly have an intrinsic connection with their referents, and one of them is the class of *onomatopoeic* words. They attempt to mimic the sounds they represent: *boom, chirp,* and *whoosh.* Even here the connection is not absolute, as different languages render these sounds in different ways; for example, the sound of a rooster is rendered *cock-a-doodle-do* (English), *cucuricú* (Spanish), *kukuliku* (Swedish), and *kokikoko* (Japanese).

Unfortunately, the relationship between a word and its referent is not usually a tidy and direct one. In some cases, the referent is a single, unique entity that the word can precisely represent, usually as a "proper noun" (*Abraham Lincoln, Eiffel Tower, Brazil*). But more often, it is really a class or category such as *cat, love,* or *uniform.* There are many different kinds of uniforms, and so the single word *uniform* cannot exactly describe each one. Rather, it represents our *concept* of what a uniform generally is like. We know that it is a standardized form of dress, but would be quite open to differences in color and insignia, for example. In fact, our concept of a uniform depends to a large extent on our exposure to uniforms of various types. Thus words are usually labels for concepts (our idea of what a uniform is), which themselves encapsulate our limited personal experience of the actual world reality (all possible uniforms) (Hirtle, 1994). For most words, therefore, we can more accurately speak of meaning as the relationship between a word and its concept, rather than its referent.

To describe the meaning of a word, then, we need to describe the concept it represents. The traditional view is that words can be defined by isolating the attributes that are essential to the relevant concept, and that taken together are sufficient to describe it. Aitchison (1987) refers to this as the "fixed meaning" view but concludes that it is not a very adequate approach. It works relatively well when the referent is unique, as with proper nouns, for example, *Sydney Opera House, Mother Teresa,* and *Egypt.* In these cases, it is not difficult to describe the attributes of a single unique entity. The approach is also suitable for *technical vocabulary.* These are terms specific to a field that have been given precise definitions so that practitioners can use them confidently without misunderstanding. *Habeus corpus* and *bail* are examples from the area of law, and *pi* and *harmonic dissonance* from engineering. These terms are often called *jargon* and are essential for operation in a particular field. Because they have been precisely defined by a field, they may be thought to have fixed meanings (Benson & Greaves, 1981).

But the majority of words do not have one-to-one relationships with a single referent and none other. As we saw above, words normally have a meaning relationship with more open-ended concepts instead. This fact brings with it problems in definition. Although it is relatively easy to precisely define a single case, as in proper nouns, it is less simple to define a category. Let us take *cat* to illuminate this point. Because the concept must encompass a wide variety of cats, a description of any one cat would be insufficient. Instead, we must determine the characteristics that describe the category of cats (these can be called *semantic features*). These semantic features are most conveniently illustrated by placing them on a *semantic grid,* and marking relevant features with a (+), inappropriate features with a (−), and questionable features with a (?). A semantic grid for *cat* is illustrated in Figure 1. If we could confidently decide on the list of semantic features for *cat,* then we might conclude *cat* has a fixed meaning. But determining the necessary and sufficient features is actually almost impossible. Obviously the most typical kind of cat has all of the (+) features, but are they really essential to being a cat? If a friend told you that her cat could not "meow," would you believe it? Probably, as the prospect of a mute cat does not seem that far-fetched. If you were told that her cat had no fur, you would think it strange, but might conclude that cats should not play near fire. In fact, one might be able to think of exceptional cases of cats that were missing any of the (+) features above (three-legged cats, declawed cats, etc.). It becomes quite difficult to find an attribute that is absolutely essential for a cat to be a cat. The other problem with the semantic features approach is deciding which features should be on the list. You probably could think of many other features that could have been put on the list, such as *has a tail* and *likes catnip.* It is difficult to decide in a principled manner which features should be included and which excluded.

In reality, any particular real-life example of *cat* is likely to have some of the above features and not others. Thus the meaning of *cat* is not fixed but has a certain amount of flexibility. Aitchison (1987) calls this flexibility "fuzzy meaning." The fuzziness becomes particularly noticeable at the boundary between words. Take the two words *walk* and *run.* Although the state of walking is easy enough to discern, as it becomes progressively faster, when does it turn into running? There is probably no place on the continuum of self-locomotion at which walking clearly becomes running. Instead, there is a fuzzy boundary. Aitchison concludes that most words have some degree of fuzziness in their meaning.

One theory that has been developed to explain how people deal with

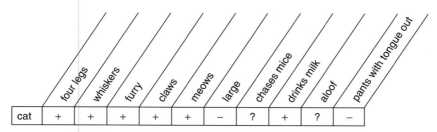

Figure 1   Semantic features of cat.

fuzzy meaning is *prototype theory*. Instead of assuming that concepts are defined by a number of semantic features, it proposes that the mind uses a prototypical "best example" of a concept to compare potential members against. Rosch (1975) found that people within a culture tend to have a relatively uniform idea of what the best examples are. For instance, Americans considered robins to be the best example of a bird, because robins represent the attributes people most commonly associate with birdiness: for example, flying, laying eggs, building nests, and singing. When compared to robins, penguins and ostriches had enough of these "birdy" features to be considered birds, although not typical ones. Although bats fly, they did not have enough other features to be considered birds. Thus, prototype theory can explain how atypical cases (three-legged cats) can be still considered as belonging to a concept. It is not without its problems, however; it has also been found that subjects judged the number 3 as being a better example of an odd number than 447 (Armstrong, Gleitman, & Gleitman, 1983), although both are equally odd. Aitchison (1987) suggests that, in addition to basic knowledge of a category, people might also be using familiarity as criterion in prototype decisions.

Prototype theory can help explain the inclusion or exclusion of members in a concept category, but how do people handle the fuzziness of the meaning boundaries between words? One way is by contrasting a word and its concept with other words and concepts. We can partially decide whether a very fast walk is still a walk by determining whether it has become a run. Thus a word's meaning is often partially determined by contrasting it with the meanings of other related words. The study of these meaning relationships, and meaning in general, is called *semantics*. The categories of meaning relationships between words are called *sense relations*. The layperson would know some of these as "oppositeness" and "similar meaning," but the field of semantics has generated technical terms to more precisely express these relationships. They are illustrated in Figure 2.

Sense Relation	Word	Attribute	Examples
synonymy	synonym	similarity	huge–gigantic rich–wealthy
ungraded antonymy	ungraded antonym	exclusive oppositeness	alive–dead pass–fail
graded antonymy	graded antonym	oppositeness on a continuum	big–little hot–cold
hyponymy	hyponym		
	superordinate (hyperonym)	more general category	<u>vehicle</u>–car <u>fruit</u>–apple
	coordinate	same level of generality	car–<u>truck</u> apple–<u>orange</u>
	subordinate	more specific category	car–<u>Ford</u> apple–<u>Crab Apple</u>
meronymy	meronym	whole–part	bicycle–wheels, handle, seat

Figure 2   Sense relations.

Especially in the case of graded antonyms, the meaning of one word is determined by the others. For example, the absolute temperature of a night in Madrid might be quite different from a night in Moscow, but both might be referred to as *cool*. *Cool* does not refer to any particular temperature in these cases, but rather stems from people's perceptions of temperature. Thus *cool* may denote differing absolute temperatures, but linguistically it will always occur between *cold* and *warm*. (See Lyons, 1977, for a fuller discussion of semantics.)

In the discussion of meaning up to this point, there has been an implied distinction between semantic features that are somehow more essential, salient, or prototypical and others that are less so. A number of commentators have made essentially the same distinction between some type of basic, fundamental meaning of a word and all of the other personal and cultural background knowledge that might be known. This distinction has been formulated with various terminology: *extension meaning* and *intension meaning* (Lyons, 1977), *denotation* and *connotation* (Hammerly, 1979), *definitional information* and *contextual information* (Stahl, 1983), and *basic domain* and *abstract domain* (McCarthy, 1990). Predating these, Katz and Fodor (1963) made the distinction with the terms *core meaning* and *encyclopedic knowledge,* which shall be used here. For the word *bachelor,* the core features of a concept might be defined as +human, +male, +adult, and −married. Encyclopedic knowledge consists of the other things one knows about bachelors: for example, they are often young, date women, and have exciting lifestyles. This encyclopedic knowledge might not be essential, but it is an important component of meaning. It can become especially significant in "fuzzy" cases. For example, is a divorced, middle-aged man with several children still a bachelor? He meets the core criteria, but one might not classify him as a bachelor without considering his lifestyle, which is connected to encyclopedic knowledge.

It is perhaps most useful to think of core meaning as the common meaning shared by members of a society. The fact that people can define words in isolation proves that some meaning information is attached to a word by societal convention that is not dependent on context. Although this information may well include a great deal of encyclopedic knowledge, it will almost certainly entail aspects of the basic, underlying core meaning, without which it would be impossible to connect with the represented concept. Encyclopedic knowledge, on the other hand, is idiosyncratic to each individual person, depending on that person's experience and personal beliefs. It may be communal to a certain extent, but will almost certainly vary to some degree from person to person. Using the *bachelor* example, everyone must agree that the person is not currently married (core meaning aspect), but there might be considerable disagreement on whether a male who is unmarried, but living with his partner, can still be considered a bachelor (encyclopedic knowledge aspect). Although the number of core features will be limited, the amount of encyclopedic knowledge one can know about a word is open-ended.

The idea of core and encyclopedic meaning can be applied to both semantic features and prototype theory. Semantic features can entail either core or encyclopedic meaning, but prototype theory suggests that the core meaning features will be the ones most important in determining membership in a concept category. Also, part of the reason why meaning is fuzzy is that different people will possess different encyclopedic knowledge for the same word.

From their review of a variety of research, Anderson and Nagy (1989) agree that word meanings cannot usually be contained by either a definition or a series of semantic features. Although these may give some sense of a word's meaning (basically core meaning), context plays a large part in filling in the other information necessary to make use of that word. Anderson and Nagy illustrate this with sentences that are uninterpretable without con-text, such as "The haystack was important when the cloth ripped," showing that words in a sentence cannot always be decoded from strictly intrinsic meaning properties. With the clue "parachutes," the reader is able to find a context that is congruent with the sentence to be deciphered. Thus, the core meaning of a word is sometimes not enough; the listener or reader needs to be able to use his/her available encyclopedic knowledge. Context can allow this to happen.

To use the potentially vast amount of encyclopedic knowledge in real time requires that it be organized and controlled in some way. This is espe-cially true in that the mind draws up more meaning information than what is finally used. An experiment by Swinney (1979) showed that when sub-jects were exposed to *polysemous* words (more than one meaning sense), such as *bug,* both the insect meaning and the spy listening-device meaning were brought up to the subconscious. Context seems to be what sets the pa-rameters of what actually reaches conscious thought. Context works in two ways: it limits what encyclopedic knowledge is finally activated, and it fills the gaps in our encyclopedic knowledge for future use. Although meanings of words in isolation can be recalled, the Anderson and Nagy (1989) "para-chute" sentence shows that strings of words generated in isolation do not always result in meaningful discourse. Context is necessary to activate the full resources of word meaning.

It seems that one way context exerts its influence on encyclopedic knowl-edge is via *schemas* (other terms used for this idea are *schemata, frames,* and *scripts*). *Schema* is knowledge of how things in a specific area of the real world behave and are organized. Schema can be activated either by a word itself in isolation or by the context it is embedded in. When a partic-ular schema is activated – say, a skydiving schema – all the encyclopedic knowledge related to this area becomes available, even before the other words related to the schema are encountered. Once the context has activated a certain schema, the schema constrains how each word's core meaning can be extended into figurative meaning (e.g., *jump* could be extended to the meaning sense of a person *jumping out of an airplane* but not to the sense of *attacking someone suddenly*) and which parts of encyclopedic knowledge are allowed to remain activated. If there is not enough context to activate a schema, then the mind must hypothesize a probable one.

Applications to teaching

The discussion above suggests that the notion of word meaning might be more complex than many teachers realize. Luckily, much of the theory mentioned above has direct pedagogical application for teaching. The first insight is that a useful distinction can be made between proper nouns and words that represent categories of things. When teaching the meaning of a proper noun, it may be sufficient merely to exemplify its referent in some way, as with a picture of the Eiffel Tower, or an explanation of it. Because the referent is a single, unique entity in the case of proper nouns, there should be little problem in delineating what the word represents. In addition, because the single referent is usually fixed and unchanging, one exemplification may be enough to adequately define that word.

On the other hand, words that represent categories usually require more information to give students an adequate understanding of their meaning. Teachers often define these words by giving a list of semantic features for that category, or by listing the subordinates of a superordinate term. In either case, it is usually necessary to give *negative* examples of what a category is not as well as *positive* information of what it is (Carroll, 1964). For example, when a student asks a teacher what *sprint* means, the teacher might well try to explain by going down a list of semantic features: *sprint* involves moving quickly, either by one's own locomotion or in a mechanical vehicle, often at the end of a race. But if the explanation stopped there, students might have the impression that a runner could sprint for a whole marathon. So teachers need to give information of what *sprint* is not (it does not usually describe a long, sustained, endurance type of effort), so that students can begin to understand the word's meaning limitations. In this way, the semantic boundary between *sprint* and *run* can start to form. For the superordinate *vehicles,* positive examples could be its subordinates *cars, buses, trams,* and *trucks,* but not *horses* or *skateboards.* The negative examples help to show that typical *vehicles* are mechanical means of transport that have motors.

As we can see, understanding the notions of semantic features and sense relations is important to teachers because they are typical means of defining new words. Teachers need to recognize their limitations, however. Teachers commonly define new words by giving synonyms and antonyms, for example, *eavesdrop = listen* or *shallow = not deep.* However, they must be aware that very few words are completely synonymous or exact opposites, and so such definitions will only be inexact representations of the word's true meaning. These are probably perfectly good methods of giving the initial impression of a word's meaning, but students will likely need more examples and exposure to these words in order to master the extent and limitations of a word's "fuzzy" meaning. In addition, once synonyms have been learned, exercises such as the following can be used to start to differentiate the nuances of meaning.

In English there are adjectives that are *normal* and adjectives that are *extreme*. For example, *good* is a normal adjective and *wonderful* is much more extreme. Here is a list of extreme adjectives. Use a dictionary to find the normal adjectives for each extreme adjective.

Normal	Extreme
1. hot	boiling
2.	enormous
3.	delicious
4.	tiny
5.	exhausted
6.	freezing
7.	awful
8.	filthy
9.	ancient
10.	wonderful

(Redman & Ellis, 1989, p. 38)

In the Introduction, it was stated that words are learned incrementally. We can see that this holds true for word meaning: because meaning is typically flexible, numerous exposures to a word in various contexts are required before it is usually mastered. This means that teachers should not make the assumption that because a word was covered once its meaning has been learned. A particular meaning sense might be learned for a particular context, but this does not guarantee that its meaning parameters will be known for other contexts.

Teachers will presumably concentrate on core meaning aspects when they first define a word, as these capture the essence of the word's meaning. When dealing with aspects that are more encyclopedic in nature, they should be aware that these can vary, and that students, particularly in mixed-culture classrooms, may have vastly different ideas about them. For example, all students should agree that *food* is something that is eaten for nourishment (core meaning), but in different cultures the word may represent very different edible substances and may be attached to quite different eating rituals.

Prototype theory was developed to explain how people deal with the fuzzy meanings of words, but its practical applications are not yet clear. It does imply that the most prototypical examples be chosen as first examples when exemplifying a category (*furniture→chair* and not *filing cabinet*), but there is no resource available to look up this information. Teachers are left with their own intuitions, which are probably valid for students from the same culture, but may not hold for students from different cultures; for example, Japanese students may believe that a *kotatsu* (low table with a heater attached underneath) is a very typical piece of furniture. In any case, less typical examples eventually need to be given to show the range of category membership.

Register

The preceding section discussed meaning in terms of the more or less explicit things one can know about a word's meaning. Core meaning refers to the most basic meaning elements, the kind that dictionaries try to capture in their definitions. This is also referred to as the *denotation* of a word meaning. In addition, there is all of the other encyclopedic knowledge that can be known about the word. To a certain extent, this extra meaning information feeds into the "unspoken" meaning aspects referred to as *connotation.* An example that illustrates this distinction is the word *skinny.* In essence it means "very thin," which is the denotation. Using only the denotation, we might assume that many people would be happy to be described as skinny. But *skinny* also carries the connotation of "so thin as too be unhealthy or unattractive." Of course, this extra meaning information constrains the contexts in which *skinny* can be appropriately used. Thus, we can use *skinny* to speak of starving children, but it is unlikely to be of use in describing the next-door neighbor. The way this important, yet implicit, extra meaning information colors the word and constrains how we use it is referred to by the cover term *register.* It describes the stylistic variations that make each word more or less appropriate for certain language situations or language purposes. Because the implicit meaning information can be of several different types, register is a somewhat broad category, as indicated by the other labels attached to it (*stylistic constraints, appropriacy*).

There have been several attempts to describe the different types of register variation. Chui (1972) (made famous by a better-known paper by Richards, 1976) suggests six areas in which there can be such variation, although some of these were mentioned as far back as 1939 by Collinson. *Temporal variation* covers the continuum of how old-fashioned or contemporary words are. Language is a living thing ever in flux; words are constantly falling out of use, while others are being created to take their place. Proficient language users sense this, and words that are archaic or becoming so gain a register marker in people's minds to signal the out-of-use status. On the other end of the spectrum, it is possible for words to have a current or cutting-edge feel, as *information technology* (IT) has for many people at the time of this writing.

A common language varies according to where it is spoken, in a kind of *geographical variation.* The variation can be divided among countries that speak the same language, in which case the variations are called *language varieties* (Indian English, Australian English). If the divisions are within a country, they are known as *language dialects.* Perhaps the most noticeable indicator of a person's home region is phonological "accent," but geographical variation refers to the lexical choices one makes. For example, where I grew up in Idaho, we call the small storage space on the passenger side of a car a *jockey box,* but my wife is from Minnesota, and she calls it a *glove compartment.* In normal situations, such lexical choices are probably not consciously manipulated, and are only noticeable when one is exposed to the spoken or written discourse of someone outside one's immediate language community.

The third type of variation is *social variation.* It is said that people in privileged classes typically have a somewhat different lexis from people in less privileged classes. The amount of social variation will probably differ from country to country, depending on the rigidity of the social class system and on perceptions of its desirability. Richards (1976) gives the example that members of privileged classes refer to a female as a *lady,* where otherwise she is referred to as a *woman* (although this example may be out of date). Other examples (in British English) include *lunch* (privileged) versus *dinner* (less privileged) and *settee* (privileged) versus *sofa/couch* (less privileged).

Social role variation covers the role of power or social relationship between *interlocutors* (people engaging in discourse), which directly affects the level of formality each uses. If one is speaking to a social superior, someone it is desirable to impress, or a stranger, polite deference is usually partially indicated by using more formal words (as well as more indirect syntactical structures) than one would use if addressing one's peers or friends. As everyone interacts with numerous people of varying relative power status, this implies that social role variation is routinely and consciously manipulated. Contrasting social role variation with geographical variation, we see that the amount of conscious control a person has is very likely to vary with type of register. Some register types seem to be largely unconscious and therefore likely to be less responsive to deliberate change in any particular situation (geographical variation), whereas others are obviously more amenable to conscious control (variation stemming from social role).

The topic being discussed can also affect the type of language used. This *field of discourse variation* stems from the fact that many fields have a *genre,* or expected style of discourse, that determines appropriate language use. This often concerns syntax (using passive voice constructions in academic discourse), but it also involves word choice constraints. In academic discourse, *we* has traditionally been preferred to *I,* even in cases of a single author, presumably because of a greater sense of objectivity. In addition, each field has its own technical vocabulary or jargon, whose use is expected, and whose nonuse can be *marked* (salient because it is not the expected norm). Gregory (1967) suggests that each field has a set of technical words restricted to people familiar with that field, and that there are also nontechnical words that are usable in many fields, but with different register ramifications in each one.

Chui's final register area is *mode of discourse variation;* that is, some words are more appropriate to written discourse than oral discourse, as the former is normally more organized and formal than the latter. For example, *yeah* is the eighth most frequent word in the CANCODE corpus of spoken English, although it is rather infrequent in written texts (McCarthy & Carter, 1997).

Halliday (1978) developed a different description of the components of register variation. His influential version divides register into three basic components: *field, tenor,* and *mode.* He uses them in an attempt to capture how vocabulary selection is constrained by the complex interactions between "the content of the message, its sender and receiver, its situation and purpose, and how it is communicated" (McCarthy, 1990, p. 61). *Field* covers the content and purpose of a message, such as an owner's manual explaining how to operate an appliance. *Tenor* refers to relationship between interlocutors, which is very similar to the social role variation discussed above. *Mode* describes the channel of communication, that is, whether the message is spoken or written, and how it is physically transferred, for example, via telephone, novel, or drum.

Halliday's description of register suggests that register competency can be viewed as *(a)* knowledge of the various kinds of register marking that a word may have, and *(b)* knowing how to apply that knowledge of a word's register marking to achieve the effect one desires linguistically. To formulate this in a slightly different way, we could say the following: for every familiar word, language users know varying amounts of (1) the above kinds of register information for the word and what the normal applications of the word are, and (2) what the effects are of using the word (with its register marking) in a number of different situations. People choose to use words with a certain type of register marking with the purpose of conforming to or diverging from their interlocutor's expectations.

Most of the time, one would choose to use words with the kind of register marking one's interlocutor expects, because this is the way to maintain communication. Benson and Greaves (1981) partially explain this by stating that, in order to have text or communication, we must have a mutually understood field of discourse. Choice of lexis gives an indication of this field (e.g., academic discourse or a car repair manual) by utilizing both lexical items that are particular to the field and more general words that have acquired a technical meaning in the field. If this flow of expected specialized vocabulary stops or is changed, then communication breaks down; if the flow is maintained, communication continues. Thus, maintaining register of the *field of discourse variation* type is an important support for continuing communication.

Any individual word can carry a number of different kinds of register marking. For example, *mosey* is not only old-fashioned but is also restricted mostly to rural American usage. Different words also carry different levels (strengths) of register marking. Some are very highly marked (*pissed, anon*), whereas others carry little, if any, marking at all. The amount of register marking is connected to the lexical specificity of the word (Cruse, 1977; 1986, pp. 153–155): more specific words tend to have more register marking, less specific words less register marking. Let us look at this in terms of synonyms, for example, *guffaw, chuckle, giggle, laugh, jeer, snigger.* In this set, *laugh* is the most essential, because it is the most frequent and because the others require its use in a definition (*chuckle* = laugh quietly) (Carter, 1982). Being the most basic word, *laugh* naturally has the least amount of register marking, because it is widely used in a variety of contexts. As one moves away from the most basic, frequent, usable item, words acquire greater and greater amounts of register marking. *Giggle* would be less likely to be used with adult males, for instance. Another illustrative example is *glass,* which is a neutral, general term. If we become more specific by speaking of its subordinates, such as *champagne glass,* or *flute* or *goblet,* we start to gain register marking. Likewise, going in a superordinate direction, toward an item such as *drinking vessel,* also increases the marking, as the situations in which this term would be naturally used are more restricted. The hyponyms *offspring – child – infant* work in a similar way, with *child* being the most neutral.

If we think of register as stylistic constraints, we can visualize how this works. The core word of the group can be used in the greatest number of situations (*glass* could be used for any meal), but as hyponyms and near synonyms have increasingly greater levels of register information attached to them, the possible situations in which they can be used appropriately decrease accordingly. For instance, *flute* has the sense of being suitable for more formal occasions and for only particular kinds of alcohol. It would probably not be suitable for the average breakfast or lunch. Thus, specific

situations require specific vocabulary; and the register information attached
to words allows language users to select the best word for each situation.

Greater register marking may also serve an interactional purpose; Robinson (1988) believes that more specific or marked words show liking, "im-
mediacy," and willingness to continue conversation.

Aston Martin.

1. Tom let me drive his new car.
2. A. I thought the film was good tonight.
   B. Yes, it was *fantastic.*
       nice.

(Adapted from Robinson, 1988)

These examples illustrate how the more marked option (in italics) may project greater involvement and interest in the topic at hand. (See McCarthy,
1984, for further discussion.)

The upshot of this is that register is a complex set of information that is
affected by a number of different factors, among them what subject field is
being discussed, who one's interlocutors are and what their social relationship is to the speaker or writer, whether the discourse is spoken or written,
and what purpose the speaker or writer has in mind. If the speaker or writer
is competent, then she or he will judge the situation and select the word from
a group of known hyponyms or near synonyms believed to have the desired
effect. When a person is not concerned with register considerations, as in
an informal conversation, then the choice will tend toward more common,
less specific words. Register becomes more salient, however, when there is
a specific purpose to be achieved by the communication – in an interview
or when writing an academic thesis, for example. But in all of these cases,
there are lexical choices affected by register constraints, whether they are
conscious or not. Some register aspects may almost always be totally unconscious, such as geographical variation, but these still carry register information, and may become more noticeable to a person as she or he gains
more exposure to a different norm of discourse (such as by living in a foreign country that uses the same language).

Applications to teaching

This section has shown that there is sometimes much more to a word than
denotative meaning, implying that teachers need to consider how to incorporate register information into their vocabulary teaching. This requires
teachers to be "tuned in" to register in the first place, and not just be satis-
fied with teaching meaning alone. It is unlikely, however, that all meaning

and register information can be taught together in a single instance, because students are unlikely to be able to absorb everything during an initial exposure to a word. This suggests that register information might be a good candidate for subsequent exposures. Thus, a reasonable way to recycle important words is to bring them to the students' attention again in order to give register information about them (see Chapter 7 for more on recycling).

Because some words have multiple register marking (as in the example of *mosey*) and others have little, if any (*walk*), teachers must decide if a target word has register constraints, and if so, whether to teach them. If the word has register marking that would stigmatize students if used in certain situations, students need to be made aware of this. Examples include "swear words" (*damn*) or words that might be considered offensive to a particular gender or race (*broad* to refer to a female, the Hawaiian term *haole* to refer to nonnative Hawaiians). Beyond this, when should a teacher highlight register? Because register is inherently related to context, the answer must depend on the situation. If a teacher is working in the United States, and her students are reading a transportation book that was written in Britain, then it is probably worth pointing out that *lorry* is the British English term for *truck*. Of course, if the teacher were working in the United Kingdom, this would probably be unnecessary. If the teacher is teaching academic English for the purpose of writing university essays, then it is useful for students to know that *acquire* may be more appropriate than *get,* because it has a more formal and academic register tone. As a general rule, the stronger the register marking, the more necessary it is for students to know, because strongly marked words can be used appropriately in relatively fewer contexts. In the following example, McCarthy and O'Dell (1994, p. 190) highlight the words that have a particularly negative loading.

Here are some examples of some slang words and expressions which you may come across. The ones which are most likely to cause offence are underlined.

Expressions for money: dough, bread, dosh, loot, brass, spondulicks
Expressions for police: pigs, fuzz, cop(pers), bill
Expressions for drunk: pissed, sozzled, paralytic, legless, arseholed
Expressions for a stupid person: wally, prat, nerd, jerk, dickhead, plonker, pillock
Expressions for lavatory: loo, lav, bog, john
Expressions for drink: booze, plonk (wine), a snifter, a snort
Drug-related expressions: a fix, dope, grass, high, stoned, snow (heroin)
Prison-related expressions: nick (prison), nark (informer), screw (warder)

A congruent idea stemming from the fact that register and context are interrelated is that register may be best taught in context. In addition to explaining register marking, it is particularly useful to tell what contexts the word would typically be used in, and perhaps give some examples of it. For instance, *anon* is an old-fashioned word mainly occurring nowadays in Shakespeare's work (*I come anon*) [soon]: *Romeo and Juliet*). This contextualization gives students a much better idea of how the word is used appropriately, and where to expect it in use than the contextless explanation of "old-fashioned word."

The notion of register also provides some guidance in determining which words to teach. First, as field-specific vocabulary is important to maintain communication in that field (Benson & Greaves, 1981), it is obviously important to teach the technical vocabulary for specific fields. Second, register is connected with the pragmatic issue of getting things done with language. If students have specific language purposes, they may need vocabulary with certain register marking in order to achieve it. For example, if students will find themselves in a power-inferior position with interlocutors from whom they desire something, then words with a polite register marking need to be taught. Much of pragmatic language occurs in *formulas* (strings of words that are commonly used to achieve some purpose, e.g., requests: "Would you please___?), so these strings with their own register marking may also be required in addition to individual words. Third, because some types of register (e.g., geographical variation) are particular to certain speech communities and are often used in a different speech community without any awareness of their effect, teachers need to watch for those words that may inhibit a student from smoothly integrating with the new speech community and help the student find alternatives that are more appropriate in the new environment. Fourth, teachers may choose to teach different words depending on whether they focus on a written or a spoken mode (see Chapter 4 for more on this). Fifth, when teaching beginners, it might be best to teach frequent words without much register marking, because these will be of the most all-around use to the students. Later, as the students progress to the point at which they are able to operate in more specific situations, they will need words with more register marking.

Word associations

We have seen that words are related to each other in various ways. Two examples are that (1) the meaning of a word depends to some extent on its relationship to other similar words, often through sense relations, and (2) words in a word family are related to each other through having a common base form, but different inflectional and derivational affixes. It seems logical to assume that these relationships are not just quirks, but reflect some type of underlying mental relationship in the mind. Indeed, assuming that there is no connection between words in the mind is tantamount to assuming that the mental lexicon lacks any organization, and that words exist totally in isolation. There is plenty of evidence to indicate that this is not the case.

One of the research paradigms that explores the organization of the mental lexicon most directly involves the use of *word associations.* In association methodology, probably best known from the field of psychology, a stimulus word is given to subjects and they are asked to respond with the first word or words that come into their mind. For the stimulus word *needle,* typical responses would be *thread, pin(s), sharp,* and *sew(s).* The assumption is that automatic responses that have not been thought out will consist of words that have the strongest connections with the stimulus word in the subjects' lexicon. Therefore, we would not expect unrelated responses such as *sky* or *study* to the stimulus *needle,* and indeed we virtually never get them. By analyzing associations, we can gain clues about the mental relationships between words and thus the organization of the mental lexicon.

Although it is unlikely that associations will ever be as explainable as other "rule-based" aspects of language, we do have a reasonable understanding of their behavior after a century of research. Perhaps the best starting point is the statement that associations from groups of respondents exhibit a great deal of systematicity. This is well illustrated by the responses to *abandon* in Table 1. The results are not random; otherwise one would expect nearly 100 different responses from the 100 British university students who responded. Rather, we find that 40% of the subjects gave the same response *leave.* The top three responses accounted for more than half of the total number. Responses that were given by two or more subjects made up more than 70% of the total. Clearly, there is a great deal of agreement among the members of this group. Of course, human beings are far too creative to be totally uniform, and the remaining 29 students gave associations that were unique to themselves. This pattern of communality has been demonstrated across numerous studies. For example, for Lambert and Moore's (1966) English-speaking high school and university subjects, the primary response covered about one third of the total responses and the primary, secondary, and tertiary responses together accounted for between 50% and 60%. This is congruent with the 57% figure reported by Johnston (1974) when she studied the three most popular responses of 10- to 11-year-olds. In sum, this pattern describes very well the distribution of responses for almost any stimulus word for almost any group: a small number of responses

Table 1   Association responses for *abandon*

Number of different answers: 38
Total count of all answers: 100

LEAVE	40	FREEDOM	1
SHIP	7	ISOLATED	1
GIVE UP	6	JUMP	1
BABY	5	LEFT	1
HOPE	4	ME	1
LOST	3	MOTHER	1
FORSAKE	2	NEGLECT	1
GAY	2	NO	1
LOSE	2	NOTHING	1
BOAT	1	NOW	1
CARE	1	PITY	1
CAST OFF	1	QUIT	1
CHILD	1	RELINQUISH	1
COMMIT	1	SAVE	1
DEFEAT	1	STOP	1
DESERT	1	SUBMIT	1
DISCARD	1	TEAR	1
DOG	1	THROW AWAY	1
EJECT	1	WEAVE	1

Source: Edinburgh Associative Thesaurus, Internet Resource.

being relatively frequent, with a larger number of responses being relatively infrequent.

Associations can be analyzed according to what category they belong to. Three of the most important categories are clang associations, syntagmatic associations, and paradigmatic associations. In *clang associations,* the response is similar in form to the stimulus word, but is not related semantically. An example is *reflect–effect.* The other two categories take into account the associations' word class. Responses that have a sequential relationship to the stimulus word are called *syntagmatic,* and usually, but not always, have differing word classes. Examples from Table 1 would be adjective-noun pairs such as *gay–abandon* or verb-noun pairs such as *abandon–ship* and *abandon–hope.* Responses of the same word class as the stimulus are labeled *paradigmatic.* Examples are verb-verb pairs such as *abandon–leave, abandon–desert,* and *abandon–eject.* Whereas syntagmatic relationships involve the contiguity (occurring in close proximity) of words in language, paradigmatic relationships are more semantic in nature.

Sometimes paradigmatic pairs are roughly synonymous (*blossom–flower*) and sometimes they exhibit other kinds of sense relation (*black–white, table–furniture*).

Analyzing the associations according to these categories gives us clues about the process in which words are acquired. Probably the most famous finding in association studies is that responses tend to shift from being predominantly syntagmatic to being predominantly paradigmatic as a person's language matures. Conversely, there is a decrease with age in clang associations. Quite early on, it was demonstrated that L1 children have different associations from adults (Woodrow & Lowell, 1916). Later, Ervin (1961) elicited associations from kindergarten, first-grade, third-grade, and sixth-grade students and found that as the students' age increased, their proportion of paradigmatic responses also increased. This syntagmatic→paradigmatic shift is not exclusive only to English. Sharp and Cole (1972) studied subjects who spoke Kpelle, an African language structurally different from most European languages, and found the same shift. The shift occurs at different times for different word classes, however. Research by Entwisle and her colleagues (1964, 1966) suggests that nouns are the first to shift, with adjectives next. The shift begins later for verbs and is more gradual.

What can we infer about the organization of the lexicon from such association research? The large degree of agreement in native responses suggests that the lexicons of different native speakers are organized along similar lines. If natives have a "normal" or "preferred" organizational pattern, then it seems reasonable that nonnatives would benefit if their lexicons were organized similarly. We do not really know how to facilitate this yet, but the fact that responses usually have either syntagmatic or paradigmatic relationships with the stimulus words suggests that these relationships might be important in vocabulary teaching and learning. As for how lexical organization changes over time, the presence of clang associations indicates that word-form similarity may initially play some role in the early lexical organization of L1 children. But formal similarity is obviously a less preferred way of organizing the lexicon, as evidenced by the rapid disappearance of clang associations as learners mature. Syntagmatic relationships are next to be focused on by the young learner, suggesting that a salient aspect of language at this point is contiguity. Later, as learners sort out the word class and sense relations of the word, their associations become more meaning-based and paradigmatic. It must be stressed that not every word passes through this progression, and as the child becomes more proficient, there will probably be no clang associations at all. Rather, the progression indicates the general evolution of lexical organization patterns as a learner's language matures.

Although most of the association research has dealt with young native speakers, it has also been applied to second language acquisition research. Meara (1980, 1983) surveyed the available research and detected several traits of L2 associations. First, although L2 learners typically have smaller vocabularies than native speakers, their association responses are much less regular and often not of the type that would be given by native speakers. This is partly because L2 responses often include clang associations. It is also presumably because the organization of L2 learners' mental lexicons is usually less advanced. Second, L2 subjects frequently misunderstand the stimulus words, leading to totally unrelated associations. Third, nonnative speakers, like L1 children, tend to produce more syntagmatic responses, whereas native-speaking adults tend toward paradigmatic responses. Fourth, L2 responses are relatively unstable. However, with increasing proficiency in the language, L2 responses seem to become more like those of native speakers. This suggests that the associations of L2 learners, like other elements of word knowledge, evolve in an incremental fashion.

These traits have been determined by comparing nonnative association responses with native ones. It would be useful to note here, however, that native association behavior itself is not necessary homogeneous. Rosenzweig (1961, 1964) found that association responses from speakers of a language can vary according to education, for example. He also found that responses differed somewhat between speakers of different languages. This means that we cannot use *any* group of native speakers for baseline data; rather, it is necessary to organize a group as similar as possible to the non-native subjects in terms of education, age, and so on. We must also take into account how stereotypical the responses of a particular L1 group are when interpreting how they compare with our native baseline norms.

Since Meara's surveys, there have been other association studies. For example, Söderman (1993) looked at Scandinavian second language learners to find out whether they would have a similar syntagmatic-to-paradigmatic shift as L1 children. She found that the number of clang and syntagmatic responses decreased and the number of paradigmatic responses increased as subjects had increasingly more exposure to the L2 through the various primary, secondary, and tertiary education levels. Similar changes were also found in relation to proficiency level. These results support Meara's earlier conclusions about more nativelike association behavior being linked to higher language proficiency.

There seems to be a connection not only between proficiency and the *type* of association produced, but also the *number* that can be produced. In a non-English study, van Ginkel and van der Linden (1996) compared the associations of Dutch learners of French with native French speakers. Using a word association task that asked the subjects to give as many associations as possible, they found that French high school students gave more associations than the Dutch high school French learners. Comparing native speakers among themselves, they found that both French and Dutch university students gave more associations than their respective high school compatriots. They conclude from this that there is "a correlation between the proficiency of the subjects and the number of association responses that they produce" (p. 31). On the assumption that a greater number of responses indicates more words connected to the stimulus word in the lexicon, this also suggests a greater level of organization.

L2 learners may have to be quite advanced before their associations become similar to native speakers, however. Schmitt and Meara (1997) studied ninety-five intermediate Japanese learners of English and found that neither their receptive nor their productive responses matched the native-speaker norms to any great degree. Even for words the learners rated as known, the match was only about 50%. When I (Schmitt, 1999) studied more advanced students (international students who were accepted into British universities) with a more developed method for calculating association scores (Schmitt, 1998a), the students' average association score was nowhere near that of the native norms. It seems that nativelike association behavior, and by implication nativelike lexical organization, is something that is not easy to acquire.

Applications to teaching

Word association responses suggest that words are indeed organized in the mental lexicon, and that they are organized in a similar manner among native speakers of a language. The fact that both syntagmatic and paradigmatic responses are common indicates that collocation is an important organizing feature in addition to meaning. This suggests that collocation might usefully be incorporated into vocabulary instruction in some way (see Chapter 5 for more on this). The responses of L1 children differ from those of L1 adults, but slowly become more like them with age. Similarly, the responses of L2 learners become more like those of adult natives, apparently as the learners increase their general L2 proficiency. On the assumption that it is desirable for L2 learners to have lexical organization similar to that of L1 natives, this is to be encouraged.

Unfortunately, association research has little to say at the moment about how to facilitate this organizational restructuring through teaching. Rather, researchers have explored whether association tests have value in measuring lexical organization and how well words are known. Examples of such tests will be discussed in Chapter 9.

Summary

Knowing a word entails having mastery over various kinds of lexical knowledge. This chapter surveyed some of the important research findings and teaching implications for meaning and register knowledge. We found that a word's meaning is normally attached to a concept rather than a discrete physical entity, and is therefore typically somewhat flexible or "fuzzy," especially at the semantic borders between words. Some meaning attributes will be essential to a particular meaning sense (core), while others are less critical and will depend on a person's experience (encyclopedic knowledge). There is register variation in the vocabulary people use, depending on where they come from, whom they are communicating with, and the content of their message.

Words are not stored at random in the mind; rather, the lexicon has organization. The chapter explored association research that indicates the nature of this organization. Word association studies provide evidence that indicates that words are organized in the mind, that this organization has similarities between native speakers, and that this organization changes as one matures (L1) or as one's language proficiency increases (L2).

One must know more than meaning to master a word, however. A person must be able to perceive or produce words in verbal or written modes. The word must also be used accurately in terms of its grammatical constraints. The next chapter looks at the written and spoken forms of a word, and the grammatical parameters within which vocabulary operates.

Exercises for expansion

1. In the introduction to this chapter, it is stated that the different kinds of word knowledge are interrelated. One example of this is that more frequent words tend to have an informal register *(ask)* while less frequent words tend to be more formal *(invite)*. Another is that knowledge of derivational suffixes is connected to knowledge of word class, because these suffixes change a word's part of speech. Can you think of any other examples of such interrelatedness?
2. Make a list of the semantic features for both *cat* and *dog*. Which features are similar? Which features distinguish the concepts? Is it difficult to find features that belong exclusively to one or the other category? Which of the features would more likely relate to core meaning, and which would relate to encyclopedic knowledge?
3. This chapter suggests that the most frequent word in a set of synonyms or hyponyms has the least amount of register marking. Look in a thesaurus and choose a set of words. Decide which word in the set is the

most common. Does it have the most general meaning and is it indeed the most neutral in terms of register? Do the less frequent words have more register marking? In what ways is their use constrained by register? What extra meaning information do they convey in addition to their denotation?

4. Give three associations for the word *illuminate.* Check with the norm list of 100 British university students in Appendix A. Did any of your responses match those on the list? If so, were they responses given frequently or infrequently by the students? What does this indicate about your knowledge of *illuminate?*

Further reading

For more on meaning and semantics: Lyons (1977), Cruse (1986), Aitchison (1987), and Hatch and Brown (1995).

For more on schema theory: Anderson and Pearson (1988), Carrell and Eisterhold (1988), and Hudson (1988).

For more details on register: Chui (1972), Halliday (1978).

For more on word associations: Jenkins and Russell (1960), Rosenzweig (1964), and Riegel and Zivian (1972).

For word association norms: Entwisle (1966), Postman and Keppel (1970), Miller and Fellbaum (1991), and Edinburgh Associative Thesaurus.

4 Aspects of knowing a word: Word form and grammatical knowledge

- How important is knowledge of the written form of a word?
- Speech doesn't have breaks between words the way writing does; all the words flow together. How do we "pick out" the individual English words?
- Is any part of a word more noticeable than other parts?
- Vocabulary and grammar are both part of language. How is grammatical knowledge connected to vocabulary knowledge?

In Chapter 3, the meaning of words, their register constraints, and the organization of the lexicon were discussed. In this chapter the focus turns to nonmeaning types of word knowledge. First we will look at the written and spoken form of a word. In some ways these can be considered among the most essential of the different kinds of word knowledge, because without the ability to recognize or produce a word, any other kind of knowledge is virtually useless. Next we will consider some grammatical aspects of vocabulary, namely, word class and derivative formation.

The written form of a word

Although many people would consider meaning the most important aspect of learning a word, there has recently been an increasing awareness that *orthographical* (written-form) knowledge, traditionally considered a "lower-level" type of knowledge, is a key component to both vocabulary knowledge and language processing in general. This awareness stems from research that has shown both that the eye fixates on most words in a text rather than skipping over many of them, and from psychological research that has shown the complexity of orthographical decoding.

Results from reading research have been particularly instrumental in showing the importance of orthographical word form. The most common cause of unsuccessful guessing from context in one study (Huckin & Bloch,

1993) was mistaking unknown words (e.g., *optimal*) for known words that were similar orthographically (e.g., *optional*). Even if the context did not support such erroneous guesses, the subjects often persisted with them all the same, supporting Haynes's (1993) assertion that word-shape familiarity can often override contextual information.

Perhaps the most basic question that can be asked about orthography is what visual information can be utilized during the recognition process. One possibility is the general outline or shape of a word (configuration):

$$\text{potential}$$

Another is the entire set of visual features of a word. There does not seem to be any strong evidence to support either of these possibilities as the primary kind of input, although they can have a supporting role (Besner & Johnston, 1989). It seems that the individual component letters of a word are the principal input used in word identification. Moreover, the position of the letters is important, with the first letter being particularly salient. For example, one experiment found that kindergarten students mainly used the first letter when recognizing the five-letter words used in the study, first graders used both shape and the first letter, while adults consistently used the first and second letters and word shape in recognizing the words (Rayner & Hagelberg, 1975).

The physical way the eye moves and fixates also determines what will be picked up when reading. The eye does not move smoothly when reading, but rather brings itself into focus on one point in the text (eye fixation) and then jumps to the next (saccade). Eye movement is very fast, measured in milliseconds (1 ms = 1/1000 of a second). The average eye fixation during reading is only about 200–250 milliseconds, during which the necessary visual information can be obtained within about the first 50 msec. The remaining time (at least 150–175 msec) is used to program the physical movement of the next saccade. The actual saccade takes from 20 to 40 msec and moves 7–9 character spaces. Fixations fall on the *preferred viewing location,* normally about halfway between the beginning and the middle of a word. This has the effect of focusing on the more informative beginnings of words.

The eye can see more than a few letters at a time, with the width of the viewing span being about 3–4 spaces to the left of the fixation and about 15 spaces to the right. Interestingly, different areas of the viewing span are used for different purposes. The area 4–8 spaces to the right of the fixation is used to identify the current word of the fixation. Beyond that, the first three or so letters of the next word are preprocessed for the next fixation. This parafoveal preview seems to perceive only the letter identities, and not other information such as shape configuration. Beyond parafoveal vision, the length of the next word is perceived by peripheral vision, which helps program the length of the next saccade. If the word to the right of the fixated word is short and can be completely identified, then it may be skipped over during the next saccade. These eye-movement characteristics dictate that the initial part of a word is the most important, both because the preferred viewing location tends toward the beginning of the word and because parafoveal vision previews the beginning of the next word.

Top-down models of reading suggested that that schema allowed the skipping of many words in a text because we could guess or predict much of the text's meaning, thus making many of the words redundant. But eye-movement research has shown that most of the words in a text are fixated upon in reading: about 80% of the content words and 40% of the function words. In addition, between 5% and 20% of the content words receive more than one fixation (i.e., we backtrack to read these words again). These figures are averages and reading a difficult text can alter them so that more words are fixated upon for a longer duration. (See Rayner & Balota [1989] for a review of eye-movement research.)

The upshot is that the eye samples most of the words on a page, and so we must be able to quickly and accurately decode these words to have any kind of fluent reading. Words for which we can do this are called *sight vocabulary*. But measuring how automatically words are recognized is not easy. For example, most of the research above was done in laboratory contexts, because sophisticated instruments were necessary to follow the eye and make measurements in milliseconds. One nonlaboratory method of determining speed of word recognition consists of measuring the time required to recognize words set in a string of characters. The following is an example where *simple* is embedded.

weolsulusimpletggiha

Meara (1986) used this format in an early experiment to study the recognition speed of L2 readers. He found that the average time required to recognize an L1 word was 1.47 seconds, but L2 recognition took longer. The L2 recognition decreased from 2.15 seconds in the seventh week of a home-study course to 1.74 in the twelfth week, and to 1.55 in the seventeenth week. Thus, the L2 subjects improved from a slow recognition time to one similar to L1 recognition, suggesting that as L2 learners progress, the automaticity of their word recognition improves. In other words, the learners were building the sight vocabulary necessary as a basis for fluent reading.

Word recognition in reading is the receptive process dealing with written word form, whereas spelling is the productive side. Teachers and students often complain that the English spelling system is filled with exceptions, fueling a debate about just how consistent it really is. Some scholars feel that the English spelling system, although it is not optimal, is reasonably systematic, and that even some of its irregularities have a functional purpose (e.g., Stubbs, 1980, Chapter 3). One example of this is that although the different members of a word family may have different pronunciations, their orthographic shape is likely to highlight their relationship, for example, *finite, infinite; Christ, Christmas; crime, criminal* (Wallace & Larsen, 1978, p. 364). On the other hand, some argue that the orthography system in place for English is not as organized and systematic as is commonly assumed, and that it is deficient in the sense that its irregularities cause problems in gaining literacy in the language (e.g., Upward, 1988). In fact, Feigenbaum (1958) states that there are 251 orthographical representations for the 44 sounds of English. From among this abundance, Upward believes that redundant characters are a major problem, and fall into three classes: (1) silent letters (*b* as in *debt*), (2) unstressed vowel sounds after stressed syllables (*e* in *chapel; o* in *atom*), and (3) doubled consonants (*committee*). He suggests adoption of a Cut Spelling System to remedy the problem, which would result in English being spelled as in the following sentence: "An importnt considration behind th Cut Speling systm is that th apearance of words shud not chanje so drasticly that peple uninstructd in th rules of CS find them hard to read" (p. 24).

   Such a system is unlikely to be embraced soon and so learners will have to cope with the English spelling system as it now stands. A close look at spelling mistakes reveals that they are not often phonological errors. Alper (1942) studied 1,340 spelling mistakes from five thousand college English compositions. Most of these made sense phonetically and followed conventional *sound-symbol correspondences* (e.g., the /r/ sound is represented by the character "r"). So, following sound-symbol rules exclusively does not guarantee accurate spelling of the exceptions in English. Some form of visual appraisal is also necessary to tell when a word "looks right." There is some evidence to suggest that lower-ability young L1 readers use primarily a visual-orthographic route to lexical access when reading, but a phonological route to generate spelling, whereas better readers use both routes in reading and spelling (Barron, 1980). The phonological route is useful for phonologically regular words, whereas the visual route is useful for the exceptions. Better readers can use the appropriate approach as needed.

   Spelling strategies seem to change with maturity, however. Between the second and fifth grades, there appears to be a major change in spelling strategy from reliance on sound-symbol correspondences toward spelling an unknown word by analogy to a known word. For example, in deciding how the vowel should be spelled in *sheep,* a learner can use knowledge of how *sleep* is spelled. This change seems to happen after the child has built up enough known words in his or her lexicon to use as models (Marsh, Friedman, Welch, & Desberg, 1980). It has also been claimed that imagery has a part to play. A mental image of a word's orthography can be generated from the visual experience of that word, and the image used to facilitate spelling, especially of familiar words:

> Findings indicate that orthographic images can be scanned like real words seen in print, that they include all of the letters in a word's spelling [and] that silent letters may have a special status in these images. Findings suggest that the presence of orthographic images in memory increases the likelihood that the spellings produced by readers resemble [the correct spelling] rather than phonetic variants. (Ehri, 1980, p. 338)

In the end, reading and spelling cannot be simplistically considered two sides of the same coin. L1 children between 7 and 10 years of age were often found to approach the reading and writing of the same words in different ways (Bryant & Bradley, 1980), and in some cases they could spell out words phonologically that they were not previously able to read (receptive knowledge does not always come before productive knowledge!). It is probably safest, therefore, not to assume that productive knowledge of a word's orthography (spelling) implies the receptive ability to recognize it, or vice versa.

Looking at second language orthographic knowledge from a crosslinguistic perspective, it is clear that a learner's L1 orthographic system plays a strong role in shaping his or her L2 processing. There are three major types of orthographic systems used in languages around the world – logographic, syllabic, and alphabetic. In logographic systems, the *grapheme* (smallest unit in a writing system) represents a concept, as in the Chinese writing system (女 = *woman*). In syllabic systems, the grapheme represents syllables, as in the Japanese *hiragana* (たまこ" [*tamago*] = *egg*). In alphabetic systems such as English, the grapheme corresponds to *phonemes* (the smallest unit of sound that can distinguish two words, e.g., pan and ban). Each of these systems leads to different processing strategies, particularly concerning the relative importance of visual versus phonological processing. It is likely that these strategies are carried over into the L2. Students learning an L2 that is similar in orthographic type to their L1 should have fewer problems with it than if it is different in type. L2 instruction should be individualized to account for these processing differences, particularly giving explicit instruction in the L2 orthographic system. (See Koda, 1997, for more on these issues.)

To illustrate such crosslinguistic orthography problems, let us consider Arabic-speaking learners of English. The problems these students often have with English orthography seems to stem from the fact that Arabic is based on triconsonantal roots, with vowels being of lesser importance. When recognition strategies based on these triconsonants are transferred into English, there can be an "indifference to vowels" that often results in misrecognized words: *moments* being confused with *monuments* (same underlying MNTS structure), and *pulls* for *plus* (PLS) (Ryan, 1994, 1997). Ryan suggests using a diagnostic test at the beginning of a course to find students who might be prone to these kinds of problems. This might be a useful idea for any L2 student who comes from an orthographic system that is different from English.

Another crosslinguistic factor of importance is how closely the orthographic and phonological systems correspond within each of the different languages. The "orthographic depth" can range from a close sound-symbol relationship (shallow language, e.g., Serbo-Croat) to a much weaker correspondence (deep language, e.g., Hebrew). Speakers of orthographically shallow languages will tend to generate phonology directly from written text, because the written form is a reliable guide to the spoken form. On the other hand, speakers of orthographically deep languages need to derive phonology from their internal knowledge of the words, because their orthographies are not reliable guides to a word's phonological form. Both methods probably exist for all languages, but their weight of usage will depend on the depth of orthography of the particular L1 (Frost, Katz, & Bentin, 1987). Learners may well carry over their L1 strategies to their L2, even if the L2 is quite different in orthographic depth, which would most likely cause problems. This certainly appears to be the case with Spanish speakers (shallow orthography) learning English (deeper orthography) (Suárez & Meara, 1989). Learners in this situation will probably need help in adopting more appropriate strategies, and this implies that L2 teachers need to be knowledgeable enough about their target language to be able to suggest what appropriate strategies might be.

Applications to teaching

The importance of the written form of words is obvious if those words are to be utilized through reading. Because research has shown that most words are actually fixated upon, it is an advantage to have as large a vocabulary as possible to recognize any word that happens to come up. But being able to recognize a word is not enough; it needs to be recognized quickly in order to facilitate fluent reading. In fact, there seems to be a threshold reading speed under which comprehension is quite difficult. This is because, in slow reading, words are decoded individually in a word-by-word manner, making it difficult to grasp the meaning and overall organization of the connected discourse. Above the threshold speed, the flow and logical progression of ideas can be appreciated. Eskey and Grabe (1988, p. 234) suggest that reading at a speed of about 200 words per minute is the minimum, with anything lower adversely affecting comprehension. This compares with an average reading rate of about 300 words per minute for a native English speaker of average education and intelligence (Nuttall, 1982, p. 36). To reach these sorts of reading speeds, the words in one's vocabulary need to be mastered at the "sight vocabulary" level.

To build up the speed of recognition, timed exercises focusing on both individual words and phrases, such as the following, are often advocated:

Underline the key word in each line as quickly as possible.

Key word

class	close	cloze	<u>class</u>	clash	crash
sold	told	bold	mold	sold	cold
book	bike	book	bake	beak	boot
worst	watch	waste	wasp	washed	worst

(Adapted from Stoller, 1986)

Underline the key phrase when it occurs.

Key phrase: <u>drive a car</u>

drive a truck	<u>drive a car</u>	drive cars
drive a bus	rent a car	car driver
dry a car	wash a car	drive a tractor
park a car	drive a truck	drive two cars
buy a car	buy a truck	drive a car
drive a car	buy a bar	drive a bus

(Adapted from Adams, 1969)

Such recognition exercises are most suitable for beginners who are at the decoding stage of reading, although they can be used as part of a program to increase reading speed at higher levels as well. They can be done for a short period at the beginning or end of every class, and have the advantage of focusing students' attention on the importance of both vocabulary and reading.

When teaching vocabulary and reading, the teacher may sometimes have to decide which will receive the major focus for a particular classroom segment. If the pedagogical aim is faster reading speed, then students can be encouraged to quickly guess or skip over unknown words in the text, as stopping to ponder them would slow down the reading. In this case, the students could be encouraged to reread the text later with the purpose of looking up the unknown words in order to learn them and facilitate future reading. The texts used in fluency exercises need to be graded for reading level, as those with a small number of unknown words are most appropriate. If the classroom segment has a focus on vocabulary learning, the teacher can either preview vocabulary in a prereading exercise, or allow students to stop and look up unknown words while reading, even though this breaks up the reading process.

When it comes to spelling, students obviously have to master the sound-symbol correspondences of a language, but it seems that developing a mental "image" of words is also important in phonologically ambiguous cases. Words with redundant characters falling into the three categories that Upward (1988) isolates as being problematical would make good candidates for such imaging. Teachers can encourage their students to imagine these words visually while they are learning to spell them. In this way they can build intuitions of whether a word "looks right" when they are spelling it. In addition, because increasingly proficient learners also use analogy to spell unknown words (Marsh et al., 1980), a valuable side benefit of having a larger vocabulary is that a person has more words to use as models. (See Bowen, Madsen, & Hilferty, 1985, Chapter 10, for numerous spelling drills.)

Given the importance of initial letters in the word-recognition process, spelling errors at the beginning of words are particularly confusing for readers, who, even if they believe a word is misspelled, will usually assume the beginning is correct. (The same is true of spell-checkers in computer word-processing programs.) This indicates that students need to be especially careful to get the initial part of the word correct in their writing.

The teacher can also take advantage of the orthographical similarities between members of a word family, even if they are phonologically different. For example, the orthographical forms make it easy to point out to students that *crime* is the base form of *criminal,* even though this might not be so obvious when spoken. Such grouping of related words is a main principle in vocabulary teaching and learning. The idea of grouping orthographically similar words can be maximally exploited by working with word families instead of single words. Instead of just teaching *indicate,* for instance, it can be useful to show that it is just a part of a wider cluster of words: *indicate, indicated, indicating, indicates, indication, indicative,* and *indicator.* Research shows that students often do not master the derivative forms of a base word (see the section titled "Grammatical Knowledge" later in this chapter), and so some extra attention to these forms may be warranted. In return for the extra investment in time, students should be better able to use the correct form in any context, rather than being limited to contexts where only the verb form *indicate* will work.

Finally, teachers should always be aware of the effect of the learners' L1 orthographical system when learning an L2. Second language learners will think and perceive orthography in ways dictated by their L1, and if it is different in kind from the L2 being taught, then explicit instruction in the L2 system will probably be necessary. There still exists the perception that orthography is a "lower-level" kind of knowledge that is easily and surely acquired, but if the L1 and L2 differ, this may be far from the truth. Ryan's (1997) suggestion that students be tested for potential problems with orthography seems a sensible one, and her test for intermediate students and above can be found as part of her paper.

The spoken form of a word

Adequate *phonological* (spoken form) knowledge of a word involves being able to separate out and understand its acoustic representation from a continuous flow of speech, as well as being able to pronounce the word clearly enough in connected speech for other people to do the same when we speak. Being able to manage these verbal input/output processes actually requires a detailed knowledge of not only the acoustic characteristics of the word as a whole, but also of its parts. First, we need to know the individual phonemes that make up a word. Second, we must know how these phonemes sound when tied together in the sequence particular to that word. Third, we need to know how the word is divided up into syllables, at least in English. If the word is polysyllabic, the syllables will not be pronounced with an equal amount of emphasis; rather, one or more will be stressed. This stressing can be accomplished by altering the pitch, volume, or length of the syllable, as well as the features of the vowel. Syllables can be unstressed as well, typically by reducing the vowel to what is called a schwa (ə) sound (the second *o* in *bottom*) or by losing its sound altogether (the second *a* in *pleasant* is virtually unspoken).

Not to minimize the problem of achieving comprehensible pronunciation, but the greater challenge for most language learners seems to lie in the act of listening. This is because learners have limited control over the rate of input, unlike reading where they can read more slowly or even reread whole passages. Understanding words in continuous speech involves two problems in particular: first isolating the sound groups that represent individual words from the speech stream, and then using those phonological representations to access lexical knowledge about the corresponding words.

Segmenting the natural flow of continuous speech into the individual component sound groups that represent words is no trivial task. As opposed to written discourse, spoken language does not have clear word boundaries. In fact, the words blend together in speech to such an extent that if one does not actually know a language, it is very difficult to pick out any individual words at all. At times, even native speakers *parse* (segment) the speech stream in the wrong place, causing a mishearing or "slip of the ear." Examples are *How big is it?* heard as *how bigoted?* and *analogy* heard as *and allergy.* Anne Cutler and her colleagues have researched the complexities of speech segmentation, and have found that, for English, stress patterns are the key. For example, Cutler and Butterfield (1992) looked at natural "slip of the ear" data and found that erroneous word boundaries were inserted much more often before strong syllables (containing full vowels) than weak syllables (containing central or reduced vowels), while boundaries were deleted more often before weak syllables than strong syllables. Additionally, when the subjects placed boundaries before strong syllables, a lexical content word followed; when placed before a weak syllable, a function word followed.

There is also evidence that the mind assumes that words do not begin with weak syllables. When presented with ambiguous strings of syllables, people used stress to determine which reading to take. If the first syllable was strong ('lɛt əs), subjects tended to choose one-word readings (*lettuce*) over two-word readings (*let us*); if the second syllable was strong (In 'vɛsts), two-word readings were normally chosen (*in vests*) over one-word readings (*invests*). Also, when people listened to words in which normally unstressed syllables were stressed, or vice versa, the words were difficult to recognize (Cutler & Clifton, 1984). All of this evidence indicates the importance of stress, and suggests that the mind assumes that strong stress indicates the beginning of a new word, and weak syllables do not begin content words.

In fact, there is good reason to believe that people assume strong syllables are word-initial. Cutler and Carter's (1987) analysis of 33,000 entries in a computer-readable English dictionary showed that 73% of them had strong initial syllables. They calculated that there is about a 3 to 1 chance of a strong syllable being the onset of a new content word, while weak syllables are likely to be grammatical words. It should be noted, however, that this discussion on stress has dealt with English as the target language. Other languages that do not feature stress, such as syllable-timed languages like

Japanese, require other strategies for determining where individual words begin.

Once the individual phonological representations have been parsed from the speech stream, how are they used to access the corresponding lexical words? A variety of theories have tried to explain how these processes work, and of these the cohort model seems to be getting its share of attention recently. Cohort models suggest that words are basically recognized in a serial manner, from left to right. Let us take the word *candle* as an example. After hearing the initial phoneme /k/ (characters in slashes indicate sounds), the mind activates all words beginning with this sound, such as *carry, chemistry,* and *cup.* After the second phoneme /æ/, which corresponds with the letter *a,* the list is narrowed to words beginning with *ca-,* such as *cam, cassock,* and *cabin.* This culling out continues with *can-* and *candl-* until the candidate list is narrowed to one, the *recognition point.* During this whole process, context is used to discard candidate words that are inappropriate. For example, if the word *candle* occurred in the context "I'll light the _____," the candidate word *cancel* would be dropped because it is a verb.

As with any model of language processing, there are the inevitable problems that need to be resolved. If we consider the serial nature of the cohort model, the first becomes obvious: the model cannot account for recognition of a word with mispronounced first phonemes, for example, a drunk saying *shigarette* instead of *cigarette.* A second problem stems from the context constraints: because "words that do not fit with the context are dropped from consideration, the model predicts that words cannot be recognized in inappropriate contexts" (Garnham, 1985, p. 57). Also, research has thrown up some contra-evidence. Longer French words (four syllables) were detected more accurately and quickly than one-syllable words when heard in fluent connected speech (Goldstein, 1983). Although the cohort model predicts that shorter words should be recognized more quickly, in fact longer words may be more easily recognized as a unit than monosyllabic words because the mind cannot be instantly sure that a one-syllable word is not part of a longer one. In other words, it is more difficult to determine the *offset* (end) of a short word (e.g., *to*) because it could easily be the beginning of a longer word (e.g., *tomorrow*).

This situation underscores an interesting phenomenon in phonological processing. In general, the speed of word recognition is very fast. Native speakers are able to recognize words in about two hundred milliseconds, which is usually before the offset of the word (Marslen-Wilson & Tyler, 1980). In contrast to this, sure identification of a word can sometimes occur only after several subsequent words have already been heard (Grosjean, 1985). This is because in connected speech it is difficult to know whether subsequent sounds are part of a longer word or the beginning of a new word. This is especially true of unstressed syllables. For example, relying strictly on phonological information, it is impossible to know where to parse the sound string /ðəlɛ j̆ Isley/. It could be part of the sentence "The ledge is laden with flowers" or "The legislature is in recess." So recognition speed is potentially fast, but is constrained by the parsing process. Of course, context usually comes into play to disambiguate such strings. Thus, it is likely that the cohort model (or any of the others) will have to incorporate a mechanism that describes the mind's ability to use a wide variety of information (including that of contextual ties, word frequency, and grammatical sequencing) in achieving lexical retrieval.

As would be expected, knowledge of spoken form is closely related to knowledge of its complement, written form, with phonological awareness being necessary for reading and using the alphabet. Knowledge of the alphabet (letter names) is necessary for L1 children to separate onsets (initial consonants or clusters) from rimes (vowels and any following consonants), which in turn seems to facilitate word recognition. This combined knowledge facilitates more complex phonological analysis. The ability to analyze onset/rime structure also fits closely with the ability to spell. So the relationship between phonological awareness and orthographical knowledge is close and interrelated; knowledge of one facilitates the learning of the other (Stahl & Murray, 1994).

Phonological awareness is also important for general vocabulary learning. Goldstein (1983) suggests that lower-level L2 learners must rely more heavily on acoustic clues than native speakers, because they cannot compensate with nativelike knowledge of semantic and syntactic constraints to predict and decode words. For example, a native speaker will seldom mistake *aptitude* for *attitude* because the context would make clear the correct choice even if one did not hear the word clearly. But weaker L2 learners might not have enough language proficiency to adequately understand the context, and so would have to rely solely on a correct hearing of the word. If the word has a number of close-sounding "neighbors," it might be difficult to decide from among the possibilities. Thus phonological similarity between words can affect L2 listeners more seriously than native listeners, making phonological awareness critical. In addition, the ability to vocalize new L2 words when learning them seems to facilitate that learning; for example, Papagno, Valentine, and Baddeley (1991) found that subjects who were prohibited from vocally or subvocally repeating new L2 words from a word list were much less able to learn those items.

In the previous section on orthography, it was stated that the beginnings of words are highly salient. Phonological research has indicated the same thing. We have all experienced the situation where we have tried to re-member a word but could not, although it was on the "tip of our tongue." Brown and McNeill (1966) induced such a state in their subjects by giving them definitions for relatively infrequent words. When this resulted in a "tip-of-the-tongue" situation, the researchers quizzed the subjects to find out what they could remember about the word. The subjects tended to re-call the beginning of words best, the endings of words next best, and the middles least best. In the case of *malapropisms* (when a similar-sounding word is mistakenly used for the intended one, e.g., *goof* for *golf*), we find a parallel phenomenon. The beginnings of the malapropisms were usually very similar to the intended word and the endings somewhat less so. The middles, on the other hand, were much less similar. Aitchison (1987) re-views this literature and concludes that there is strong evidence for a "bath-tub" effect. Imagine a person lying in a bathtub with their head well out of the water at the front end of the tub and their feet slightly out of the water at the bottom. This is a visual metaphor for our memory for words. The be-ginnings of words are the most prominent and are remembered best, with their endings somewhat less so. Conversely, the middle of a word is not re-membered so well in comparison.

Although the "bathtub effect" is a robust effect in English, it probably does not hold for some other languages. For example, the ends of Spanish words carry a great deal of grammatical information in the form of inflec-tions; English does not. Thus, one would expect Spanish speakers to give relatively more attention to the ends of Spanish words than English speak-ers would to the ends of English words. Thus, ESL learners from L1s with a different saliency structure from English may well find themselves fo-cusing on the less informative parts of English words.

Applications to teaching

Perhaps the most obvious implication from phonological research is the need for students to be attuned to word stress if they are to successfully parse nat-ural, connected English speech. This means that teachers need to highlight this stress information when dealing with vocabulary. Once students have a sense of the rhythm of the English language, they can fall back on the strat-egy of assuming that strong stress indicates new words if they find themselves unable to parse a verbal string of discourse. Once the string is parsed, know-ing the stress patterns of the individual words should help in decoding them.

The teacher can give stress and other phonological information by pro-nouncing a word in isolation, but it should be realized that words can sound somewhat different when spoken together. Because of this, it is probably advantageous to also pronounce the word in the larger context of a phrase or sentence. There are several advantages for the students if this is done. First, it allows them to hear the more natural intonation that comes from speaking in connected speech. Students will usually hear the word in connected speech in the real world, so it is important that they be exposed to connected pronunciation in the classroom. Second, this gives students practice in parsing out the word from connected speech in a situation where they have the advantage of knowing that it will occur. Third, the teacher can use this opportunity to give a context that helps illustrate the meaning of the word, thus allowing the example to do double duty.

Given the bathtub effect, teachers can anticipate that learners will have the most trouble remembering the middle of words. It is not clear what should be done about this, but teachers can at least make their students aware of the phenomenon, and let them know that if they are having trouble remembering the form of a word, their impressions are likely to be the most accurate about its beginning.

Grammatical knowledge

In Chapter 2, I suggested that lexical knowledge and grammatical knowledge are inextricably interrelated in a kind of lexicogrammar. Such an integrated view is supported by corpus evidence that is now showing the extent of lexical patterning in discourse. Hunston, Francis, and Manning (1997) believe that most words can be described in terms of the pattern or patterns in which they typically occur. For example, they found that about twenty verbs have the pattern "VERB *by* _____ ING":

1. those that mean either "start" or "finish": *begin, close, end, finish, finish off, finish up, open, start, start off, start out.*

    I would therefore like to finish by thanking you all most sincerely for helping us.

2. those that mean either "respond to" or "compensate for something": *atone, compensate, counter, react, reciprocate, reply, respond, retaliate.*

    It would retaliate by raising the duty on U.S. imports.

3. those that mean "gaining resources": *live, profit.*

    Successful businessmen can see the opportunity to profit by investing in new innovations.

Thus, these verbs fall into three meaning groups that take the same syntactical patterning. This highlights the key point that "groups of words that share patterns also tend to share aspects of meaning" (p. 211). Hunston et al. went on to analyze more than two hundred verbs that take the "VERB *at* NOUN PHRASE" pattern and found that they too fell into ten recognizable meaning groups. Among these are the following:

1. verbs meaning "shout" or "make a noise": *bark, hiss, scream, yell, blow up.*

   All I seem to do is scream at the children and be in a muddle.

2. verbs meaning "make a facial expression or gesture": *grin, smile, frown, scowl, wave.*

   He turned to wave at the waiting photographers.

3. verbs meaning "look": *glance, gaze, look, peer, stare.*

   She glanced at her watch.

4. verbs meaning "react": *laugh, rage, shudder, grumble, marvel.*

   Jane shuddered at the thought of being stranded here.

Again we see the connection between verbs and their meanings and the patterning that they take. From this kind of evidence, Hunston et al. argue that patterns like these are key elements in language, and might even be considered its building blocks. Lexical patterning is one of the most exciting new strands of current vocabulary study, and will be expanded upon throughout the next two chapters.

However, from a more traditional view, two of the most obvious aspects of lexis/grammar are word class and morphology. (Others include notions such as countability and valency.) Let us look at each in turn.

Word class

Word class (alternatively *part of speech*) describes the category of grammatical behavior of a word. There are a number of potential word classes, but the majority of language research has concentrated on the four major categories of noun, verb, adjective, and adverb. The results from a number of studies suggest that certain word classes are easier to learn than others. In an early study, Morgan and Bonham (1944) looked at these classes and found that nouns were clearly the quickest to be learned, with adverbs being generally the most difficult part of speech. The subjects in Phillips's (1981) study learned nouns better than verbs or adjectives, but the difference decreased with the increase in the learners' proficiency. For subjects learning Russian-English pairs of words, pairs in which the Russian word was a noun or an adjective were easier to learn than pairs in which the item was a verb or an adverb (Rodgers, 1969). Thus it would appear that nouns are the easiest word class, adverbs the most difficult, with adjectives and verbs occupying the middle ground. This conclusion is somewhat tentative, however, as Laufer (1997) points out weaknesses in these studies and concludes that word class has no clear effect on the ease or difficulty of learning a word.

Regardless of whether any particular word class is easier or more difficult than others, there does not seem to be any doubt that word class is involved in the learning and storage of vocabulary. Let us look at the psycholinguistic evidence for this statement. When malapropisms are made, the errors almost always retain the word class of the intended target word.

I looked in the *calendar* (catalog).
The tumour was not *malicious* (malignant).
It's a good way to *contemplate* (compensate). (Aitchison, 1987, p. 99)

Similarly, "tip-of-the-tongue" guesses also tend to retain word class. This suggests that words from the same word class are closely linked, with nouns having the strongest affinity. In contrast, words from different word classes are relatively loosely linked. Certain *aphasics* (person who has lost some language ability because of brain damage) retain their use of nouns, but are largely unable to utilize verbs, indicating at the very least that nouns and verbs are stored somewhat differently.

Improving knowledge of a word's part of speech is related to nongrammatical aspects of lexical knowledge. We have already seen one example of this on page 40: word associations tend to shift from being syntagmatic to paradigmatic. Brown and Berko (1960) gave subjects an association task and a word-class awareness test. Both the paradigmatic tendency of the associations and the scores on the awareness test increased with age and were closely related to one another. This suggests that the syntagmatic→paradigmatic shift may well be a manifestation of a developing appreciation of syntax.

It is obvious that most native speakers possess and can utilize knowledge of a word's part of speech, even if they are not able to explicitly name the word class. (Interestingly, Alderson, Clapham, & Steel [1997] found it is quite common for native speakers to be unable to explicitly name a word's part of speech.) But is the same true of nonnative speakers? The common assumption seems to be that word-class knowledge easily transfers from the L1 to the L2. Odlin and Natalicio (1982) established that this is not necessarily true. They found that intermediate and advanced ESL students did not always know the word class of words they knew the meaning of. They claim that "acquisition of the semantic content of target language words does not always entail acquisition of the target language grammatical classification of those words" (p. 35). However, on the positive side, both intermediate and advanced L2 students were able to identify the word classes by name about 75% of the time, albeit for target words of a relatively high frequency. The conclusion is that nonbeginner L2 learners are likely to know the word class of at least the more frequent words, but there is also the possibility that they will not know it even if they know a word's meaning.

There is also some evidence that more advanced learners seem to recognize the value of knowing word class. In a survey of Japanese learners of English, 55% of junior high school students indicated that using part of speech to help remember words is a helpful strategy. For high school students, this percentage increased to 67%, while 85% of university and adult learners rated it as helpful (Schmitt, 1997).

Morphology

Whereas Laufer (1997) suggests that it is not clear how word class affects vocabulary learning, she identifies *morphology* as an aspect with definite effects. Morphology deals with affixes and how they are attached to the base forms of words. Laufer suggests that if derivational affixes are transparent, then learning is facilitated. For example, if students know the meaning of *-ful,* it should not be too difficult to recognize the meaning of new words such as *useful* or *careful* if the base forms are already known. However, a lack of consistency can cause problems even if the affix is transparent. Someone having a special skill is a *specialist,* a person who is pragmatic is a *pragmatist,* but a person who acts on stage is an *actor* not and **actist.* (An asterisk before a word indicates that it is inappropriate, ungrammatical, or otherwise nonstandard.) This is more likely to cause problems in production than comprehension, although learners do confuse affixes receptively as well, for example, believing that *cooker* means a person.

Laufer points out a similar problem in word compounding. In what she terms "deceptive transparency," words consisting of apparently meaningful and transparent parts can cause considerable confusion for unwary learners. She gives the example of *outline,* where *out* does not mean *out of.* Yet many students in her experiments (Laufer & Bensoussan, 1982; Bensoussan & Laufer, 1984) interpreted *outline* as *out of line*. Other confusing words were *discourse,* glossed as *without direction* and *falsities* as *falling cities.* The learner assumption in these cases is obviously that the word equaled the sum of meanings of its components. Although making this assumption can be a useful strategy in many cases, with deceptively transparent words, it unfortunately leads to incorrect guesses. Unsurprisingly, in a later experiment Laufer (1989) found that subjects made more errors with deceptively transparent words than with nondeceptively transparent words. So words that look simple to analyze, but are in fact not, are more difficult to learn.

PROCESSING OF AFFIXES

The manner in which the mental lexicon handles affixes depends partly on what kind of affixes they are. Inflections generally seem to be added to base forms in the course of speech. The exceptions are words that are most commonly used in their inflected forms, such as *peas* and *lips.* These words may be "welded together" and stored as wholes as a result of massive exposure. On the other hand, derivations seem to be stored as single units (*resentful*), which can be analyzed into their components (*resent + ful*), if necessary. As for prefixes, if they are obligatory (*rejuvenate*), they are stored as part of the word. Nonobligatory prefixes (*unhappy*) probably are as well, or there would be more cases of prefix errors (**dishappy, *nonhappy*). Also, if cohort versions of word search are correct, the beginnings of words need to be consistent and reliable, suggesting the fixation of prefixes. (See Aitchison, 1987, for a summary of the affix processing literature.)

RELATIVE DIFFICULTY OF VARIOUS AFFIXES

The idea that morphemes might be learned in a particular sequence (thus implying individual degrees of difficulty) began with the "morpheme studies" of Dulay and Burt (1973, 1974). They studied Spanish- and Chinese-speaking children aged 6 to 8 and found a similar ordering in the children's acquisition of morphemes. These results were broadly confirmed by Larsen-Freeman's 1975 study of L1 adults. But it was difficult to set the order for individual morphemes, and Krashen (1977), after reviewing more than a dozen studies, hypothesized that the morphemes clustered into the following levels:

Acquired earlier

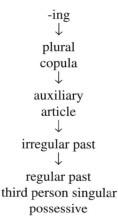

Acquired later

The methodology of the various morpheme studies was called into question (see Long & Sato, 1984, for a review,) but by 1991, Larsen-Freeman and Long had concluded that there was simply too much evidence of some kind of ordering to be ignored. At the same time, results from studies carried out by Pienemann and his colleagues suggested that the underlying basis for the ordering was cognitive processing constraints (e.g., Pienemann, 1984).

Bauer and Nation (1993) used linguistic instead of acquisitional criteria to inform a hierarchy of affixes. They focused on the ease or difficulty of understanding affixed words when encountered in written texts. Their linguistic criteria resulted in the following seven levels:

Level 1. *Each form is a different word.* Each derivative is counted as a separate type.

Level 2. *Inflectional suffixes.* Base words and their inflections are considered part of the same word family. Affixes include the plural, third person singular present tense, past tense, past particle, *-ing*, comparative, superlative, and possessive.

Level 3. *The most frequent and regular derivational affixes.* The affixes include *-able, -er, -less, -ly, -ness, -th, -y, non-*, and *un-*.

Level 4. *Frequent, orthographically regular affixes.* The affixes are *-al, -ation, -ess, -ful, -ism, -ist, -ity, -ize, -ment, -ous*, and *in-*, all with restricted uses.

Level 5. *Regular but infrequent affixes.* These affixes are not general enough to add greatly to the number of words that can be understood. They include *-age, -al, -ally, -an, -ance, -ant, -ary, -atory, -dom, -eer, -en, -ence, -ent, -ery, -ese, -esque, -ette, -hood, -ian, -ite, -let, -ling, -ly, -most, -ory, -ship, -ward, -ways, -wise, anti-, ante-, arch-, bi-, circum-, counter-, en-, ex-, fore-, hyper-, inter-, mid-, mis-, neo-, post-, pro-, semi-, sub-*, and *un-*.

Level 6. *Frequent but irregular affixes.* These affixes cause major problems in segmentation. Some of these affixes are already listed above; those can be considered the transparent cases, whereas these are the opaque cases. They include *-able, -ee, -ic, -ify, -ion, -ist, -ition, -ive, -th, -y, pre-,* and *re-*.

Level 7. *Classical roots and affixes.* Bauer and Nation do not deal with these roots and affixes, except to suggest that they should be explicitly taught to learners, and to note that many frequent English prefixes belong here, such as *ab-, ad-, com-, de-, dis-, ex-,* and *sub-*.

Bauer and Nation have succeeded in creating a useful hierarchy of affixes that can be used in the discussion of vocabulary, but we must be careful not to assume that their ranking of affixes (achieved on solely linguistic criteria) necessarily translates directly into a psycholinguistically valid statement of learning difficulty. Indeed, when I compared my learners' knowledge of affixes with the Bauer and Nation hierarchy, there was little correspondence other than inflections being easier than derivations (Schmitt, 1995b).

Applications to teaching

There seems to be an implicit assumption among teachers that if a word's meaning is learned, all of the other "lower-level" kinds of lexical knowledge will follow in due course. As with spelling, we find this is not always the case with knowledge of word class and morphology. It is probably worth explicitly giving the word class of an item when teaching it, especially for less frequent words that may not be met often enough for this information to be easily acquired from context. It is also important not to confuse knowing the word class for a word with the ability to use that word in a grammatically correct manner. A student may be able to use a word correctly, but still not know its metalinguistic label (noun, verb, etc.). Conversely, the student may know the label but still not be able to use it properly.

As for morphology, I have found in several studies that knowledge of a base form did not mean that all the derivative forms were mastered (Schmitt, 1998b, 1999; Schmitt & Meara, 1997). Inflections did not seem to be much of a problem, but derivative forms were generally not well known. This indicates that teachers should consider giving a higher profile to derivative forms in their instruction.

If affixes are transparent and behave as would be expected, then their acquisition should be facilitated, as Laufer (1997) claims. But affixes that are not regular can clearly cause problems. The Bauer and Nation (1993) affix list can be used as a helpful (but not infallible) guide as to which affixes should be easier and which more difficult to learn. Nation (1990, p. 48) suggests that, in general, exceptions should not be introduced until any rule or regularity in patterning has been acquired. This implies that the most regular affixes in the first levels should be taught initially, and only after students are comfortable with them should the more irregular affixes be focused on. This is assuming that affixes should be taught in the first place. Nation (1990, pp. 168–174) argues that they should be, because using word parts is one of three major strategies that can help students become independent vocabulary learners (guessing from context and memory techniques are the other two) and so is definitely worth explicit attention from the teacher. He illustrates a number of exercises that focus on morphology, including a form of Bingo in which students build complete words from a given prefix or stem. Another good reason for focusing on suffixes in particular is that they facilitate the learning of word families. As mentioned in the section on orthography, teachers should consider having students work with word families instead of just single words; an understanding of derivational suffixes makes this possible.

Using word parts can be a very useful strategy, but it occasionally has pitfalls (e.g., *discourse* does not mean "without direction"). When students use word parts as an initial word-guessing strategy, they must be careful to check the surrounding context to see if their guess makes sense. Haynes (1993) found that students sometimes made an incorrect guess about what an unknown word meant in a text, and then stuck with that meaning even though it made no sense in the context. For this reason, Clarke and Nation (1980) suggest that word parts might best be used as a confirmatory strategy to verify guesses made from context.

Summary

This chapter has stressed that the form of a word is important for its effective use. Receptively, automatic reading requires a great deal of sight vocabulary. Productively, learners need to develop "visual images" of words that are exceptions to spelling rules in addition to their knowledge of sound-symbol correspondences. In this way, they have two spelling strategies available to use with difficult words.

The beginnings of words seem to be particularly salient, both orthographically and phonologically, with the ends of words slightly less so. This "bathtub effect" indicates that the middle of words is usually the least easily remembered. The mind uses the saliency of word beginnings to parse words from the speech stream. As most words in English have a strong or secondary initial stress, the mind assumes that a strong stress in the speech stream indicates the beginning of a new word.

Grammatical knowledge of a word can consist of many things, but this chapter concentrated on word class and morphology. It seems that nouns are generally the easiest word class to learn. Knowledge of suffixes is particularly important as this allows learners to use the different members of a word family. A list that presented affixes in order of difficulty, based on linguistic criteria, was presented.

The next chapter will discuss the role of corpus research in lexical studies. Because frequency and collocation have mainly been studied through corpus evidence, these last two types of word knowledge will be covered there.

Exercises for expansion

1. Compile a list of "slips of the ear" that you notice yourself and other people making. Does the mis-segmentation of word boundaries have anything to do with stress, as indicated in this chapter? If the language you are working in is not English, does the stress-parsing connection hold in your language?
2. Consider the orthographic depth of your L1 and another language you have learned. Are they similar or different? If different, can any difficulty in learning your L2 be attributed to this difference? Could you recommend ways for another learner studying your L2 to avoid these difficulties?
3. The following are items from Ann Ryan's (1997) Word Discrimination Test. The testees must find any mistakes in the sentences, underline the word that is wrong, and write the correct word above it. One third of the sentences are already correct.

   He won the rice by running very fast.
   We had delicious hot soap for dinner.
   How much do you earn each month?
   Step making so much noise.
   There was a horse and two cows on the farm.
   Can you get some broad if you are going to the baker's?

   How useful do you think a test like this is for discovering language learning problems that are mainly orthographically based? What type and level of student would it be most appropriate for?
4. If possible, listen to a language you are not familiar with. Can you discern where the words begin and end? Does the strategy of assuming that strong stress begins a new content word work with this language?

5. Keep track of any "tip-of-the-tongue" experiences. What can you remember about the form of the word you cannot quite retrieve? Does the "bathtub effect" hold, especially if the language you are using is not English?

Further reading

For more on spelling: Venezky (1970), Frith (1980), Carney (1997), and Shemesh and Waller (1999).

For information about other theories of lexical access: the bin model (Forster, 1976); logogen model (Morton, 1979); cohort and spreading activation models (Aitchison, 1987); visual word recognition (Balota, 1994).

For more detail on how word class is involved in the learning and storage of vocabulary: Aitchison (1987).

For more on morphology: Aitchison (1987), Matthews (1991), Nagy, Diakidoy, and Anderson (1993).

5 *The use of corpora in vocabulary studies*

- "Language" is such a big subject that it is almost impossible to get my head around it. Is there a way to conveniently obtain language data so that I can study particular words or structures?
- Some words are relatively common, and others are relatively rare. What difference does this make?
- Many words seem to "fit together" in combinations, for example, *sweep* a *floor.* What am I to make of this?

The vast improvement of corpora has been one of the most significant developments in vocabulary studies in recent years. *Corpora* or *corpuses* (singular: *corpus*) are simply large collections or databases of language, incorporating stretches of discourse ranging from a few words to entire books. The exciting thing about corpora is that they allow researchers, teachers, and learners to use great amounts of real data in their study of language instead of having to rely on intuitions and made-up examples. Insights from corpus research have revolutionized the way we view language, particularly words and their relationships with each other in context. In particular, the two remaining kinds of word knowledge in Nation's (1990) list, frequency and collocation, have been studied almost exclusively through corpus evidence. Because research into large databases of language is necessary in order to make any meaningful statements about these two lexical aspects, they will be covered in this chapter. Finally, *lexicography* (dictionary writing) has also been fundamentally affected, with the four major learner dictionary publishers all relying on corpus input to set their word definitions and examples.

Corpora and their development

Some of the earliest corpora began appearing in the first third of the 1900s, the products of thousands of painstaking and tedious hours of manual labor. Extracts from numerous books, magazines, newspapers, and other written sources were selected and assimilated into these corpora. Working in this manner, corpora of one million words were considered huge at the time. Even in the early age of computers, one million-word corpora were on the large side, because the written texts still had to be manually typed in. Two good examples of corpora at this point of development are the Brown University Corpus (Kučera & Francis, 1967) focusing on American English, and its counterpart in Europe, the Lancaster-Oslo/Bergen Corpus (LOB) (Hofland & Johansson, 1982; Johansson & Hofland, 1989) focusing on British English. Decades before these two efforts, Thorndike and Lorge (1944) combined several existing corpora to build an eighteen million-word corpus, which was colossal at the time.

It was when texts could be quickly scanned into computers that technology finally revolutionized the field. With the bottleneck of manually typing and entering texts eliminated, the creation of immensely larger corpora was possible. We now have "third-generation" (Moon, 1997) corpora that can contain hundreds of millions of words. Three important examples are the COBUILD Bank of English Corpus, the Cambridge International Corpus (CIC), and the British National Corpus (BNC). The Bank of English Corpus has more than 300 million words, and the CIC and BNC each have more than 100 million. These corpora are approaching the size at which their sheer number of words allows them to be reasonably accurate representations of the English language in general. This is partly because their larger size means that more infrequent words are included.

To get some idea of what these numbers mean, let us consider how many words people are exposed to in real life. Simpson (1988) estimates that the average person is exposed to around one million words per day. This figure stretches the bounds of credibility, but does take into account repeated exposure to the more frequent words. At this rate, that person would be exposed to thirty million words per month; that is, the Bank of English Corpus would represent about ten months of exposure. Based on other estimates, Stubbs (1995) arrives at a much lower exposure rate of about one million words per month, which would mean that the Bank of English Corpus represents 25 years' total exposure. Either way, these kinds of figures mean that the larger current corpora can equal, at least in numerical terms, a substantial part of the language an average person might be exposed to in daily life.

Numerical size is not everything in corpus design, however. There is also the important question of *what* goes into the corpus. A corpus that consisted of only automotive repair manuals would contain only a very specific kind of language, even if it grew to one billion words. It could be extremely representative of the kind of language appearing in such manuals, but it would not represent language in general use to any great extent. Although there are corpora concentrating on certain areas, such as journalism (Zettersten, 1978), scientific English (Johansson, 1978), and applied linguistics (which I am currently compiling), most corpora are designed to represent language as a whole, including all topics and spheres of use. To be truly representative of such global language, a corpus must be balanced to include all of the different genres of a language (sermons, lectures, newspaper reports, novels, etc.) in proportions similar to that of their real-world occurrence. At the moment, this idealistic goal is unattainable, because no one knows exactly what those percentages are. In fact, the best source of information on this subject comes from existing corpora, which were put together without the aid of this information. The best that can be done is to incorporate large amounts of language from a wide range of genres, on the assumption that this diversity will eventually lead to a sample of language representative of the whole.

There are other issues in balancing a corpus as well. With a worldwide language such as English, one must consider what proportions, if any, to include of the various international varieties of English (North American, British, Australian, Indian, etc.). But a more important issue is that of written versus spoken discourse. It is technically much easier to work with written text and this has led to most corpora having a distinct bias toward written discourse. Spoken discourse must first be taped, then manually transcribed, and finally entered into the computer before it can be used. This has inevitably led to smaller percentages of spontaneous spoken data compared to written (e.g., approximately 11% for the BNC, 6% for the Bank of English Corpus). However, technology may eventually eliminate this imbalance by automatizing the input of spoken data. Computer programs for automatically transcribing spoken discourse into a written form are being developed, and in the future we may find corpora with ratios approaching that of real-world language use. (Note that these ratios are yet to be determined.)

There is already a great deal of interest in purely spoken corpora, spurred on by the realization that spoken discourse exhibits quite different behavior from written discourse. Early spoken corpora include the 500,000-word *Oral Vocabulary of the Australian Worker* (OVAW) Corpus (Schonell et al., 1956) and the 250,000-word corpus from which the Davis-Howes Count of Spoken English (Howes, 1966) was taken. An example of a more recent spoken corpus is the Cambridge and Nottingham Corpus of Discourse English (CANCODE), which was developed expressly for the purpose of developing a grammar of the spoken English language (Carter & McCarthy, in press).

By carefully considering the issues above, corpus linguists have succeeded in developing modern corpora that are arguably reasonably representative. Still, it must be remembered that no corpus is perfect, and that each will contain quirks that are not typical of language as it is generally used in the world. Thus, one must maintain a critical eye and a certain healthy skepticism when using this and other language tools.

Applications of corpora

Once a corpus has been compiled, it needs to be analyzed to be of any value. The computer revolution has also changed this aspect, with powerful new programs that can explore the corpus and isolate more aspects of language behavior than ever before. The three major kinds of information these programs can provide about language are how frequently various words occur, which words tend to co-occur, and how the structure of language is organized. The last aspect has much to do with the recurring lexicogrammatical theme running through this book, and will be expanded upon in the next chapter. Of the other two aspects, let us look at frequency first.

Frequency

Probably the most basic thing that can be learned from studying the language contained in a corpus is how frequently any particular word occurs. In fact, because counting frequency of occurrence is such a basic procedure, this was the major form of information that came out of the earlier corpora. To derive this frequency information, the computer program simply counts the number of occurrences of a word (in any combination of its base, inflected, and derivative forms) in a corpus and shows the result on the screen in a matter of seconds. Figure 1 illustrates frequency lists from three different corpora. The first is from the CIC corpus, and indicates the fifty most frequent words in the English language. The second list comes from the CANCODE corpus of spoken language, and represents the most frequent words in spoken English discourse. The third list shows which words are most frequent in the specialized genre of automotive repair manuals (Milton & Hales, 1997).

Word counts like these have provided some very useful insights into the way the vocabulary of English works. One of the most important is that the most frequent words cover an inordinate percentage of word occurrences in language. As we can see from the frequency lists in Figure 1, *the* is the most frequent word in general and spoken English, making up approximately

General English (CIC)	Spoken English (CANCODE)	Car manuals (AUTOHALL)
1. the	the	and
2. of	I	the
3. to	you	to
4. and	and	of
5. a	to	in
6. in	it	is
7. that	a	or
8. is	yeah	with
9. for	that	remove
10. it	of	a
11. was	in	replace
12. he	was	for
13. on	is	oil
14. with	it's	be
15. I	know	valve
16. as	no	check
17. at	oh	engine
18. be	so	from
19. by	but	if
20. his	on	on
21. but	they	gear
22. have	well	install
23. from	what	rear
24. are	yes	when
25. said	have	not
26. not	we	bearing
27. they	he	assembly
28. you	do	it
29. this	got	cylinder
30. an	that's	brake
31. had	for	as
32. has	this	that
33. or	just	at
34. one	all	by
35. which	there	clutch
36. will	like	shaft
37. were	one	piston
38. their	be	front
39. who	right	system
40. we	not	air
41. would	don't	switch
42. all	she	pressure
43. she	think	transmission
44. her	if	rod
45. more	with	removal
46. been	then	side
47. about	at	note
48. there	about	out
49. when	are	seal
50. its	as	ring

Figure 1   The most frequent general, spoken, and automotive words.

6–7% of all word *tokens* (occurrences). Figures from the CIC indicate that, for general English, the top three words make up about 11.5%, the top 10 words 22%, the top 50 words 37%, the top 100 words 44%, and the top 2,000 words about 80% of all tokens. Considering that estimates of the total size of the English language vary from 54,000 word families (Nation & Waring, 1997) to millions of words (Bryson, 1990), we find that a relative handful of words do the bulk of the work, while the others occur rather infrequently. Although this data is for English, other languages would yield similar figures. This insight about high-frequency words has immediate practical ramifications. Because these very frequent words are so widely used, it is essential that they be learned if one is to be able to use language. However, because the most frequent content words are also the most likely to be polysemous, students must learn more than 2,000 meaning senses if they are going to have control over this important vocabulary. In addition, these words make up the majority of tokens in any discourse, so if they are not known, language users will be unable to make accurate guesses about the meanings of the remaining less frequent words, many of which are likely to be unknown.

A second insight is that the most frequent words in English tend to be *grammatical words,* also known as *function words* or *functors* (words that hold little or no meaning, and primarily contribute to the grammatical structure of language). This stems from the commonsense fact that such grammatical words are necessary to the structure of English regardless of the topic. Articles, prepositions, pronouns, conjunctions, forms of the verb *be,* and so on, are equally necessary whether we are talking about cowboys, space exploration, botany, or music. The three frequency lists in Figure 1 indicate that this holds true regardless of whether the language in the corpus is general (CIC) or more specific (AUTOHALL), and whether it is primarily written (CIC) or spoken (CANCODE). In fact, we must go down to the twenty-fifth position to find the first *content word* (one that does carry meaning), *said,* in the general English frequency list. In contrast to grammatical words, however, content words are affected by the type of corpus. We can see that automotive-specific words such as *valve* and *engine* are extremely common in the AUTOHALL corpus but do not appear in the most frequent words of general English.

The third insight is that spoken and written discourse differ considerably. A close look at the frequency lists above suggests the nature of some of these differences. In particular, a number of content words, such as *know, well, got, think,* and *right,* appear much higher on the spoken list than on the written list. On closer inspection, it turns out that these words are not content words at all, but actually elements of interpersonal phrases (e.g., *you know, I think*), single-word organizational markers (*well, right*), smooth-overs (e.g., *never mind*), hedges (e.g., *kind of/sort of*), and other kinds of discourse items that are characteristic of the spoken mode (McCarthy & Carter, 1997). Therefore, the first difference is that spoken language makes frequent use of these types of discourse markers, whereas they rarely occur in written language. A second difference is that the same word may take different meanings the two modes. McCarthy and Carter (1997) show that *got* is used mainly in the construction *have got* in the CANCODE as the basic verb of possession or personal association with something. In addition, they highlight the following two sentences from the corpus, which are indicative of other meanings:

1. I've got so many birthdays in July.
2. I've got you.

In Example 1, the speaker means something like "I have to deal with," because she is referring to the obligation of sending numerous birthday cards. In Example 2, *I've got* seems to mean "I understand you." Neither of these meaning senses would be common in the formal written mode.

A third difference is that the most frequent fifty words cover a greater proportion of the tokens in spoken discourse than in written. If we look at typical written texts and typical spoken conversations, we find that spoken discourse usually uses a smaller variety of individual words. An analysis of the OVAW corpus of Australian spoken English (Schonell et al., 1956) suggests that a person can largely function in everyday conversation with a vocabulary of 2,000 words. On the other hand, scholars believe that a person needs to know far more words to be able to read an average text. The estimates in L2 situations range from 3,000 word families (Laufer, 1992) to 3,000 to 5,000 word families (Nation & Waring, 1997), and up to 10,000 word families (Hazenberg & Hulstijn, 1996). Thus, one clearly needs more words to function adequately in the written mode than in the spoken one.

The notion of frequency has also been utilized to analyze individual texts. One of the ways of determining a text's difficulty is to ascertain the diversity of the vocabulary in that text. If most of the words are repeated several times, then fewer different words (*types*) need to be known. On the other hand, if few words are repeated, then more types will be included in the text. The degree of lexical diversity is often expressed as a *type-token ratio,* calculated by the following formula:

$$\text{Lexical variation} = \frac{\text{number of different words (types)}}{\text{total number of words in the text (tokens)}} \times 100$$

(Laufer & Nation, 1995)

The lower the ratio, the more repetition there is, and the fewer types need to be known to understand the text. An example will help illustrate how this ratio works. This paragraph contains 245 tokens (total words), but only 132 types (different words). This makes the type–token ratio 53.88 (132 ÷ 245 × 100). Compare this to 245 words taken from a more advanced teacher reference book on vocabulary (Schmitt & McCarthy, 1997, Chapter 2.2 by Nick Ellis). Its type–token ratio is 58.24, suggesting a lexically more complex treatment. Ure (1971) found that spoken texts generally had ratios under 40. Written texts generally had ratios over 40, although they ranged from 36 to 57. Of course, the type–token ratio is rather simplistic, and one might think of cases in which it would not be very indicative of difficulty, such as a scientific journal that contains a great deal of repetition of very technical vocabulary. On the other hand, a children's story can have rather simple vocabulary but at the same time a relatively high type–token ratio; for example, the English translation of the Japanese children's story *My Neighborhood Totoro* (Miyazaki, 1992) produced a type–token ratio of 55.59. In addition, the length of a text greatly affects the type–token ratio, because, as texts get longer, the number of types does not normally increase as fast as the number of tokens. This leads to increasingly low ratios solely owing to the length factor.

Of course, not all words in a text are equal, and another measure of lexical complexity, *lexical density,* takes into consideration the number of content versus grammatical words present. It is calculated with the following formula:

$$\text{Lexical density} = \frac{\text{number of content words}}{\text{total number of words in the text (tokens)}} \times 100$$

(Laufer & Nation, 1995)

Texts with a higher proportion of content words are said to be lexically dense, whereas those with few content words have low lexical density (Ure, 1971). Using the same three text samples as above, we find that the lexical density figures for the paragraph above is 66.12, Ellis's paper 61.60, and the children's extract 57.59. Thus, lexical density seems to better indicate the relative simplicity of the children's story, but it does not capture the complexity of Ellis's paper. The discrepancy between the type–token ratios and lexical density figures for these three text samples highlights the weaknesses of such basic lexical analyses. More sophisticated methods of analyses are available that do a much better job of capturing the complexity of lexis in texts, but they are beyond the realm of this book. (Interested readers can consult Laufer & Nation, 1995; Malvern & Richards, 1997; and

Read, 2000, for more on these.) Nevertheless, these two basic methods have served to illustrate the ways an analysis of lexis has been used to indicate the overall difficulty of a text. (See Chapter 9 for more on these.)

Word counts drawn from corpora provide objective data concerning frequency of occurrence. Of course, people have always had intuitions about how frequent various words are, and Nation (1990) lists such intuitions as one of the eight types of word knowledge. Still, until the advent of corpora, no one really knew how accurate those intuitions were. Research that compares people's intuitions of frequency with corpus word counts indicates that native speakers are reasonably accurate in their intuitions, and that advanced nonnatives can be as well (Shapiro, 1969; Arnaud, 1989, 1990; Schmitt & Dunham, 1999). There is also some evidence that accurate intuitions are related to level of education (Schmitt & Dunham, 1999). This suggests the possibility that these intuitions are enhanced by the greater exposure that students normally gain from extensive reading. In any case, intuitions of frequency are surely important for proficient word use. At the most basic level, they give a person a sense of how often to use a word. One of the reasons L2 learners do not sound native may be that they overuse certain relatively infrequent words and underuse certain relatively frequent words. At a more sophisticated level, frequency is tied to such notions as register, in that more formal words tend to be less frequent and colloquial words more frequent.

Collocation

The second major area of insight into the nature of vocabulary that can be gained from corpus research concerns *collocation*. Collocation refers to the tendency of two or more words to co-occur in discourse, and is the last of Nation's (1990) eight types of word knowledge to be covered. J. R. Firth first brought this notion into prominence in 1957, and it has become increasingly important since. Perhaps the best place to start a discussion of collocation is with Sinclair's (1991) distinction between the *open-choice principle* and the *idiom principle*. The open-choice principle tries to cover the idea that language is creative, and in most instances there is a wide variety of possible words that could be put into any "slot." This is the traditional way of viewing language, and Sinclair states that "virtually all grammars are constructed on the open-choice principle" (p. 110). However, complementary to this freedom of choice, he notes that language also has a systematicity that constrains vocabulary choice in discourse, constraints that the open-choice principle does not capture. To some extent, this systematicity merely reflects real-world phenomena: *fishing* is often done in close physical proximity to a *lake,* so the words expressing these concepts will naturally co-occur as well. But much of the systematicity is strictly linguistic: there is no reason why we do not say **to put something on fire,* but fluent members of the English-speaking speech community know that the appropriate phrase is *to set/start something on fire.* The idiom principle highlights the fact that there are regularities in how words co-occur with each other; collocation is the term that covers this notion.

Two factors are key to the notion of collocation. The first is that words co-occur together and the second is that these relationships have varying degrees of exclusivity. A commonly given example of collocation involves the word *blonde. Blonde* occurs almost exclusively with the word *hair* and a few other animate nouns like *woman* or *lady.* But it never occurs with words like *paint* or *wallpaper,* even though there is no reason semantically why they should not fit together. Because *blonde* has such an exclusive relationship with *hair,* they are said to collocate strongly. Most words do not collocate this robustly, however. Sometimes the collocation can be much weaker, as in the case of the word *nice.* It commonly occurs with almost any noun that one would want to associate with pleasantness, such as a *nice view, nice car,* or *nice salary.* These combinations could be said to collocate weakly. Some words combine so indiscriminately that there is not enough exclusivity to warrant the notion of collocation. An example is the word *the,* which co-occurs with virtually every nonproper noun. So to collocate, words must co-occur in discourse, but there must also be an element of exclusiveness.

Most authors agree that there are two basic kinds of collocations: grammatical/syntactic collocations and semantic/lexical collocations (Benson, 1985; Biskup, 1992; Bahns, 1993). Grammatical collocations are the type in which a dominant word "fits together" with a grammatical word, typically a noun, verb, or adjective followed by a preposition. Examples are *abide by, access to,* and *acquainted with.* Lexical collocations, on the other hand, normally consist of combinations of two basically "equal" words such as noun + verb (*ball bounces*), verb + noun (*spend money*), and adjective + noun (*cheerful expression*), in which both words contribute to the meaning (Benson, 1985). In addition to these two basic collocational categories, Allerton (1984) proposes a third, consisting of collocations that are not based on grammatical or semantic patterning. The relatively arbitrary prepositions attached to time fit in this category, because there does not seem to be any logical reason why we should say _at_ six o'clock, but _on_ Monday.

However, it is becoming quite clear that more than just single words collocate; strings of words do as well. Research by Nattinger and DeCarrico (1992) and Sinclair (1991) suggests that there is much more lexical patterning and widespread collocation in language than has been realized before, and when one word is selected, it can constrain lexical choice several words away. Nattinger and DeCarrico (1992, p. 22), for instance, believe that we must look more than five words away to find every collocational relationship. In fact, the realization that words act less as individual units and more as part of lexical phrases in interconnected discourse is one of the most important new trends in vocabulary studies. These lexical phrases in language reflect the way the mind tends to "chunk" language in order to make it easier to process.

Cowie and Howarth (1995) suggest that such lexical phrases can be placed on a 4-level scale of complexity (Figure 2).

At Level 1, idioms are multiword lexemes that have frozen collocation. If any variation is inserted into the idiom, it ceases to exist as a unit. In the idiom *kick the bucket,* the meaning "to die" would be lost if even one element was changed. To show this, note how *kick the pail, boot the bucket,* and *kick a bucket* all lose the idiom's meaning. Thus idioms are the least complex because they allow no variation. Moving to Level 2, the collocation is still fixed, but the meaning is not idiosyncratic any longer; rather it is more transparent because it is composed from the meanings of all of the component words. This level is somewhat more complex because the meaning has to be composed from several lexemes, rather than coming from a single one as in Level 1. Level 3 has a slot that can be filled from a limited list of words, most of which are similar in meaning. This choice introduces both variation and complexity. Level 4 has two slots instead of one, adding increased variation and complexity. Thus each level contains increasingly more variation, and therefore complexity.

Most of this discussion on collocation is based on evidence from corpora that was analyzed with computer programs called *concordancers.* These concordancers look for all the instances of a target word/string in the corpus being used and show the lines of text in which they appear. To make these text lines easier to read and analyze, the target word/string (also called *node* or *keyword*) is lined up in the center of the screen. Figure 3 illustrates the output, which is called a *concordance.*

The concordances in Figure 3 exemplify another phenomenon brought to light by corpus research: that words may habitually collocate with other words from a definable semantic set (Stubbs, 1995). The words in these semantic sets may carry either positive or negative connotations. For example, Stubbs reports how *cause* typically collocates with unpleasant things such as *problems, trouble, damage, death, pain,* and *disease. Provide,* on the other hand, collocates mainly with positive things such as *facilities, information, services, aid, assistance,* and *money.* Using the col-

LEAST COMPLEXITY AND VARIATION

1. IDIOM
   bite the dust, shoot the breeze

2. INVARIABLE COLLOCATION
   break a journey, from head to foot

3. COLLOCATION WITH LIMITED CHOICE AT ONE POINT
   take/have/be given precedence [over noun phrase]
   give/allow/permit access to [noun phrase]
   have/feel/experience a need [for noun phrase]

4. COLLOCATION WITH LIMITED CHOICE AT TWO POINTS
   as dark/black as night/coal/ink
   get/have/receive a lesson/tuition/instruction [in noun phrase]

MOST COMPLEXITY AND VARIATION

Figure 2   Levels of collocational complexity.

locate *work* with both of these words further illustrates the difference: *cause work* is usually considered a bad thing, while *provide work* is usually looked upon favorably. The term *collocational prosody* is used to describe this phenomenon. We can find the same collocational prosody in the concordances in Figure 3, even though they were taken from a different corpus than was used by Stubbs.

So far, the discussion has been based on corpus evidence. One might also ask if collocation has psycholinguistic reality. There has been much less research from this perspective, but what evidence there is suggests that collocational links are "powerful and long-lasting" links between words in the mind (Aitchison, 1987, p. 79). In association tasks, collocations are the second most common response type after coordinates (Jenkins, 1970). Aphasics retain collocational information fairly well, even though they have lost much of their other use of language (Goodglass & Baker, 1976). These collocational links do not seem to fade as people grow older (Howard, McAndrews, & Lasaga, 1981). So it does seem that collocations are a psycholinguistic reality and that the mind does organize words according to their collocational links to some extent.

Although it is not clear how collocational knowledge is acquired, it seems to be relatively difficult to achieve. This difficulty means that collocational knowledge is something that normally distinguishes native speakers from nonnative speakers. In an unpublished study, Levenston found that when native speakers responded to a completion task, they relied on collocational criteria to a large extent. On the other hand, even advanced L2

have searched for a single	cause	of aging–a critical gene, hor
s in property lending will	cause	a serious credit crunch – compa
lit second nobody moves?	Cause	we're looking at the dolly-bird
ith in the fast lane is no	cause	for driving without due care and
ion so far available gives	cause	for concern about the circumstan
of 70–90 mph expected to	cause	structural damage. The forecaste
aming. If untreated it can	cause	permanent damage to hearing."
urder came not from any	cause	worth the name but from the very
e in prison without good	cause	, he says. The Foreign Office has
es of martyrdom ina noble	cause	. He said they had been granted "
South West Water] did not	cause	the problem is no defence at all
obviously bleeding, could	cause	blood to seep from veins and art
justice is the Palestinian	cause	and right of the Palestinian
d the relevant details may	cause	an underpayment and perhaps resu
onous toxins which could	cause	kidneys to fail. This could happ
e of the information liable to	cause	serious injury to the nation wi
ity and its strength gives	cause	for optimism for the prospects
ng legislation which could	cause	considerable problems for compan
t in a situation likely to	cause	unnecessary suffering, and permi
on of schools is likely to	cause	ministers more problems than it
ffice staff, said the main	cause	of recruitment problems was low
inspectors are the biggest	cause	of poor reading standards. "Some
mmit criminal damage, and	cause	public disorder, yesterday were
dence in you is total. Our	cause	is just. Now you must be the thu
in 1987 for conspiracy to	cause	explosions, was yesterday refuse

e opportunity, rather than	provide	it. The House of Lords amended
and Outdoor World might	provide	the breath of fresh air that i
t horrendous, a swap can	provide	a route into areas where there
and the venues which can	provide	such facilities will no doubt
major car-hire companies	provide	cars with mounted phones. Amer
ed out. The motion was to	provide	an access gate into the city
show is being prepareed to	provide	training throughout England an
he said. The bill aims to	provide	the first coherent framework
said: "What we earn and	provide	for ourselves is only one part
er international action to	provide	places for safety for refugees
BARCLAYS Bank is to	provide	a year's paid maternity leave,
s to encourage people to	provide	their own pensions, by offerin
Plans to	provide	power for the southwest of
mming pool operators, to	provide	lifeguards or any other
any occasion declined to	provide	the resources that are require
st time in British history	provide	statutory guarantees for the
tish Constitution does not	provide	for an Act of War to be approv
0 vehicles. We have had to	provide	a site for them. It has just
a litre would be needed to	provide	enormous killing power."
oops, the specialists will	provide	support to medical and nursing
ns are run by BR staff to	provide	tourist trips and do not compe
hedules will be cleared to	provide	continuous news coverage for
(1,770–2,017m), which can	provide	skiing from December until ear
says. The government will	provide	extra hostel beds if necessary
million every two years to	provide	safe storage facilities for th

Figure 3   Concordances of cause *and* provide *from the CIC corpus.*

learners were much less likely to respond with collocationally based answers. Granger (1998) found that French learners of English used some collocational combinations far more than did native English speakers, in particular amplifiers such as *very, completely, highly, dazzlingly,* and *strongly.* The nonnatives tended to overuse those words that collocated most freely with a wide variety of other words. She suggests that this liberal use of "all-rounders," especially *very,* is a "safe bet" strategy designed to minimize error. She also found that the natives were much more confident in identifying the most common collocates and that the most appropriate collocational combinations are often not very salient for nonnatives.

A final finding was that most of the English collocations used by the French learners were congruent with collocations in their L1, and so might have transferred. Bahns (1993) suggests that this is exactly what happens. If this is so, it could help to address the problem of how to teach collocations. One of the main pedagogical hurdles is the sheer number of collocational possibilities to deal with. Bahns suggests that learners are able to transfer directly translatable collocations from their native language to the target language, making it necessary to address only the collocations with no direct translation equivalents. This would still leave the problem of identifying these nontranslatable collocations, and in any case the number remaining would be massive.

From the discussion above, we see that collocation manifests the strong link between lexis and grammar in one of its most obvious forms. In Chapter 6, we will explore this connection further, in terms of lexical phrases and even longer sequences of discourse.

Corpus input into dictionaries

It is worth briefly noting that the practical area in which corpora have made the most tangible impact to date is lexicography. All of the major learner dictionaries are now based on corpus evidence, including the *Cambridge International Dictionary of English,* the *Collins COBUILD English Dictionary,* the *Longman Dictionary of Contemporary English,* and the *Oxford Advanced Learner's Dictionary* (all 1995). Corpus input has been particularly informative about the meaning, register, and collocation elements of dictionary entries (Scholfield, 1994, 1997). Where dictionaries have traditionally been seen as "prescriptive" depositories of language that identified "the 'best' usage, on the grounds of beauty, logic, history or the like," corpus input has now allowed an accurate "descriptive" treatment of the way language is actually used (ibid., p. 283). At the time of writing, computerized dictionaries are just starting to become available, making possible a lexical resource that contains more detailed information, but in a compact and user-friendly format. These developments are certainly exciting, and years from now we may even look back upon this time as the golden age of lexicography.

Applications to teaching

Because we can access "hard data" about real language in use from corpora, it is not surprising that this has led to very practical applications in pedagogy. Word-frequency lists are one important linguistic tool to come out of corpus research. They can be used to great effect to improve vocabulary teaching, but instructors also need to be aware of their limitations. Any corpus contains only a tiny sampling of the type of language it strives to represent, and so will inevitably include quirks. If teachers encounter a bit of corpus evidence that seems totally counterintuitive, it is well to question whether it is truly representative of the targeted language type, or just an artifact of the makeup of the corpus. In other words, teachers should always run corpus results through the filter of common sense. (See Cook, 1998, for more on the limitations of corpora.)

Unless the teacher has access to frequency lists from spoken corpora, the lists available will likely be heavily biased toward written language. These types of lists need to be used with caution as a reference for spoken language. As the CIC and CANCODE lists in this chapter show, frequency lists of general English do not always give an accurate indication of the frequency of some of the most common words (*yeah*), and, by extension, phrases (*never mind, sort of*), occurring in spoken discourse. We have also seen that frequency lists of general language do not indicate the specialized vocabulary of a particular field, such as auto mechanics, and so a specialized corpus is needed for this. For example, if a teacher were teaching English for academic purposes (EAP), a general frequency list would be useful in showing the high-frequency words that are common to most subject areas, but a specialized EAP list would also be required to illustrate vocabulary dominant in academic areas. In this case, a specialized list has already been compiled, the University Word List (UWL), and is available as an appendix in Nation (1990). An updated version, called the Academic Word List (AWL), is also now available (Coxhead, 1998; the list is reproduced in Appendix B).

In many cases, though, a specialized list will not exist or be accessible. One way around this problem is to compile a custom corpus oneself that includes only the type of language desired. This is now within the reach of any school that has a computer with a moderately sized hard disk, a scanner, and a hundred dollars for (1) an optical character recognition (OCR) software program (which translates the scanned image into text) and (2) a concordancing program. The teacher can then scan in (with the permission of the copyright holders) any number of written texts that are relevant to the area. (See Tribble & Jones, 1990, for a detailed explanation of how to compile and use one's own corpus.) Corpora could also be compiled for beginning students by scanning in the simplified readers used at a particular reading level. It is not necessary to do this to obtain frequency lists, as most simplified series include such lists in their documentation, but the resulting concordance data should provide useful insights into how words are used in the actual texts the students are reading.

The procedure above is feasible for compiling a small corpus of written language, but unfortunately compiling a corpus of spoken language is probably too involved for anyone but large institutions. A great number of conversations have to be tape-recorded, then transcribed into written form, and finally entered into the computer. This process is expensive in both time and money. For the moment, teachers will probably have to rely on the "authorities" for an analysis of spoken data, through corpus-based dictionaries such as the four mentioned above and reference books on the grammar of spoken discourse (Brazil, 1995; Carter & McCarthy, 1997).

Coming back to the original point, teachers need to be sure that the word lists they use truly represent the language targeted. Nation (1990, p. 20) lists several other problems to be aware of when using frequency lists to inform pedagogy. The first is that many important words do not occur early in frequency lists of general language. For example, such words as *pencil, eraser,* and *blackboard* do not occur in the most frequent words of general English, though they are frequent and essential in a classroom context. This indicates that we cannot use frequency lists as a strict prescription of the order in which to teach words. They can be a useful guide, but teachers need to be free to add what other words they feel are necessary for their students to know. Conversely, Nation notes that many of the most frequent words in general English might not be suitable for beginning students, for example, *company, issue,* and *labor.* To this one could add the fact that the most frequent words of all in English are grammatical words. One cannot envision teaching functors like *the, of,* and *with* until a number of content words are learned. Only then can functors be taught in any context that will make sense to students. Two last points Nation adds to the caveats already mentioned are that word lists often disagree with one another, and they are less reliable as they move toward lower-frequency words.

Nevertheless, as long as teachers keep these limitations in mind, frequency lists can be an extremely useful pedagogical tool. The most frequent words occur so often in general language that they are essential for any real language use. Utilizing a cost/benefit perspective, Nation (1995) argues that the most frequent words are so important that they are worth whatever time and effort is required to learn them. Therefore, although the words may not be taught in the exact order on the list, and although other words may be added, the most frequent words of a language need to be taught sometime during the beginning of a student's course of study. The most frequent two to three thousand words are often mentioned as forming a realistic target for basic language use (Meara, 1995; Nation & Waring, 1997). In addition, the order of words on the lists gives some indication of a desirable order of teaching in the classroom.

The discussion so far has centered on how frequently words occur, but many words carry more than one meaning sense. How is a teacher to know which meaning of a word should be taught first? If the word appears in a story or in some other contextualized situation, then the context determines the appropriate meaning sense. But if the teacher is involved in vocabulary building that is not tied to any particular context, then a frequency list of meaning senses would be a useful aid. The General Service List (GSL) (West, 1953) is just such a resource. It includes about two thousand of the most useful words in English, and gives information about the relative frequency of their various meaning senses. The entry for *block* looks like this:

BLOCK, n. 184e (1) *(mass)*
　　　　　　　　　　A block of stone, wood *etc.*　　　　　　　　**34%**
　　　　　　　　　(2) *(houses)*
　　　　　　　　　　A block of houses, flats　　　　　　　　**21%**
　　　　　　　　　(3) *(obstacle, stoppage)*
　　　　　　　　　　Stumbling block　　　　　　　　**1%**
　　　　　　　　　[*Various technical uses:* Butcher's block;
　　　　　　　　　picture block; block and tackle, 6%]
block, v.　　　　　　　The road is blocked
　　　　　　　　　　Block up the doorway　　　　　　　**28%**

From this example, a teacher would know that the meaning sense of *mass* occurs the most frequently, and so should probably be taught before the other, less frequent meaning senses. On the other hand, West suggests that the meaning senses in brackets are not worth teaching. The meaning sense of *obstacle* occurs so rarely that the teacher needs to consider whether it is worth teaching. However, the low figure for the *obstacle* meaning sense seemed counterintuitive to me, so I checked with the BNC to see if it confirmed these results. Of a random set of 100 concordance lines, 6% had the meaning sense of *obstacle*. I also found a significant new meaning sense that is not in the GSL entry: a use of *block* in computers, as in "blocking some text in order to cut and paste it in a word processor program." The other meaning senses of *block* indicated in the GSL are still important but produced somewhat different percentage figures. These discrepancies highlight the GSL's major shortcoming: it is based on written corpora compiled before 1936. Happily, a revised version based on modern corpora should be available by the time this book comes out. I would suggest using the GSL as a guide to the teaching order of meaning senses in conjunction with the teacher's own intuitions. You might note that the GSL also gives information on the absolute frequency of the word *block;* in this case, it occurs an estimated (e) 184 times per 5 million words.

Other than frequency, corpus evidence can be used to illustrate the collocations between words. Without a corpus and concordancing program, teachers are left with written references, such as *The BBI Combinatory Dictionary of English* (Benson, Benson, & Ilson, 1986) and the *LTP Dictionary of Selected Collocations* (Hill & Lewis, 1997), as sources of collocation information. These have limited usefulness, as I find they often do not contain the word I am looking for, and the "BBI" mainly illustrates grammatical collocations. They also do not give information about things like collocational prosody. There is probably no substitute for having first-hand access to a corpus and concordancer. Luckily, these are becoming much less expensive. The Oxford *Wordsmith Tools* concordancer (Scott, 1997) is a good case in point. It is inexpensive, will run on virtually any computer, and is relatively easy to use. Programs like this are so user-friendly that they have opened up the possibility of having students use them as part of their study. Ellis (1992) has promoted giving students language data and letting them derive the underlying grammatical rules in an inductive learning approach. The same approach can be used with a focus on lexis. Students can be given key words to learn and can find their meanings and behavior in context by looking at numerous concordance examples. Tribble and Jones (1990, p. 59) give an example of an exercise sheet that can guide students in their investigations of target words, in this case adverbs. Note that most concordancers can sort the words on either side of the keyword in either forward or reverse alphabetical order, and that the following exercise takes advantage of this facility.

Keyword: ┌──────────────────────────────┐ adverb
         └──────────────────────────────┘

Left sort
Are there any words (or word classes) that appear frequently before the key-word? Write any you find in the box below:

┌──┐
│   │
│   │
│   │
└──┘

Right sort
Are there any words (or word classes) that appear frequently after the key-word? Write any you find in the box below:

┌──┐
│   │
│   │
│   │
└──┘

Are there any grammar rules that you think might work for this word? Write them in the box below and then decide how you can test your idea by study-ing further examples.

┌──┐
│   │
│   │
│   │
└──┘

With most words having numerous collocates, the number of possible col-locations for even a limited number of words is colossal. There needs to be some principled way to reduce the total to a more manageable number. Bahns's (1993) suggestion of not teaching collocations that can be trans-ferred from the students' L1 is a good start, but it only works in classes where students share the same native language. Collocation can probably be considered a more advanced type of word knowledge, and so may be best left to higher-level students who are enhancing and consolidating vocabu-lary that has already been partially learned. This is because appropriate col-location is something that can give away better learners as being nonnative speakers, and so is worth the effort for them to work on. Beginners, on the other hand, need to focus on developing larger vocabularies and better grammatical and pragmatic mastery of language.

There is no reason to focus on collocation for idioms and fixed phrases, because the collocation is frozen and therefore not really an issue. The problem with other collocational combinations is that there does not seem to be any principled reason behind many of them, and so they need to be learned individually in a piecemeal fashion. A noticeable exception is when a word or string collocates with members of a lexical set, such as *flag down* a *bus/taxi/tram*. Cowie (1978) suggests using exercises that exploit this kind of item that has collocates clustering in some recognizable group or pattern. For example, students can be made aware that the object of *flag down* is usually a vehicle. Note also how the following exercise not only attempts to make the collocational regularity salient, but also tries to make the learner aware of other, sometimes unusual, possibilities.

i. Look at some of the nouns which can combine with *flag down* (= stop by waving with a flag or the hand):

flag down . . . a car, a bus, a taxi

What do the nouns have in common? All are *powered vehicles, controlled* by a driver, travelling on *roads,* equipped to carry *passengers.* Now say which of the following could equally well combine with *flag down:*

coach, hitch-hiker, tram, swimmer

Say why you accept some words and reject others.

ii. Try to explain why the following nouns, which are rather unusual choices for *flag down,* might still be used:

lorry, steam-roller, water-bus, horse and carriage, elephant

(Cowie, 1978, p. 42)

Although it is very plausible that exercises like this will help students with collocations that have a degree of regularity, it is difficult to imagine how they could work with the large number of combinations that are not as transparent, consistent, or predictable (*play basketball, play chess,* but **play skiing*). The fact is that we have little idea of the best way to teach collocations. The majority of current collocation exercises are variations of a basic matching task, often requiring learners to fill in blanks in grids like the one in Figure 4. This example is complete, but some or all of the markers would be eliminated before giving it to students as an exercise.

The problem with such exercises is that if students do not know the col-

	bike	motorcycle	car	truck	horse	camel
drive a	−	−	+	+	−	−
ride a	+	+	−	−	+	+

Figure 4   Collocational grid for drive a _____ *and* ride a _____ .

locations on grids like this one, they have no option but to guess. This makes these exercises more suitable for consolidation with students who already have partial knowledge of the words than initial teaching for students who do not. If students are learning new words, it might be better to give them completed grids so that they can study the appropriate collocational pairings rather than merely guess blindly. Another problem is that grids comprehensive enough to cover all of the main collocational possibilities may be too large to be learnable. Thus the problem remains: the type of unpredictable collocations that learners are likely to have the most trouble with are precisely those for which there are no obvious teaching approaches. In fact, the key question remains unanswered: should teachers spend time on collocations at all, or should they be content to let collocations be learned implicitly through language exposure?

Summary

Corpora provide a convenient source from which to obtain evidence of the behavior of many different facets of language: lexical, grammatical, and pragmatic. The computer resources required to use this tool are now within the reach of many schools. Corpus evidence has shown that a very limited number of words do the bulk of the work in language. This means that it is absolutely crucial for learners to master these high-frequency words, as they will be required regardless of the topic students wish to deal with. As such, they are worth explicit teaching. On the other hand, the rest of language is made up of words that occur relatively infrequently. It would be impossible to give all of these words explicit attention. Word-frequency lists can inform teachers how frequent words are, which gives a key indication of their importance.

Corpus evidence has also shown that words tend to collocate. Some words have a collocational prosody that derives from a word's collocates having either positive or negative undertones. Collocation is an advanced type of vocabulary knowledge that is difficult to know how to teach, but two pieces of advice seem helpful. Bahns suggests that we limit instruction to nontransferable collocates, and Cowie advises us to teach collocations when they involve a relatively transparent lexical set.

Overall, corpus evidence has yielded considerable insight into the working of lexis. This is true not only of single words, but also of multiword strings that seem to act as a single lexeme. In fact, a major direction in vocabulary studies today is researching these multiword units through corpus evidence to establish their frequency and behavior. This is part of a move from lexis as individual words to be considered in isolation toward viewing them as integral parts of larger discourse. We will expand our perspective of words' behavior in the next chapter and explore the role of vocabulary in context.

Exercises for expansion

1. Look at the following words and consider how frequently they occur in general English. Rank them in order of frequency. Next, compare the frequencies of these words with the benchmark word *disaster.* If a word is more frequent than *disaster,* judge how many times more frequent it is. For example, if you think it is twice as frequent as *disaster,* write 2, if it is 100 times more frequent, write 100. If you think a word is less frequent than *disaster,* write how much less, for example, 1/2 as frequent or 1/100 as frequent. Then look at the frequency figures taken from the CIC and BNC corpora in Appendix C. How accurate were your intuitions? How easy was it to rank the words in order of frequency compared to fixing numerical estimates to each word?

	Rank in order of frequency	Judge frequency in relation to *disaster*
age	_____	_____
and	_____	_____
brainy	_____	_____
complication	_____	_____
device	_____	_____
disaster	_____	___1___
effort	_____	_____
emblem	_____	_____
vanquish	_____	_____
wine	_____	_____

2. If there were discrepancies between your estimates of the word frequencies in Exercise 1 and the corpus figures, it should not be automat-

ically assumed that the corpus figures are more accurate. Is it possible to build a reasonable argument that your intuitions in fact provided a better estimate of the frequency of these words in general English than the corpus figures?

3. Find three texts of approximately the same length: one that you consider quite difficult, one that is relatively easy, and one that is in between. Calculate the token–type ratios for each. Then calculate lexical density figures. (For convenience, you may assume that the first fifty words from the CIC word list in Figure 1 [except *said, one, all,* and *more*] represent the class "grammatical words," although a complete listing would be much longer.) Your judgments of difficulty are likely to be based on a number of factors, including those lexical, grammatical, and pragmatic. Which of the two lexically based measures best fits with your judgments? Is either measure powerful enough to be useful in judging the difficulty of your texts, or might a focus on lexis simply be too narrow to provide a good indication of a text's complexity?

4. Dictionaries are the essential vocabulary reference aid. But the inevitable space constraints limit how much information can be given about each word. This makes decisions about both the dictionary format and what to include for each word critical. Consider the following entries for the word *bank* taken from four major learner dictionaries. Analyze the entries with regard to the concordance that follows them. It contains fifty instances of *bank* from the CIC corpus. How well does each entry capture the information exhibited in the concordance? Are the most frequent meaning senses always listed at the beginning of the entries? Which dictionary format do you like best and why?

bank ORGANIZATION /bæŋk/ *n* [C] an organization where people and businesses can invest or borrow money, change it to foreign money, etc., or a building where these services are offered • *The banks have been accused of exploiting small firms.* • *The bank that Shaun works in is in the town centre.* • *You should keep your savings* **in** *a bank.* • *This bank has branches* (= buildings and offices that form part of it) *all over the country.* • *I had to take out a bank* **loan** *to start my own business.* • *I got an angry letter from my* **bank manager** (= the person in charge of a bank) *the other day.* • A bank of something, such as blood or human organs for medical use, is a place which stores these things for later use: *a blood bank* ○ *a sperm bank* • In GAMBLING, the bank is money that belongs to the owner and can be won by the players. • A **bank account** is an arrangement with a bank where the customer puts in and removes money and the bank keeps a record of it. • Your **bank balance** is the amount of money that you have in the bank. • **Bank charges** are sums of money paid by the customer for the bank to perform various services: *When my statement came I noticed some unexpected bank charges.* • *(Br)* A **bank holiday** is an official holiday when banks and most businesses are closed for a day. • The **bank rate** is the amount of INTEREST that a bank charges, esp. the lowest amount that it is allowed to charge, when it lends money. • A **bank statement** is a printed record of the money put into and removed from a bank account. • LP〉 **Money** Ⓘ Ⓣ

bank *(obj)* /bæŋk/ *v* • *I used to bank* **with** *Lloyd's* (= keep my money there). [I] • *You ought to bank that money* (= put it in a bank) *as soon as possible.* [T]

bank-a-ble /ˈbæŋ.kə.bl̩/ *adj* • *She is currently Hollywood's most bankable actress* (= Her films make large profits).

bank-a-bi-li-ty /ˌbæŋ.kəˈbɪl·ɪ·ti, $-ə.t̬i / *n* [C] • *His bankability* (= ability to make money) *as a pop star decreased as he got older.*

bank-er /ˈbæŋ.kəʳ, $-kɚ/ *n* [C] • *She was a successful banker* (= someone with an important position in a bank) *by the time she was forty.* • The banker in GAMBLING games is the person responsible for looking after the money. • **Banker's card** is another name for a **cheque card.** See at CHEQUE. **Banker's order** is another name for a **standing order.** See at STANDING PERMANENT.

bank-ing /ˈbæŋ.kɪŋ/ *n* [U] *The intricacies of international banking* (= the business of operating a bank) *remained a mystery to him.*

bank RAISED GROUND /bæŋk/ *n* [C] sloping raised land, esp. along the sides of a river, or a pile or mass of earth, clouds, etc. • *By the time we reached the opposite bank, the boat was sinking fast.* • *These flowers generally grow on sloping* **river** *banks and near streams.* • *A dark bank* **of** *cloud loomed on the horizon.* • A bank of buttons or switches on a machine is a large number of them, usually arranged in rows. • ⓘⓣ

bank *(obj)* /bæŋk/ *v* • *The snow had banked* (= formed into a mass) *in the corner of the garden.* [I] • *We banked* **up** *the fire* (= put more coal on it) *to keep it burning all night.* [M]

bank TURN /bæŋk/ *v* [I] (of an aircraft) to fly with one wing higher than the other when turning • *We felt the plane bank steeply as it changed direction.* • ⓘⓣ

(*Cambridge International Dictionary of English,* 1995)

---

bank 1 finance and storage

bank /bæŋk/ **banks, banking, banked**

◆◆◆◆◆

1 A **bank** is an institution where people or businesses can keep their money. *Students should look to see which bank offers them the service that best suits their financial needs... I had £10,000 in the bank.*   N-COUNT

2 A **bank** is a building where a bank offers its services.   N-COUNT

3 If you **bank** money, you pay it into a bank. *Once you have registered your particulars with an agency and it has banked your cheque, the process begins.*   VERB / Vn

4 If you **bank** with a particular bank, you have an account with that bank. *My husband has banked with the Co-op since before the war.*   VERB / V *with* n

5 You use **bank** to refer to a store of something. For example, a blood **bank** is a store of blood that is kept ready for use. *...Britain's National Police Computer, one of the largest data banks in the world.*   N-COUNT: with supp, usu n N

6 If you say that the cost of something will not **break the bank,** you mean that it will not cost a large sum of money. *Prices starting at £6 a bottle won't break the bank.*   PHRASE: V inflects

bank 2 areas and masses

bank /bæŋk/ **banks**

◆◆◇◇◇

1 The **banks** of a river, canal, or lake are the raised areas of ground along its edge. *...30 miles of new developments along both banks of the Thames. ...an old warehouse on the banks of a canal.*   N-COUNT: usu N *of* n =side

2 A **bank** of ground is a raised area of it with a flat top and one or two sloping sides. *...resting indolently upon a grassy bank.*   N-COUNT =knoll

3 A **bank** of something is a long high mass of it. *On their journey south they hit a bank of fog off the north-east coast of Scotland.*   N-COUNT: N *of* n

4 A **bank** of things, especially machines, switches, or dials, is a row of them, or a series of rows. *The typical laborer now sits in front of a bank of dials.*   N-COUNT

5 See also **banked.**

bank 3 other verb uses

bank /bæŋk/ **banks, banking, banked.** When an aircraft **banks,** one of its wings rises higher than the other, usually when it is changing direction. *A single-engine plane took off and banked above the highway in front of him.*   VERB V

(Reproduced from *Collins COBUILD Learner's Dictionary* with the permission of HarperCollins Publishers Ltd. © HarperCollins Publishers Ltd 1996. Updated from the Bank of English. Based on the COBUILD series, developed in collaboration with the University of Birmingham. COBUILD® and Bank of English® are registered trademarks of HarperCollins Publishers Ltd.)

bank¹ /bæŋk/ *n* **1** (a local office of) a business organization which performs services connected with money, esp. keeping money for customers and paying it out on demand, or lending money to customers: *The major banks have announced an increase in interest rates.* | *She works at the bank in the High Street.* | *I think she's a lot more interested in your* **bank balance** (= your money) *than your personality!* **2** a place where something is kept until it is ready for use, esp. products of human origin for medical use: *a kidney bank* | *Hospital blood banks have saved many lives.* **3** (a person who keeps) a supply of money or pieces for payment or use in a game of chance – see also **break the bank** (BREAK¹ (23)) and CLEARING BANK, MERCHANT BANK

bank² *v* **1** [T] to put or keep (money) in a bank **2** [I (**with**)] to keep one's money (in the stated bank); *Who do you bank with?*

  bank on/upon sbdy./sthg. *phr v* [T] to depend on; trust in: *I'm banking only̲ou̲on your help.* [+v-ing] *We mustn't bank on getting their agreement.* [+obj+to-v] *I'm banking on you to help me with the arrangements.* [+obj+v-ing] *We were banking on John knowing the way.*

bank³ *n* **1** land along the side of a river, lake, etc.: *the left bank of the Seine* | *the banks of the River Nile* – see SHORE (USAGE) **2** a pile or RIDGE of earth, mud, snow, etc.: *They sat on a grassy bank at the edge of the field watching the game of cricket.* **3** a mass of clouds, mist, etc.: *The banks of dark cloud promised rain.* **4** a slope made at bends in a road or racetrack, so that they are safer for cars to go round **5** a SANDBANK: *the Dogger Bank in the North Sea*

bank⁴ *v* [I] (of a car or aircraft) to move with one side higher than the other when making a turn

  bank up *phr v* [I;T(=**bank** sthg. ↔ **up**)] to form into a mass or pile: *The wind had banked the snow up against the wall.* | *At night we bank up the fire so that it's still burning in the morning.*

bank⁵ *n* [(**of**)] a set of things arranged in a row, esp. a row of OARS in an ancient boat or of KEYS ON A TYPEWRITER

(*Longman Dictionary of English Language and Culture,* Second Edition. © Addison Wesley Longman Limited 1998, reproduced by permission of Pearson Education Limited)

bank¹ /bæŋk/ *n* **1** the land sloping up along each side of a river or canal; the ground near a river: *Several people were fishing from the river bank.* ∘ *My house is on the south bank (of the river).* ⇒ note at COAST¹. **2** a raised slope at the edge of sth or dividing sth: *low banks of earth between rice-fields* ∘ *flowers growing on the banks on each side of the country lanes.* **3** = SANDBANK. **4** an artificial slope in a road, etc that enables cars to keep going fast round a bend. **5** a mass of cloud, snow, etc., esp one formed by the wind: *The sun disappeared behind a bank of clouds.*

bank² /bæŋk/ *v* (of an aircraft, etc) to travel with one side higher than the other, usu when turning: [V, Vpr] *The plane banked steeply (to the left).* PHRV **bank up** to form into piles, esp because of wind: *The snow has banked up against the shed.* **bank sth up 1** to make sth into piles: *bank the earth up into a mound.* **2** to stop the water in a river, etc from flowing by piling up earth, mud, etc: *bank up a stream.* **3** to pile coal, etc. on a fire so that the fire burns slowly for a long time: *We banked up the fire before going out for a walk.*

bank³ /bæŋk/ *n* **1** an organization or a place that provides a financial service. Customers keep their money in the bank safely and it is paid out when needed by means of cheques, etc: *My salary is paid directly into my bank* (ie the bank where I keep my money). ∘ *the **high street banks*** (ie the major ones, with branches in most town centres) ∘ '*a bank manager* ∘ *a ·bank account* ∘ *a ·bank loan* (ie money borrowed from a bank). **2** a supply of money or counters (COUNTER²) used in certain games for payment, etc. **3** a place where sth is stored ready for use; a supply: *build up a bank of useful address/references/information* ∘ *a ·blood bank* ∘ *a ·data bank.* IDM **break the ·bank** (*Brit*) **1** (in gambling) to win more money than is in the bank³(2). **2** (*infml*) to cost more than one can afford: *Come on! One evening at the theatre won't break the bank.* **laugh all the way to the bank** ⇒ LAUGH.

■ **·bank balance** *n* the amount of money that sb has in their bank account at a particular time: *My bank balance is always low at the end of the month.*

·**bank-book** (also **passbook**) *n* a book containing a record of a customer's bank account.

·**bank card** *n* = CHEQUE CARD.

·**bank draft** *n* (a document used for) the transferring of money from one bank to another.

‚**bank ·holiday** *n* **1** (*Brit*) a day on which banks are officially closed and which is usu a public holiday (eg Easter Monday, Christmas Day, etc): *New Year's Day is always a bank holiday.* ⇒ note at HOLIDAY. **2** (*US*) any day on which banks are closed by law.

·**bank rate** *n* the rate of interest¹(5) in a country, fixed by a central bank or banks.

·**bank statement** *n* a printed record of all the money paid into and out of a customer's bank account within a certain period: *The bank sends me a bank statement every month.*

bank⁴ /bæŋk/ *v* **1** to place money in a bank: [Vn] *bank one's savings/takings.* (**with sb/sth**) to keep one's money at a particular bank: [Vpr] *Who do you bank with?* [V] *Where do you bank?* PHRV ·**bank on sb/sth** to rely on sb/sth: *I'm banking on your help/banking on you to help me.* ∘ *He was banking on the train being on time.*

▶ **banker** *n* **1** a person who owns or manages a bank³(1) **2** a person who looks after the bank³(2) in certain games. ‚**banker's ·order** = STANDING ORDER. **banking** *n* [U] the business activity of banks (BANK³ 1): *choose banking as a career* ∘ *She's in banking.*

bank⁵ /bæŋk/ *n* a row or series of similar objects, eg in a machine: *a bank of lights/switches* ∘ *a bank of cylinders in an engine* ∘ *a bank of oars.*

Fifty-item concordance for *bank* from the CIC corpus

my money's sitting in the	bank	earning lots of lovely interest.
was bordered by a grassed	bank	
Palestinians from the West	Bank	Palestinian sources gave glowing
ent career disruption. The	bank	is also allowing staff time off
to have been carrying out	bank	robberies in the southwest of
uch more difficult to open	bank	accounts and building society acc
ourt. I've got to keep the	bank	manager happy first and foremost,
h port. They still owe the	bank	over 500,000, and ended last year
rticle 2 of the EC Central	Bank	Governor's draft statutes for the
l's occupation of the West	Bank	and Gaza Strip. "I am very happy
at any branch of Barclays	bank	, and credit card donations can be
rs involved in an abortive	bank	robbery. The raiders were filmed
rs of the American Express	Bank	in Athens early today, police sai
ies like Glaxo and NatWest	bank	. The study says the top half of
million may mean less to a	bank	than 100 to an old man or single
so from the east, over the	bank	of the Tigris. "Today is an ideal
of the National Investment	Bank	, emphasised in earlier policy doc
riggers its collapse. Each	bank	has a central "intensive care uni
t remains depressed but if	bank	base rates fall to 12 per cent or
eform. Withdrawing the top	bank	notes overnight caused panic and
itical troubles by cutting	bank	base rates from 14 to 13.5 per ce
cut. The Treasury and the	Bank	of England indicated there was ov
s and could sue a Canadian	bank	for the return of a valuable stat
iva, presently in a London	bank	after being seized by police in
e found at Blackfriars and	Bank	tube stations.
City the three-month inter-	bank	rate fell to a fraction over 13
itish company crashes. The	bank	expects to lose 703 million of la
o have stabilised. But the	bank	was seeing more personal bankrupt
and the future of the West	Bank	and Gaza Strip. It gives his coal
y refuse her permission to	bank	them. The tape usually ends up at
ther from husband or sperm	bank	, is the simplest form of assisted
corridor linking the West	Bank	and Gaza. Second, there might be
concerts at London's South	Bank	Centre in August, entitled Mozart
f nothing but a huge earth	bank	," says Anne Moralee. "We won't se
e bodyguards and a wad of	bank	notes, had driven to their positi
signal a half point cut in	bank	base rates to 12.5 per cent. The
investment ate into firms'	bank	accounts, this was the third cons
ongly critical. Dr William	Bank	, of the University of Pennsylvani
een found washed up on a	bank	of the Thames near Tower Bridge,
is, they agreed to provide	bank	guarantees of around 10 million
t Friday. He has asked the	bank	for more details, including an a
d only be able to restrict	bank	mortgages. Any meaningful steps w
s from the Governor of the	Bank	of England for curbs on mortgage

f the French-owned Paribas	bank	in Luxembourg. In 1984 he returne
an, aged 24, from the West	Bank	town of Bethlehem, was the
ended to the setting up of	bank	accounts for the British forces
te Jerusalem from the West	Bank	. But there was a rare openness an
already released. A World	Bank	official has warned that there is
lion residents of the West	Bank	and Gaza Strip have not been issu
ommitment to guarantee all	bank	deposits up to $100,000, but has

Further reading

For more on corpora: Sinclair (1991), Crowdy (1993), Barnbrook (1996), McEnery and Wilson (1996), McCarthy (1998), and http://info.ox.ac.uk/bnc/corpora.html.

For access to corpora: COBUILD http://www.cobuild.collins.co.uk/, BNC http://info.ox.ac.uk/bnc, and Aston and Burnard (1998).

For published word counts: Thorndike and Lorge (1944), West (1953), Kucera and Francis (1967), and Johansson and Hofland (1989).

For more information on frequency intuitions: Shapiro (1969) and Schmitt and Dunham (1999).

For a fuller treatment of collocation: Benson (1985), Sinclair (1991), and Howarth (1998).

For more on dictionaries: Summers (1988), Landau (1989), Scholfield (1997), and Carter (1998).

6 *Vocabulary in discourse*

- Vocabulary is made up of more than just single words. What about these multiword units?
- The traditional view is that vocabulary just fits into the slots in a syntactic construction. But how do words really connect with the larger discourse?
- Vocabulary obviously carries meaning, but what can it add to the cohesion and style of a text?

In the previous chapters, we looked at lexemes as individual words in order to explore the kinds of knowledge it is necessary to know about vocabulary. But stopping at this level of discussion would be misleading because words exist and are used in the environment of context. As such they have connections far beyond the place where they reside in that context. This chapter will explore the relationship of lexis to discourse by discussing how vocabulary operates beyond the level of single words. I will first discuss how English lexemes are often made up of multiple orthographic words. These multiple word units make up a good percentage of English, and are attracting increasing attention. The next topic, lexical patterning, is just beginning to be explored, but will probably become a key linguistic notion in the future. Corpus evidence is beginning to show how choosing one word in discourse often affects the lexical choices for the surrounding text. We are finding a surprising amount of lexical patterning, and we may have to start thinking of vocabulary more in terms of lexical clusters than individual words. Finally, vocabulary is manipulated in various ways by skilled writers and speakers to construct smooth and coherent discourse and to create various emotive effects. We shall look at some ways that this is done.

Multiword units in English

In his "idiom principle," Sinclair (1991) states that words tend to cluster together in systematic ways. We have already seen this in the collocational patterning of words. But sometimes the patterning becomes so regular that the resulting cluster seems to be more than simply words with collocational ties. Rather, the words take on aspects of a single entity, that is, a string of words acts as a single lexeme with a single meaning. When this happens, those lexemes are called *multiword units* (*MWUs*). There are a great variety of MWUs, and to give some flavor of this, Carter (1998, p. 66) presents the following list:

as a matter of fact	to smell a rat
as old as the hills	honesty is the best policy
spick and span	for good
if I were you	bottoms up
a watched pot never boils	a good time was had by all
light-years ago	how do you do?
as far as I know	no way
you can say that again	in no uncertain terms
a stitch in time saves nine	I thought you'd never ask
by and large	like it or lump it
down with the Social Democrats	
further to my letter of the _____th	

The definition of a "string of words with a single meaning" seems to describe the group as a whole, but there are clearly huge differences between different MWUs. Moon (1997) suggests that three criteria come into play when defining multiword units more precisely: *institutionalization, fixedness,* and *noncompositionality.* A MWU must be conventionalized in a speech community, that is, everyone must recognize it as a unit that regularly reoccurs in language and does so with the same meaning. To the extent that language speakers use a MWU in a similar and consistent way, it is institutionalized.

A MWU is also fixed to various degrees. Idioms tend to be among the most fixed of MWUs; as we saw in the last chapter, *kick the bucket* would lose its meaning if any component were changed – for example, *punt the bucket.* The same thing happens if the idiom is modified with an adjective or a plural grammatical marker (*kick the big bucket, kick the buckets*). But it is interesting to note that in another way this idiom is not absolutely fixed: one of the components is used to create an equally colloquial derivative for dying – *kick off.* If an idiom is institutionalized, people know its basic form well, which allows imaginative speakers to "play" with it and create interesting variations. So it is better to think of idioms as having a relatively great degree of fixedness rather than being absolutely frozen. Other types of MWUs have more variation, but all must be fixed to some extent, or else they would just be a string of words held together by the rules of syntax.

Finally, MWUs differ in the degree in which their meaning can be derived from a word-by-word analysis. Some MWUs are relatively transparent (*running on all cylinders* as a description of a smoothly operating machine or operation), whereas idioms are totally opaque. If we look at the three individual words in the idiom *kick/the/bucket,* it is impossible to derive the idiomatic meaning of dying; this is noncompositionality.

These are useful criteria, but, as we have seen, they must be considered clines along which MWUs vary. The variation is particularly noticeable along the fixedness continuum. In fact, Moon (1997) suggests that there is so much variation along this continuum that we should think in terms of "preference of form" or "preferred lexical realization" rather than "fixedness of form." She looked at expressions in an eighteen-million-word corpus, and found that 40% of the items she studied regularly varied in the form they took (Moon, 1998). Some examples of this variability follow.

British/American variations:
    not touch someone/something with a bargepole (British)
    not touch someone/something with a ten-foot pole (American)
    hold the fort (British)
    hold down the fort (American)

varying lexical component:
    burn your boats/bridges
    throw in the towel/sponge

unstable verbs:
    show/declare/reveal your true colors
    cost/pay/spend/charge an arm and a leg

truncation:
    silver lining/every cloud has a silver lining
    last straw/it's the last straw that breaks the camel's back

transformation:
    break the ice/ice-breaker/ice-breaking
    blaze a trail/trail-blazer/trail-blazing

(Moon, 1997, p. 53)

In some cases, Moon found little fixedness at all. There only seemed to be some semantic core idea upon which expressions could be built with varying realizations. In the following example, that semantic core is the idea of "dirty laundry" signifying unsavory secrets.

wash your dirty linen/laundry in public (mainly British English)
air your dirty laundry/linen in public (mainly American English)
do your dirty washing in public (British English)
wash/air your dirty linen/laundry
wash/air your linen/laundry in public
dirty washing/linen/laundry

(Ibid.)

Types of multiword unit

Several people have categorized MWUs, including Alexander (1984), Nattinger and DeCarrico (1992), and Moon (1998). Some of the more common categories include compound words, phrasal verbs, fixed phrases, idioms, proverbs, and lexical phrases. Let us now look briefly at each.

The first category of MWU is *compound words.* Compounds are created when two or more words are combined to make a single lexeme. This lexeme can be written as multiple orthographic words, hyphenated words, or as a single orthographic word. In many cases, there is no standardized spelling, with the result that the written representation can vary from person to person, or from time to time. For example, *freeze dry* can be rendered as *freeze dry, freeze-dry,* or *freezedry.* Compounding is an important method of new word formation, which has led to the existence of a large group of compounds in the English language. Some examples from McCarthy (1990, p. 101) include *blackmail, Walkman, drop by,* and *off-day.*

Phrasal verbs are another very common category of MWU in English. In fact, they are so frequent that many publishers have dictionaries/workbooks focusing on this type of item alone, for example, the *Cambridge International Dictionary of Phrasal Verbs* (1997) and the *Phrasal Verb Organizer* (Flower, 1993). Phrasal verbs are usually made up of a monosyllabic verb (e.g., *go, come, take, put, get*) and an adverbial or prepositional particle (e.g., *up, out, off, in, on, down*) (Moon, 1997). Sometimes phrasal verbs can be readily understood from their components (*give away*), but quite often their meaning is uninterpretable (*give up* [quit doing something]). This idiomaticity makes phrasal verbs a particular problem for learners, with learners often relying on single-word equivalents (*confuse*) even though a native speaker might use a phrasal verb in its place (*mix up*) (Dagut & Laufer, 1985).

Fixed phrases may not be particularly difficult to figure out, but their sequencing is frozen. With *binomials,* two key words conventionally occur in only one order: *to and fro, back and forth,* and *ladies and gentlemen.* *Trinomials* are similar, but consist of three major components: *ready, willing, and able; morning, noon, and night,* and *hook, line, and sinker* (McCarthy, 1990). Semantically, there would be nothing wrong with changing the order of these fixed phrases – for example, saying *gentlemen and ladies* – but this would sound very awkward because these expressions have been institutionalized and any deviation would not be expected. Note, however, that different languages may well use similar phrases, but with a different order. An example of this is the German equivalent of *back and forth,* which is *hin und her* (forth and back) (Carter & McCarthy, 1988, p. 25).

Idioms have been one of the more discussed types of MWU, probably because of their "puzzle" aspect of noncompositionality. McCarthy (1990, pp. 6–11) suggests that all languages have idioms and that, in English, certain words are more likely to be "idiom-prone" than others, such as *bite:*

to bite the dust	[to die]
to bite the bullet	[to become very serious about something, even if painful]
to bite off more than you can chew	[to attempt something you are incapable of]
bitten by the love bug	[fallen in love]

In addition, certain kinds of genres seem to have a strong preference for idioms, such as journalism and informal conversation (Moon, 1997). We can see this heavy use of idiom in the following horoscope taken from a daily tabloid:

Whatever slight resentments you may harbour against those who are pulling the purse strings, you are managing to smile. You have a plan up your sleeve which with a little subtle footwork will bring you more control and probably quite a few compliments. Friends are on hand if you need support. (*The Express,* January 12, 1999)

Using idioms correctly is one of the things that sets apart fluent speakers of a language, and, realizing this, students are often keen to learn them. As with phrasal verbs, there are a number of dictionaries/workbooks dedicated to idioms, for example, the *Oxford Learner's Dictionary of English Idioms* (Warren, 1994) and the *Collins COBUILD Dictionary of Idioms* (1995).

Proverbs differ from idioms in that they display shared cultural wisdom. Thus proverbs are usually tied to common situations in a culture. In Japan, conformity is highly prized, and so a proverb such as "The nail that sticks up is hammered down" makes perfect sense when speaking of an individual made to adapt to society. In Western culture, the meaning is not immediately apparent, because different values are held. But many situations are universal, and in these cases, proverbs often have equivalents across languages:

English:	*Out of sight, out of mind.*
Arabic:	*Il-ba 'iid 'an il-'een ba 'iid 'an il-'alb.*
Japanese:	*Saru mono wa hibi ni utoshi.*
Italian:	*Lontano dagli occhi, lontano dal cuore.*

(Hatch & Brown, 1995, p. 203)

Lexical phrases/lexical chunks

The last category comes not from an attempt to describe the linguistic classification of MWUs but from the perspective of analyzing language production. We now know that native speakers tend to use a great deal of language that is formulaic in nature. These formulaic expressions are so common that they become memorized. They then act as prefabricated language units that can be used as wholes, rather than being composed through vocabulary + syntax. These prefabricated units go by several names – *holophrases* (Corder, 1973), *prefabricated routines* (Bolinger, 1976), *routine formulae* (Coulmas, 1979), *gambits* (Keller, 1979), *conventionalized language forms* (Yorio, 1980), and *lexical chunks* (Lewis, 1993) – but I will refer to them as *lexical phrases* (Nattinger & DeCarrico, 1992). These phrases can be made up of MWUs from the categories above (phrasal verbs, fixed phrases, etc.), or they can be composed of any string of words that are commonly used together. Lexical phrases are likely to have an increasingly prominent role in the discussion of vocabulary, so let us look at them in more detail.

It is believed that lexical phrases comprise a considerable part of a person's total vocabulary. Pawley and Syder (1983) state that a mature English speaker will probably know many thousands of these phrases. This is not insignificant given Goulden, Nation, and Read's (1990) estimate that an average native-speaking university graduate has a vocabulary of around twenty thousand word families. One reason lexical phrases are so common is that they are typically related to functional language use. For example, *to make a long story short* is often used in summarizing, and *Have you heard the one about . . .?* is reserved for beginning a joke or humorous story. Such lexical phrases are institutionalized as the most efficient and most familiar linguistic means to carry out language functions. As such, they facilitate clear, relevant, and concise language use. Because of their functional usage, knowledge of lexical phrases is essential for pragmatic competence.

There is a good psycholinguistic basis for believing that the mind stores and processes lexical phrases as individual wholes. (To keep this psycholinguistic perspective separate from the descriptive one, I shall call lexical phrases as they exist in the mind *lexical chunks*.) The main reason stems from the structure of the mind itself (Pawley & Syder, 1983). It can store vast amounts of knowledge in long-term memory, but it is able to process only small amounts of it in real time, as when one is speaking. In effect, the mind makes use of a relatively abundant resource (long-term memory) to compensate for a relative lack in another (processing capacity) by storing a number of frequently needed lexical chunks as individual whole units.

These can be easily retrieved and used without the need to compose them on-line through word selection and grammatical sequencing. This means that there is less demand on cognitive capacity because the lexical chunks are "ready to go" and require little or no additional processing.

Some lexical chunks have "slots" that can take different words according to the situation, providing a scaffold for quick, but flexible, language use. For example, "_____ [person] *thinks nothing of* _____ *ing* [verb]" can provide the preformulated platform for many different realizations, such as *Jon thinks nothing of playing guitar for hours on end* or *She thinks nothing of jogging eight miles a day.* The ability to use preformed lexical chunks allows greater fluency in speech production. The use of lexical chunks can aid the listener as well. Because lexical chunks can be recognized as individual wholes, this spares the listener some of the processing effort required to interpret an utterance word by word.

Lexical patterning in discourse

The discussion of lexical phrases has taken us some way toward the idea of words acting in unison and affecting one another in stretches of discourse. So far, the MWUs discussed have had some identifiable factor that serves to tie the words together in a unit, either a single meaning (e.g., idioms) or because an expression is commonly used to express a function (e.g., lexical phrases). However, one of the latest insights to come out of corpus research is that lexical patterning extends beyond these identifiable units, and probably affects the use of most words in discourse.

John Sinclair (1996, 1998) is the father of research into this wider lexical patterning. Through his access to the COBUILD corpus, he has found that choosing a particular word guides and constrains the lexical choices several words away from the initial one. To illustrate his insights into the patterning of language, let us consider the word *sorry*. By itself, it occurs in a variety of contexts and patterns, such as the following:

We are	**sorry**	there was no index to help in the search for these.
acknowledges that GE has put up a	**sorry**	performance in having only four women among its
I am	**sorry**	to say I have such a headache at this very moment
Some of them were a	**sorry**	sight!

Looking at concordance lines for *sorry,* we find that one of its collocates is *so,* creating the sequence *so sorry.* When we examine concordance lines for *so sorry,* however, we find that the patterning is much more restricted.

Oh, I'm	**so sorry**.	
id shrugging on my jacket, 'I'm ever	**so sorry**.	
	So Sorry.	
We are	**so sorry**!	
I was ever	**so sorry**.	
	"So sorry."	
Oh, ducks, I'm	**so sorry**."	
"I'm	**so sorry**	," Anna said into the receiver, 'Mr Bouverie is out
them on for Mary Lou because I'm	**so sorry**	anyone should play at such a dirty trick.
'I'm	**so sorry**	," Eline said, the enormity of the tragedy sweeping
'I'm ever	**so sorry**	, but I've forgotten your name."
It is I who am	**so sorry**	for disturbing you.
I've always felt	**so sorry**	for her."
I felt	**so sorry**	for him.
said, he talked about his boys and I felt	**so sorry**	for him.
'A little jealousy will stop him feeling	**so sorry**	for himself!"
I do not often feel	**so sorry**	for myself, I assure you.
I feel	**so sorry**	for that dead boy's family.
We felt	**so sorry**	for you at the shareholders' meeting.
I'm ever	**so sorry**	for you both but of course I'm ever so relieved.
'Gosh, I'm	**so sorry**	I'm late, I've had a terrible journey and on top of
'I am	**so sorry**	if I've offended you."
'I'm	**so sorry**	, Josh, this is all my fault."
"I'm	**so sorry**	, so very sorry.
At that the king's son was	**so sorry**	that he nearly died himself.
'I'm really ever	**so sorry**	to do this to you," apologized Mildred humbly
'I'm	**so sorry**	to have kept you, but we had a little emergency!"
I'm	**so sorry**	to have troubled you.
'I was	**so sorry**	when you had it cut.
He thought: You're going to be	**so sorry**	you ever said that, you ridiculous fop, you silly

This concordance is indicative of the behavior of *so sorry,* which occurs in two main patterns: *so sorry for* and *so sorry to.* If we look slightly further afield with *so sorry to,* we find that it is almost always followed by some form of inconvenience that the speaker regrets having caused (e.g., having been late, troubling someone). *So sorry for* is usually followed by a reference to people (e.g., dead boy's family, her), although occasionally other animate things are referred to, such as an *injured horse.* Also, it normally clusters with some form of the verb *feel.* In the cases where these two patterns do not apply, we still find a great deal of regularity in the sense that there is usually some inconvenience caused, or some unfortunate situation in place that is regretted. In almost all cases, the subject is a person, with the first-person singular *I* being by far the most common. Thus, *so sorry* is the core of an expression that essentially means "expressing regret about something." This is unsurprising, but what *is* fascinating is the strength of patterning in the realization of this concept. Below are the basic forms:

PERSON(S) (be) *so sorry* UNFORTUNATE SITUATION EXISTS
PERSON(S) (be) *so sorry to* CAUSE INCONVENIENCE
PERSON(S) (feel) *so sorry for* PERSON(S)

Therefore, there are four key elements pertaining to the use of *so sorry.* The first is mandatory and is a "sense of regret" (R). The rest are optional and include the person(s) expressing regret (P), the undesirable situation (S), and the inconvenience caused (I). Here are some examples of how they can be combined:

R   So sorry.
RS   So sorry things didn't work out for you.
PR   Oh, I'm so sorry.
PRS I'm so sorry anyone should play at such a dirty trick.
RI   So sorry to have to ask you these personal questions.
PRI "I'm really ever so sorry to do this to you," apologized Mildred
     humbly.

If we are empathizing with someone, then the form *feel so sorry for* is used and three elements are mandatory: person(s) empathizing (P), sense of empathy (E), and the person(s) being empathized with (P2).

PEP2 I feel so sorry for that dead boy's family.
PEP2 We felt so sorry for you at the shareholders' meeting.

From this perspective, we see that words are not chosen in isolation, but have ramifications some distance from their actual placement. Sinclair believes that if you pick a target word and a collocate of that word, you will almost inevitably find another word in the pattern. This suggests that language is not constructed word by word, but key word by key word, each with its own patterns. Whereas the usual approach to language is paradigmatic and meaning-based, this approach highlights the importance of syntagmatic systematicity.

If we step back to get an overview, we find that this kind of thinking forces a totally different perspective of the makeup of language. The old view relied on the traditional categories of grammar and semantics to form creative language, with fixed expressions being placed in a peripheral category on the side.

Old view

Grammar and Semantics	Fixed expressions

Sinclair's view is radically different. He sees structures like those in the *so sorry* example making up the bulk of language. Although syntagmatically structured, these organized strings allow enough variation to fit the many contextual situations we might need them in, thus his term *variable expressions*. Grammar and semantics can still be used to compose totally creative language, but Sinclair believes this is likely to comprise only a small percentage of language overall. Likewise, the number of fixed expressions that are totally frozen is also likely to be limited. Thus, variable expressions are the major category in this perspective of language.

Sinclair's view

Grammar and Semantics	Variable expressions	Fixed expressions

Cohesive and stylistic effects of vocabulary in discourse

Cohesive effects

Sinclair's view is perhaps the most complete realization of lexicogrammar to date. However, the idea that the systematicity of language includes a lexical element is not new. Halliday and Hasan (1976) incorporated a similar notion in their explanation of how language coheres together, arguing that a considerable part of text cohesion comes from lexis. In this section we will consider how vocabulary patterning across the wider discourse aids in holding that discourse together.

Lexical cohesion stems to a large degree from the way lexis is varied in discourse. When speaking about a topic, we need to refer to the same things again and again. We could use the same word each time (*exact repetition*), but it is considered inelegant to do so. Notice how this makes the following text sound stilted.

A: I really like *fast cars.*
B: Yes, I'd like to buy a *fast car* myself. But *fast cars* are too <u>expensive</u>.
A: You have a good job. Wouldn't the bank lend you money to buy a *fast car?*
B: Maybe. But don't forget the maintenance on *fast cars* is also <u>expensive</u>.

Although some exact repetition is normal, people naturally try to vary their vocabulary to avoid sounding like an inarticulate machine. One way of doing this is by using *proforms* (forms that can substitute for other elements in language, such as pronouns). These grammatical words can replace the words that we do not want to repeat exactly. See how their use makes the text sound more natural.

A: I really like *fast cars.*
B: Yes, I'd like to buy *one* myself. But *they* are too <u>expensive</u>.
A: You have a good job. Wouldn't the bank lend you money to buy *one?*
B: Maybe. But don't forget the maintenance on *them* is also <u>expensive</u>.

This sounds better, but we still have the awkward repetition of *expensive,* and the fact that proforms do not help if we want to talk about a specific brand of car. Halliday and Hasan (1976) found that language users also introduce variation by substituting one content word for other, often by using superordinate or nearly synonymous terms. Introducing this *relexicalization* further improves the naturalness of the text.

A: I really like *fast cars.*
B: Yes, I'd like to buy a *BMW* myself. But *they* are too <u>expensive</u>.
A: You have a good job. Wouldn't the bank lend you money to buy *one?*
B: Maybe. But don't forget the maintenance on *Beamers* is also <u>costly</u>.

This "elegant variation" improves the style of a text, but an additional effect of these connections between words is to tie discourse together. If we highlight each of these connections, it is soon apparent that lexical cohesion is really a spiderweb of grammatical and semantic relationships between a large number of words in the text. To illustrate this, let us plot the connections in the following short extract of conversation.

A group of people are talking about the ferry crossing on their recent holiday:

A: but it was ⟨lovely⟩ our one with the (nightclub) and we had, we

had a [super cabin] which was just (below) the (nightclub),

utterly [soundproof] you know, when you think of what houses are

like, when we shut our [cabin] door you wouldn't know there

was anything outside and yet there was a (nightclub) pounding

music away, just one immediately (overhead) and we were

the [cabin] next to it and you [couldn't hear] at all

C: good heavens

B: that's ⟨good⟩, very ⟨good⟩

A: and it's, of course we could say to the children we'll just be

(upstairs) and they knew they just had to put their dressing

gown on and come (up) if they wanted us and that was ⟨super⟩

C: were you, did you have a car with you?

(Crystal & Davy, 1975, p. 52)

We can see from this extract that there are numerous threads of lexis running through the conversation. They focus on the cabin (light squares), the noise (dark squares), the nightclub (light circles), location (dark circles), and an evaluation of the situation (diamonds). McCarthy (1990) calls these threads *lexical chains,* and suggests that they are one mechanism that enables people maintain a topic during conversation. For example, these chains maintain the topic until C's last turn, during which they are broken and a new topic, cars, is introduced. Lexical chains can go dormant and then be picked up again after a considerable break. In this conversation, the word *children* in A's last turn is taken up much later ("I mean it's probably worth it with *kids*"). So the way vocabulary is used not only allows the avoidance of repetition and establishment of lexical cohesion; it also facilitates the maintenance and manipulation of meaning flow, in the form of topic control.

Stylistic effects

In addition to its cohesive function, vocabulary can be manipulated to cause a stylistic effect. One way writers do this is by exploiting *lexical ambiguity*. This occurs when there is more than one possible meaning for a word or phrase. For example, newspaper writers often use lexical ambiguity to create engaging headlines.

THREE BATTERED IN FISH SHOP
EIGHTH ARMY PUSH BOTTLES UP GERMANS
MOUNTING PROBLEMS FOR YOUNG COUPLES
FIELD MARSHALL FLIES BACK TO FRONT

(Carter, Goddard, Reah, Sanger, & Bowring, 1997, p. 80)

The multiple possible meanings grab attention and create interest, which is the essential purpose of a headline. For example, the first headline could mean either that the three people were physically assaulted in a restaurant or that they were dipped in the flour-and-water mixture that fish are cooked in. The other headlines play on the fact that some words can be used as more than a single word class (e.g., *push* is intended as a noun here, but could be read as a verb). Once customers have been amused by the ambiguity, they are more likely to buy the newspaper and read the story. This same principle is used in the names of shops and businesses. The names below play on phrases having more than one possible meaning.

A PIECE OF CAKE	*Wedding cakes*
COOL FOR CARS	*Air conditioning*
CUTS BOTH WAYS	*Unisex hairdressers*
HEADLINES	*Wig and toupees*
NEW WAVE	*Television and satellite antennas*
SOUNDS ELECTRIC	*Musical instruments*
TAKE ONE	*Video rental*

All of these business names are identifiable with the particular service offered, but they also have secondary meanings that potentially make the business more attractive or memorable. For instance, *a piece of cake* has a literal meaning of a physical section of cake, but it is also an idiom meaning "something very easy to do."

Another way to affect the style or tone of discourse is to use words with strong connotations. Grammatical words, very high-frequency words, and technical words (*the, a, it; building, show, vehicle; phoneme, transmission, orbit*) normally do not carry much connotative loading, but many words do. Some have very negative connotations for most people (*torture, bankruptcy, starve, slum*), while others have positive ones (*treasure, freedom, joy, sunshine*). Use of loaded words can have a dramatic impact on the tone of a text. Compare the two passages below, which both report on alleged European Union corruption. The first is from a respected newspaper and gives the story a fairly neutral treatment. The second is from a more sensational tabloid, which uses a large number of negatively loaded words (e.g., *outcry, fiddles, scams, hoodwink*) to create an overwhelmingly critical tone.

The crisis began last July, when the French press began publishing stories about her [Edith Cresson's] dentist being hired by the commission to assess Europe's programmes to prevent the spread of Aids. The same man, René Berthelot, had also been hired by the Perry-Lux group of companies, now the subject of police enquiries, which was until last year the biggest single recipient of commission contracts. . . . Belgian MEP Nellies Maes filed a lawsuit in the Belgian courts last week alleging serious irregularities in the Leonardo education programme, for which Mme Cresson is responsible. (*Guardian*, January 12, 1999)

The crisis rocking the EU to its foundations has been sparked by massive fraud and corruption. It is estimated that it costs European taxpayers, including us, £3 Billion a year. The latest outcry came when an official investigating EU corruption was sacked after claiming more than £500 million was creamed off in backdoor deals with Mafia gangs. Dutchman Paul van Buitenen said that since he spoke out he has been sent death threats. His allegations are the latest in a long line of fiddles and sleaze sensations that have rocked the EU. Here Paul Gilfeather highlights ten of the most amazing scams to hoodwink bungling Euro bosses. (*Sun*, January 12, 1999)

We all write and speak in different ways depending on our purposes and who the intended audience is. One register parameter that we routinely manipulate is level of formality. Of course, the more intimate and relaxed we are with our interlocutors, the more informal our language, and vice versa. One way we can vary the level of formality is with the words we choose to use. We found in the section on register in Chapter 3 that more frequent words are generally more colloquial, whereas less frequent words are generally more formal. This also has a historical dimension. Although most of the words in the English language have been borrowed from other languages, there does seem to be a difference in usage between Old English and Greco-Latin vocabulary. Words that modern English has retained from Old English are often monosyllabic and tend to have a relaxed, informal feel, whereas loanwords borrowed from Latin and Greek give discourse a more formal or academic tone. To see how this can affect the nature of a discourse, read the following extracts from two speeches. A high proportion of the content words in the first one are loanwords (underlined), whereas the second uses more forms from Old English (italicized).

We're <u>approaching</u> the end of a bloody <u>century</u>, <u>plagued</u> by a <u>terrible invention</u> – <u>totalitarianism</u>. <u>Optimism</u> comes less <u>easily</u> today, not because <u>democracy</u> is less <u>vigorous</u>, but because <u>democracy's enemies</u> have <u>refined</u> their <u>instruments</u> of <u>repression</u>. Yet <u>optimism</u> is in order because day by day, <u>democracy</u> is <u>proving</u> itself to be not at all a <u>fragile flower</u>.

I have a *dream* that *one day* on the *red hills* of Georgia the *sons* of *former* slaves and the *sons* of *former* slave *owners* will be able to *sit down together* at the *table* of *brotherhood* . . . I have a *dream* that my *four little children* will *one day live* in a nation where they will not be judged by the color of their *skin* . . .

(Adapted from Carter et al., 1997, p. 113)

Everyone is aware that vocabulary carries the meaning of language, but this section has suggested some of the other "work" vocabulary does, namely, supporting cohesion and affecting the tone of a discourse. As with other aspects of lexis, it seems that the more we look at its behavior in detail, the more we find that it is the dominant element of language.

Applications to teaching

This chapter has suggested that vocabulary operates in discourse in complex and interesting ways. In pedagogical terms, this can cause difficulties for learners, but it also offers creative teachers the substance for intriguing teaching tasks.

Phrasal verbs have long been recognized as a particular problem for students, but they are so arbitrary that no one has yet been able to offer a truly satisfactory way of teaching them. Gairns and Redman (1986) give the sensible advice to treat them as regular items, and teach them if their frequency and utility make it worthwhile. They believe that it is possible to group some phrasal verbs to good effect for teaching purposes if the adverbial particle has a consistent influence on the root verb (e.g., those with – *off*, such as to *break off* [become detached], to *take off* [be removed], to *turn off* [be disconnected], etc.). But for most phrasal verbs, there is not enough consistency for grouping to help students, and presenting several unrelated phrasal verbs together may even cause confusion.

The existence of multiword units such as phrasal verbs and idioms was always apparent to language professionals, and so were incorporated (with varying degrees of success) into traditional descriptive systems. The consequence of this was that these MWUs have been addressed in language teaching materials. However, the more expansive lexical patterning was largely invisible to traditional approaches to vocabulary, and only became discernible through the window of corpus evidence. We are just on the threshold of exploring Sinclair's vision of variable expressions, and although this notion is likely to be important, it is probably too soon to derive pedagogical implications.

On the other hand, we have been aware of lexical phrases for long enough to consider their importance and implications. The description of lexical chunking indicates that there are processing advantages to using chunks, and the ability to rely on them is one factor that allows native speakers to be fluent. However, this does not downplay the importance of grammar in language use or in language teaching. Rather, the point is that language ability requires not only the ability to produce language through syntactic generation (via grammatical competence), but also the ability to use lexical chunks. This is especially true if learners hope to gain the pragmatic fluency that comes from knowing the right lexical phrase for the right functional situation. Ultimately, language learners need both abilities to use language well.

This importance suggests that we need to include instruction on lexical phrases in our language teaching. Nattinger and DeCarrico (1992, p. 121) argue that knowledge of lexical phrases is important for communicative competence because these phrases "provide the patterns and themes that interlace throughout its [conversation's] wandering course." They believe that existing material dealing with interactional aspects of language learning can be used to focus on lexical phrases, without creating a whole new program. In an example exercise taken from Keller (1979), one student uses lexical phrases to interrupt his partner (*excuse me for interrupting, I might add here, may I ask a question?*), while the partner answers and then tries to get back on topic as quickly as possible with lexical phrases such as *to return to* and *where was I going?*

Nattinger and DeCarrico also suggest using *exchange structures* (sequences of utterances that relate to each other in expected ways) to illustrate appropriate language for particular contexts. The first examples would be typical of conversations between friends (1), and the second between acquaintances or strangers (2).

Exchange structure: closing–parting
1. (It's been) nice talking to you. – (Well), so long (for now).
2. It's been nice talking to you, but I must be going. – Goodbye.

asserting–accepting
1. Word has it that X. – No kidding.
2. It seems (to me) that X. – I see.

Lewis (1993, 1997) presents an approach to incorporating lexical phrases into language teaching, advocating a focus on inducing lexical patterns from language input and favoring exercises that concentrate on larger lexical phrases rather than individual words. His proposals are beginning to generate interest, but it must be said that at this point neither his nor Nattinger and DeCarrico's pedagogical ideas have been empirically tested for effectiveness in the classroom.

One implication of lexical chunking is multiple storage in the mental lexicon. A large number of lexical chunks are likely to be fully analyzed, even though they are retained in longer-term memory because of their utility. Thus, it is possible that the production of a frequent sequence of words can stem from the retrieval of a lexical chunk, or from the syntactic generation of the string from individual words. (Of course, it is likely that the lexical chunk approach will be used when possible because of the lower cognitive load.) This means that if a learner produces a sequence of words that contains an error, the source of the error might be a weakness in lexical or grammatical construction, or it might be that a lexical chunk has been acquired in a faulty manner. If the language error is the result of a faulty lexical chunk, then any amount of grammar-based correction would seem unlikely to remedy the error. What would be required is a relearning of the correct form of the lexical chunk. Thus, different psycholinguistic sources of language may require different types of corrective feedback.

If Sinclair is right, then it is less than optimum to teach single words or even single collocations. The best way to demonstrate the way language actually works would be to draw students' attention to the variable expressions, or at least to teach lexical items in a broader context. This implies two possibilities. The first is that language teachers would need to make extensive use of concordance data in their classrooms, because it is only with numerous examples available that variable expressions can be discerned. The teachers could use deductive techniques in which the variable expressions were pointed out, but the concordancing data would also be ideal for inductive learning approaches. The second possibility is that publishers will incorporate this perspective into their future textbooks, using their research connections and computing power first to identify the most important variable expressions, and then to present them in a systematic way. Two well-known authors, Dave and Jane Willis, are pursuing just such a course. But even if one or both possibilities are taken up, it will probably take considerable time for this research insight to filter down into mainstream teaching methodology.

When teaching learners about the organization of language, it is probably useful to introduce them to the idea of lexical cohesion. This approach is already standard practice in Discourse Analysis, and exercises from this discipline would be very useful to get students thinking about vocabulary not as discrete words, but as interrelated members of a cohesive discourse.

Summary

Vocabulary is more than just individual words working separately in a discourse environment. Rather, once words are placed in discourse, they establish numerous links beyond the single orthographic word level. A relatively local form of link is when several orthographic words from a single lexeme. These multiword units come in a variety of guises, and can be classified into several different categories. Sometimes the multiword unit is an expression used to achieve a functional purpose in language. Such lexical phrases are so useful that the mind often stores them as a single unit of information (lexical chunk) in order to speed up the processing and use of language.

A more global form of link between words is the lexical patterning that John Sinclair is finding in his corpus evidence. He believes that most language is made up of variable expressions that have much more syntagmatic structure than imagined before. In this view, lexis and grammar are not distinct, but are combined into a single lexicogrammatical force.

Vocabulary also has great effect on the style and tone of a discourse. Skilled interlocutors manipulate a number of lexical variables in order to achieve a desired effect. A number of these were discussed in this chapter, including lexical ambiguity, connotation, and the effect of Old English words versus loanwords on the formality of a text.

Exercises for expansion

(See Appendix D for suggested answers to this section.)

1. Take the word *plain.* One of its main collocations is *make/made/making it plain.* Write down your intuitions about how this phrase patterns. Are you aware of any variable expressions? Now look at the concordance lines for *made it plain* in Appendix D. Are any variable expressions obvious from the concordance lines?

2. We have already seen that there are numerous connections between words and phrases in spoken conversation. One would expect a similar situation in written discourse. Below is a passage from Howatt (1984, p. 247) that describes Michael West's use of higher-frequency words in place of lower-frequency ones. Mark the connections between related words in the text, including exact repetition, relexicalization, and the various forms of co-reference.

It seemed to West that there were two main ways in which the reading texts could be improved in order to help the children to achieve more. The first was to simplify the vocabulary by replacing old-fashioned literary words by more common equivalents. For example, West discovered words like *plight, mode, isle, nought, ere,* and *groom* and substituted more frequent items such as *state, way, island, nothing, before,* and *servant* instead. This principle, which could be called a *lexical selection* principle (though West did not use the term), was to become a dominant one during the next twenty years.

3. This chapter covered only some elements of lexical systematicity; there are numerous others. One example is the ordering of modifiers before nouns. All of the following modifiers can be used together in a 5-unit string to describe the related noun. Put them in the most natural order. Then see whether you can develop a "rule" for their ordering.
   a. electric
      old
      splendid
      those
      two
      ————, ————, ————, ————, ————, trains
   b. big
      brown
      cuckoo
      noisy
      that
      ————, ————, ————, ————, ————, clock

Further reading

For an overview of multiword units: Moon (1997, 1998).

For a book-length treatment of lexical phrases: Nattinger and DeCarrico (1992).

For an accessible introduction to elements of lexical stylistic behavior, including numerous exercises: Carter et al. (1997).

For an explanation of discourse analysis techniques for exploring the interconnections in discourse, including those lexically based: Coulthard (1985) and McCarthy (1991, 1998).

For more on lexis and discourse: Hoey (1991), Carter (1998), *Collins COBUILD Grammar Patterns I: Verbs* (1996), and *Collins COBUILD Grammar Patterns II: Nouns and Adjectives* (1998).

For an Internet site focusing on phraseology:
http://www.ims.uni-stuttgart.de/euralex/bibweb

7 *Vocabulary acquisition*

- How do we learn words?
- What does L1 vocabulary acquisition have to tell us about L2 acquisition?
- How is memory related to vocabulary acquisition?
- How can learners become independent of teachers in their vocabulary learning?

In Chapter 1, we found that the average educated adult native speaker of English knows between fifteen and twenty thousand word families. Many L2 learners of English also know thousands of word families. This chapter will explore the intriguing question of how language learners are able to acquire such an impressive amount of vocabulary. Tens of thousands of word families are probably too many to be learned solely from formal study, so most L1 vocabulary knowledge has to be "picked up" through simple exposure during the course of language use. This suggests two main processes of vocabulary acquisition: *explicit learning* through the focused study of words and *incidental learning* through exposure when one's attention is focused on the use of language, rather than the learning itself. Second language learners acquire vocabulary through these same processes, but their learning context usually differs markedly from children learning their native language.

In fact, there are so many different variables that affect second language vocabulary acquisition, such as L1, age, amount of exposure, motivation, and culture, that it is very difficult to formulate a theory of acquisition that can account for them all. Nation (1995, p. 5) summarizes the situation as one in which there are still many more questions than answers:

[T]there isn't an overall theory of how vocabulary is acquired. Our knowledge has mainly been built up from fragmentary studies, and at the moment we have only the broadest idea of how acquisition might occur. We certainly have no knowledge of the acquisition stages that particular words might move through. Additionally, we don't know how the learning of some words affects how other words are learned. There are still whole areas which are completely unknown.

Because we cannot physically see or track words in the mental lexicon, all research evidence must necessarily be indirect, making it difficult to arrive at unequivocal conclusions on which an overall theory could be based. (Notice how many of the statements in this book must be hedged with terms such as *probably* and *likely*.) In the end, we may not have a definitive understanding of the vocabulary acquisition process until neurologists are finally able to physically trace words in the brain. But although we do not have a global theory that can explain vocabulary acquisition, models have been proposed that attempt to describe the mechanics of acquisition for more limited aspects of lexis, such as how meaning is learned. Much of the research contributing to this understanding has been with L1 learners, but a great deal of this can be applied to second language learning. Numerous studies have also focused on L2 vocabulary learning itself. This chapter will highlight some of the most important insights from both of these research strands.

The incremental nature of vocabulary acquisition

One point this book has repeatedly stressed is that vocabulary acquisition is incremental in nature. We have seen that complete mastery of a word entails a number of component types of word knowledge, not all of which can be completely learned simultaneously. Experience has shown that some are mastered before others, for example, learners will surely know a word's basic meaning sense before they have full collocational competence. Even before the level of mastery, learners are likely to know more about certain word knowledge aspects than others at any point in time. But at the moment it is difficult to confidently say much about how the different word knowledge types develop together, simply because there is a lack of studies that look at the acquisition of multiple types of word knowledge concurrently. Still, I believe the following account is representative of how the acquisition of different word knowledge aspects actually occurs: On the first exposure to a new word, all that is likely to be picked up is some sense of word form and meaning. If the exposure was verbal, the person might remember the pronunciation of the whole word, but might only remember what other words it rhymes with or how many syllables it has. If the exposure came from a written text, the person may only remember the first few letters of the word. Because it was only a single exposure, it is only possible to gain the single meaning sense that was used in that context. It is also possible that the word class was noticed, but not much else. As the person gains a few more exposures, these features will be consolidated, and perhaps some other meaning senses will be encountered. But it will probably be relatively late in the acquisition process before a person develops intuitions about the word's frequency, register constraints, and collocational behavior, simply because these features require a large number of examples to determine the appropriate values. This account allows for a great deal of variability in how words are learned, but the key point is that some word knowledge aspects develop at different rates than others.

But each of these word knowledge types is also mastered to greater or lesser degrees at any point in time. Henricksen (1999) provides a good description of the various aspects of incremental development in her discussion of vocabulary knowledge. She proposes three dimensions of knowledge, all of which can be acquired to various degrees. She first suggests that for any lexical aspect, learners can have knowledge ranging from zero to partial to precise. This would mean that all word knowledge ranges on a continuum, rather than being known versus unknown. Even knowledge as seemingly basic as spelling can behave in this manner, ranging on a cline something like this:

| can't spell word at all | knows some letters | phonologically correct | fully correct spelling |

←——————————————————————————————————→

I found evidence for these partial/precise degrees of knowledge, and for some word knowledge types being learned before others in a study I made of advanced L2 learners at university level (Schmitt, 1998b). I followed how well they knew the spelling, meaning senses, grammatical behavior, and associations of eleven words over most of an academic year. The students had little problem with spelling, regardless of what else they knew about the words, generally being able to derive the spellings from sound-symbol correspondences. This suggests that spelling is one of the first aspects of lexical knowledge to be mastered for these students. However, they rarely knew all of the words' derivational forms or meaning senses. They normally knew the word class of the stimulus word and one derivation, but rarely all of the four main forms (noun, verb, adjective, adverb). Likewise, they normally knew the core meaning sense, but almost never all of the possible senses. Thus, these two word-knowledge types are clearly mastered after spelling, as one would expect. Similarly, Bahns and Eldaw (1993) found that their subjects' collocational knowledge lagged behind their general vocabulary knowledge. The association scores for my students generally became more nativelike over time, indicating that the words were gradually becoming better integrated into the students' mental lexicons. Again, this word-knowledge type took time to develop.

Henricksen's second dimension is essentially the same as our discussion of word-knowledge types: depth of knowledge requires mastery of a number of lexical aspects. I have already suggested how some of these may develop before others.

The third dimension, receptive and productive mastery, brings up a long-standing lexical distinction. Traditionally, the view has been that words are first learned receptively, and then develop to become known productively. But Melka (1997) argues that this is too simplistic and that receptive and productive mastery should be seen as poles of yet another continuum. Meara (1990, 1997), on the other hand, wonders whether this dimension is subject to a threshold effect, that is, words are receptively known until they reach a point or threshold where they "jump" to being fully productive. At the moment, it is difficult to settle this question empirically because different definitions of receptive and productive knowledge and different methods of measuring these two notions can lead to quite different results.

Unsurprisingly, studies have generally shown that learners are able to demonstrate more receptive than productive knowledge, but the difference between the two may be less than commonly assumed. Melka (1997) surveyed several studies that claim the difference is rather small; one estimates that 92% of receptive vocabulary is known productively. Takala (1984) suggests that the figure may be even higher. Highlighting the problem of measurement, Waring (1998) found that indications of receptive knowledge could be either higher or lower than productive knowledge, depending on whether the measures used for each were relatively easy or difficult. For example, if a relatively demanding receptive measure was used, then subjects' receptive scores were lower than their productive ones. Thus, we will not have clear answers on receptive versus productive knowledge until we develop standardized testing instruments for the two modes (see Chapter 9 for more on testing). Waring's results do suggest, however, that an initial ability to use a word productively, at least in a limited way, precedes full mastery of its receptive aspects. Thus productive knowledge does not occur sequentially after receptive; there seems to be some overlap.

If we look at lexical knowledge from a word-knowledge standpoint, it is clear that all knowledge does not have to be either receptively or productively known at the same time. For example, it is easy to find students who can produce a word orally without any problems but cannot read it receptively. Likewise, students can often give the meaning(s) of a word in isolation but cannot use it in context for lack of productive collocation and register knowledge. So instead of thinking of a *word* being known receptively or productively, it may be better to consider the degree of receptive/productive control of the various *word-knowledge aspects*.

To sum up the discussion in this section, we see that not only is vocabulary acquisition incremental, but it is incremental in a variety of ways. First, lexical knowledge is made up of different kinds of word knowledge and not all can be learned simultaneously. Second, each word-knowledge type may develop along a cline, which means that not only is word learning incremental in general, but learning of the individual word knowledges is as well. Third, each word-knowledge type may be receptively or productively known regardless of the degree of mastery of the others. Taken together, this indicates that word learning is a complicated but gradual process.

Incidental and explicit learning of vocabulary

I have suggested that explicit and incidental learning are the two approaches to vocabulary acquisition. Explicit learning focuses attention directly on the information to be learned, which gives the greatest chance for its acquisition. But it is also time-consuming, and for all but the most diligent student, it would be too laborious to learn an adequately sized lexicon. Incidental learning can occur when one is using language for communicative purposes, and so gives a double benefit for time expended. But it is slower and more gradual, lacking the focused attention of explicit learning. One may have to read a great deal of text or converse for quite some time to come across any particular word, especially if it is relatively infrequent. For example, *spur* is within the most frequent five thousand words of English, according to the BNC, but can you remember the last time you actually heard or saw it being used?

A person should be able to start learning incidentally from verbal conversation almost from the beginning, but when it comes to reading, a certain amount of explicit study is probably necessary as a prerequisite. Not only must one learn to read, but written language typically makes more use of infrequent vocabulary than does spoken language. These less frequent words are less likely to be known, leading to a higher proportion of unknown words on a page. Unless a high percentage of words on a page are known, it is very difficult to guess the meaning of any new words. The upshot is that some explicit learning is probably necessary to reach a vocabulary size "threshold" that enables incidental learning from reading. To start reading authentic texts meant for adult native speakers, the threshold is somewhere between three and five thousand word families (Nation & Waring, 1997), but one can access the easiest simplified readers with only a few hundred. (See Chapter 8 for more details on reading and vocabulary learning.)

The consensus is that, for second language learners at least, both explicit and incidental learning are necessary, and should be seen as complementary. Certain important words make excellent targets for explicit attention, for example, the most frequent words in a language and technical vocabulary. Nation (1995) thinks we should consider vocabulary teaching in terms of cost/benefits, with the value of learning such words well worth the time required to teach them explicitly. On the other hand, infrequent words in general English are probably best left to incidental learning.

The field of psychology (which actually has very close ties with the area of language learning and processing) has given us an important concept related to explicit language learning: the more one manipulates, thinks about, and uses mental information, the more likely it is that one will retain that information (*depth [levels] of processing hypothesis*). In the case of vocabulary, the more one engages with a word (deeper processing), the more likely the word will be remembered for later use. An example of an explicit learning technique that requires relatively deep processing is the *Keyword Method* (Hulstijn, 1997). This technique works by combining elements of phonological form and meaning in a mental image. Let us say that an English speaker wants to remember the Japanese word for sword (*katana*). First, a word with a phonological similarity to *katana* is found in English, for example, *cat*. Then a mental image is conjured up combining the two, such as a samurai cat waving a sword. When the person hears the word *katana,* he or she is reminded of *cat,* which activates the mental image. This in turn leads to the meaning of "sword." Use of "deep processing" techniques such as the keyword method has been shown to help fix target words in memory. Conversely, techniques that only require relatively shallow processing, such as repeatedly writing a word on a page, do not seem to facilitate retention as well.

Words not explicitly focused upon can be learned incidentally from exposure, facilitated by the use of vocabulary learning strategies (discussed later in this chapter). Another way to expedite incidental learning is to increase the amount of exposure, because lack of exposure is one of the most common problems facing second language learners. This was demonstrated in an interesting line of research involving *extensive reading* in the South Pacific islands. Students read extensively (or were read to) from a large number of books, but were given little or no explicit supplementary linguistic instruction; that is, the focus was on the meaning of the stories. The average student's language proficiency increased much more from this increased input than from an audiolingual program with which it was compared. These results indicate the value of such a "book flood" in providing the kind of exposure to the target language that learners need (Elley, 1991).

In an L1, incidental learning is the dominant way of acquiring vocabulary. This really has to be the case because parents do not "teach" their children most of the vocabulary they acquire, although they do simplify their speech to make it more comprehensible (*motherese* or *caretaker talk*). But the children are the beneficiaries of a massive amount of input, which allows them to enter school at age 5 with vocabularies of around four to five thousand word families. In fact, children are exposed to their native language even before they are born. Research has shown that embryos become accustomed to the *prosody* (rhythm, flow, and stress of a language) of their mother's speech while still in the womb.

It appears that some kinds of word knowledge are particularly responsive to either explicit or incidental learning. For example, reliable intuitions of collocation can only come from numerous exposures to a word in varied contexts, which suggests incidental learning as an acquisition vehicle. Ellis (1997) suggests that mastery over the orthography and phonology of a second language is also gained incidentally, for the most part. Of course, spelling and pronunciation can be facilitated by an explicit focus, such as the spelling rule "i before e except after c." But Ellis believes that learning mainly consists of an implicit tuning in to the orthographic/phonological regularities that exist in any language system. For example, in English the consonant cluster *sch* can begin a word (*school*), but *hsc* cannot. Early conscious learning (if any) eventually becomes automatized, with the speed and overall proficiency of the orthographic input (reading) and output (spelling) systems mainly acquired by the repetitive practice of actually using the target language. Further evidence for this comes from Thomas and Dieter (1987), who found that the act of writing a word enhances memory of its orthographic form.

Certain factors can facilitate or inhibit this acquisition, especially in an L2 context (Ellis & Beaton, 1995). The orthography is easier if the L1 and L2 use the same orthographic characters and they are read in the same manner (left to right, right to left, up to down in vertical columns, etc.). Similarly, use of the same sequential letter probabilities (consonant clusters) facilitates learning (e.g., *sch* is an acceptable cluster in English, but may not be in another language). The closer the correspondence between the graphemes and the phonemes they represent (sound-symbol correspondences), the easier it is to learn. If the L1 and L2 words have similar orthographies based on etymological or loanword reasons (English *hound;* German *hund*), this also facilitates learning. Last, shorter words are easier than longer words, partly because shorter words occur more frequently.

In contrast to the incidental acquisition of word form, Ellis (1997) suggests that meaning is one lexical aspect amenable to conscious learning, particularly by means of guessing a new word's meaning from context, using imagery, and utilizing appropriate strategies for connecting meanings to word forms. (I will discuss these strategies later in the section titled "Vocabulary learning strategies.") Because meaning is so central to vocabulary learning, let us now discuss how it is acquired.

Acquisition of word meaning and grammatical knowledge

To illustrate the process of lexical acquisition, this section will examine the learning of two lexical aspects in some detail: first meaning and then grammatical/morphological knowledge.

Meaning

Children acquiring their native language seem to easily learn elements of the core meaning of words in a kind of "fast mapping" between word and concept, but it may take much longer to come to a refined understanding of all of a word's meaning features (Carey, 1978). Similarly, Miller and Gildea (1987) observe that children acquire word meaning in two stages: a fast initial stage in which novel words are fitted into categories (*logo* is a kind of sign), then a slower stage in which the words within the categories are differentiated (*logos* usually identify companies and are attached to those companies' products, whereas *emblems* represent a particular person, group, or idea). Aitchison (1987) summarizes the process of meaning acquisition in L1 children in three basic stages: (1) labeling (attaching a label [word] to a concept), (2) categorization (grouping a number of objects under a particular label), and (3) network building (building connections between related words).

Once learners have acquired the core meaning, they then learn from additional exposure to the target word in context how far the meaning can be extended and where the semantic boundaries are. This is an ongoing process, as each exposure to a novel usage of a word further defines its boundaries. It seems that L1 children categorize novel words with others of a like kind, but the criteria for "likeness" appear to change with a child's development. Initially, perceptional similarity (particularly shape similarity) is paramount, but gradually coordinate relationships (*necklace–ring;*

cake–pie; see Figure 2 on page 26) become more important (Imai, Gentner, & Uchida, 1994). Children often overextend their first nouns to things outside the category, such as using *dog* to refer to any four-legged animal. They may also underextend objects that are not typical members of a class and exclude them from the concept, as in believing that Chihuahuas are not dogs (deVilliers & deVilliers, 1978). Eventually, enough input is gained to clarify the word boundaries. But those boundaries often remain fuzzy to some extent, for the reasons described in Chapter 3, and even very well read native adults are constantly learning new applications for words they already know.

Part of this will include learning new meaning senses for words. Many or most words in English have two or more meaning senses (polysemy)–for example, *spur* = cowboy apparel, to encourage someone, a side road or track, and so on–and native speakers will be exposed to these new meaning senses throughout their lifetimes. From among the different meaning senses for each word, one is usually the most basic, frequent, neutral, or substitutable (Carter, 1998, Chapter 2), and can be termed the *core meaning sense.* For example, the word *cream* can mean a color or the best part of something, but by far the most common meaning sense is that of a part of milk. West (1953) puts the relative percentages of usage at 14%, 14%, and 48%, respectively, clearly indicating that the "milk" sense is core. It is important not to confuse the distinction being made between *core meaning sense* and *core meaning* (Chapter 4). For any meaning sense, there can be core meaning features and additional encyclopedic knowledge. But from among the many senses of a polysemous word, only one will be the most fundamental; this will be the core meaning sense.

In L2 vocabulary acquisition, it seems that learners acquire the core meaning sense of a word before more figurative senses, and that much L1 meaning information is transferred over to the L2. Ijaz (1986) found that the core meaning senses of words are transferred, whereas nontypical meaning senses are not. In addition, literal L1 meaning senses (*break* a stick) are more likely to be transferred to an L2 than figurative meaning senses (*break* a heart) (Kellerman, 1978). Levenston (unpublished manuscript) found that Hebrew learners of English tended to know the literal meaning senses of words that are used both literally and figuratively, even if native speakers used the figurative meanings almost exclusively. Similarly, Lovell (1941) found evidence that knowledge of multiple meaning senses of a word is closely related to understanding the most common meaning sense. All of these pieces of evidence suggest that words have a core meaning sense that is relatively universal and is likely to be acquired before other more figurative senses.

English	French	Danish	Swedish
tree	arbre		träd
wood (material)	bois	træ	trä
wood (small forest)	bois		
forest	forêt	skov	skog

Figure 1   Semantic space for tree and wood.

Like L1 children, L2 learners must define the boundaries of word meaning, but they usually have the advantage of already knowing the concepts. Thus, L2 learners seldom over- or underextend basic words, but may have trouble initially setting the meaning boundary between two or more related words that are less common, such as *job, career,* and *vocation*. This is partially because there is not always a one-to-one correspondence between words in different languages. For example, it is often the case where one language has one word for a semantic space, and another two or more for the same area. Swan (1997, p. 158) illustrates this for the words *tree* and *wood* in Figure 1. Learners have to assimilate enough additional features to disambiguate similar words that may have almost the same core meaning, but with subtle differences. Sonaiya (1991) contends that this is one of the most difficult and important aspects of learning new words, and that it is a continuous process.

Grammatical/morphological knowledge

Nagy and Anderson (1984) estimate that the average upper primary school student encounters a minimum of 1,000 new word families per year while reading, with better readers being exposed up to a possible 3,000–4,000 new vocabulary items. Nagy, Diakidoy, and Anderson (1993) estimate the figure to be closer to 10,000 new words per year. This is a large number, but Nagy and Anderson point out that most are related to words already known through prefixation, suffixation, or compounding. Thus a knowledge of morphology is crucial in handling the flood of novel words being met at this time. But how and when do L1 children gain this morphological knowledge? To some extent, it depends on the type of morphology. Inflections and compounding seem to be acquired before derivational suffixes (Berko, 1958). In fact, students are able to recognize the base forms within a suffixed word before they understand the function of the derivational suffix it-self, with this ability more or less acquired by the fourth grade (Tyler & Nagy, 1989).

One obvious reason why inflections are learned before derivational suf-fixes is that inflections are more rule-based and consistent. But another rea-son is that derivational suffixes are more common in the written mode than the oral mode, and are particularly associated with formal and academic dis-course (Chafe & Danielewicz, 1987). Therefore, children simply have more exposure to inflections than derivational suffixes. It seems that, as their ex-posure to written language increases, so does their knowledge of deriva-tional suffixes. Nagy, Diakidoy, and Anderson (1993) found that most of the improvement in suffix knowledge came between the fourth grade and the seventh grade, although it continued to improve into high school. But even by high school, the students' knowledge of the suffixes was not complete, as they still were not able to judge the word class of suffixed items as well as they were the base-form items. As with other kinds of language knowl-edge, morphology seems to be incrementally acquired, and may not be fully mastered until quite late.

It has been commonly assumed that once a base form is known, its in-flections and derivations can be learned with minimum effort. This is ex-emplified by Bauer and Nation's (1993) vision of word families, which states that "once the base word or even a derived word is known, the recog-nition of other members of the family requires little or no extra effort" (p. 253). This intuition of the connection between knowledge of a base word and ability to learn other members of its word family does have some em-pirical backing. In a laboratory setting, Freyd and Baron (1982) found that subjects learned nonwords (*skaffist-thief*) faster when they had previously been exposed to the meaning of the nonword stem (*skaf-steal*). Sandra (1988) found that it did not make any difference whether Dutch learners of English were explicitly told to notice the stems of transparent suffixed words while learning them or not; their level of retention was the same. To do as well as the "noticers," the "nonnoticers" must have unconsciously re-lied on morphological information to learn the novel words. However, when the meaning of the stem to the overall suffixed word meaning was not trans-parent, cluing subjects in to the connection helped them to learn the suffixed word (Sandra, 1993; cited in Sandra, 1994). So it seems that knowing the stem word does help facilitate the learning of its derivations.

This does not mean, however, that we can assume that acquiring the der-ivations is easy or that it will be accomplished almost automatically. Indeed, we have seen that even native speakers do not have full mastery over mor-phology until at least high school (Nagy, Diakidoy, & Anderson, 1993). If it takes that long to develop in natives, with their advantage of maximum exposure, then L2 learners are likely to have difficulties in their morphological acquisition. A study exploring the suffix knowledge of intermediate Japanese learners of English showed that they were able to produce, on average, only 60% of the possible inflected forms of base words (Schmitt & Meara, 1997). Furthermore, they were largely unable to produce the derivations of the base words (only 15%). On a recognition task, they did better, but still generally recognized much less than 50% of the legal derivational suffixes as being allowable. This is hardly surprising: whereas inflections are rule-based, derivational suffixes are much more idiosyncratic and need to be individually memorized (for example, *stimulate→stimulative, reflect→reflective*, but not *disclose→*disclosive*). Schmitt and Meara concluded that their subjects did not have very good mastery of suffix knowledge in general, even for words that the Japanese learners rated as known.

This discussion shows that we have some idea about the acquisition of meaning and morphological knowledge. But there are other types of lexical knowledge about which we have virtually no idea regarding their acquisition behavior–for example, the acquisition of register and collocation are unexplored mysteries. Until we are able to describe these processes to some minimal degree, an overall theory of lexical acquisition is impossible (at least within the constraints of our current conceptualizations of vocabulary).

MWUs in vocabulary acquisition

In Chapter 6, we found that much lexis consists of multiword units (MWUs). These MWUs act as chunks that facilitate fluent language use with less cognitive overhead. MWUs also have important ramifications for the acquisition of vocabulary. To illustrate this, we need to first introduce the idea of *item learning* versus *system learning*. In language acquisition, learning seems to take place in two ways in phonology, morphology, and other linguistic aspects:

1. Item learning: learning individual units, such as the words *sled* and *walked*
2. System learning: learning the system or "rules," such as *sl = s+l* and *walked = walk+ed*

Lexical chunks clearly fall into the category of item learning, because their key feature is that they are wholes. Grammar, on the other hand, falls into the category of system learning. But these two types of learning are not mutually exclusive; rather, they feed into one another. Thus, once a chunk is known, it can be analyzed and segmented into its constituent words. In this way, unanalyzed chunks can be analyzed to provide additional vocabulary. Hakuta (1974) was the first to suggest that chunks could be analyzed into words plus grammar. Wong-Filmore (1976, p. 640) also believes that L2 children use many prefabricated chunks that "evolve directly into creative language." Peters (1983) presents the argument in its most considered form, proposing that learning vocabulary from lexical chunks is a three-part process. First, chunks are learned that are frozen wholes with no variation possible. At this point they are unanalyzed and are single lexemes. Common examples are idioms (e.g., *kick the bucket, burn the midnight oil*) and proverbs (e.g., *An apple a day keeps the doctor away, A stitch in time saves nine*). Also included are some expressions that are tightly related to a functional use (e.g., *Ladies and gentlemen,* which is a typical opening address in a formal situation).

Second, a language learner may realize that some variation is possible in certain chunks, and that they contain open slots. For example, after having heard the phrase *How are you today?* several times, it may be acquired as a chunk with the meaning of "a greeting." However, the learner may later notice the phrases *How are you this evening?* or *How are you this fine morning?* and, at that point, may realize that the underlying structure is actually *How are you _____?*, where the slot can be filled with most time references. It is then possible for the learner to perceive that what fits in the slot is a separate lexical unit from the rest of the phrase, which opens the door to learning that lexical unit. Thus chunks can be segmentalized into smaller lexical units, oftentimes individual words. Lexical chunks at this stage are partly fixed and partly creative.

Third, this segmentation process can continue until all of the component words are recognized as individual units by use of syntactic analysis. When this happens, every word in the chunk is potentially available for learning. This does not mean that the segmentation process has to continue to this point; in fact, it can stop at any stage. There are some lexical chunks that the learner may never start to analyze, and that may be retained only as unanalyzed wholes. Likewise, learners may or may not realize that certain lexical chunks contain variability and slots. When the variability is realized, it is possible that only the slots are analyzed; the rest of the pattern may remain unanalyzed. Still, it seems safe to assume that many, if not most, of the lexical chunks a learner knows will eventually become fully analyzed, and Peters (1983) suggests that much of a learner's vocabulary is learned in this way. This is especially true because learners are likely to eventually know numerous lexical chunks, seeing how they are easy to learn, efficient to use, and cover a wide variety of lexical content.

This segmentation process can lead to more than lexical knowledge, however. Segmentation also requires grammatical information, which focuses attention on syntax as well as lexis. Ellis (1997) argues that grammar can be learned through the implicit recognition of the patterns in strings of language, some of which are bound to include lexical chunks. In this line of reasoning, innate grammar would not consist of an inborn understanding of grammatical rules, but rather a facility for recognizing the systematic patterns in language input. A perceptive ability to recognize such patterning does seem to be a sufficient condition for at least some types of grammar acquisition; a model developed by Kiss (1973) demonstrated that simply calculating which words occur sequentially eventually provides enough input to distinguish their word class.

Role of memory in vocabulary acquisition

Memory has a key interface with language learning. In fact, Ellis (1996) suggests that short-term memory capacity is one of the best predictors of both eventual vocabulary and grammar achievement. I have already brought up the memory-language relationship in the discussion of MWUs and language processing, but there are other, more general, memory issues worth touching on in a discussion of vocabulary acquisition.

It must be recognized that words are not necessarily learned in a linear manner, with only incremental advancement and no backsliding. All teachers recognize that learners forget material as well. This forgetting is a natural fact of learning. We should view partial vocabulary knowledge as being in a state of flux, with both learning and forgetting occurring until the word is mastered and "fixed" in memory. I found that advanced L2 university subjects (Schmitt, 1998a) improved their knowledge of the meaning senses of target words about 2.5 times more than that knowledge was forgotten (over the course of one year), but this means that there was some backsliding as well. Interestingly, most of the forgetting occurred with words that were only known receptively; productive words were much less prone to forgetting.

Of course, forgetting can also occur even if a word is relatively well known, as when one does not use a second language for a long time or stops a course of language study. In this case, it is called *attrition*. Studies into attrition have produced mixed results, largely because of the use of different methods of measuring vocabulary knowledge. In general, though, lexical knowledge seems to be more prone to attrition than other linguistic aspects, such as phonology or grammar. This is logical because in one sense vocabulary is made up of individual units rather than a series of rules, although we have seen that lexis is much more patterned than previously thought. It appears that receptive knowledge does not attrite dramatically, and when it does, it is usually peripheral words, such as low-frequency noncognates, that are affected (Weltens & Grendel, 1993). On the other hand, productive knowledge is more likely to be forgotten (Cohen, 1989; Olshtain, 1989). The rate of attrition appears to be independent of proficiency levels; that is, learners who know more will lose about the same amount of knowledge as those who learn less. This means that more proficient learners will lose relatively less of their language knowledge than beginning learners. Overall, Weltens, Van Els, and Schils (1989) found that most of the attrition for the subjects in their study occurred within the first two years and then leveled off.

This long-term attrition mirrors the results of research on shorter-term forgetting, i.e., when learning new information, most forgetting occurs soon after the end of the learning session. After that major loss, the rate of forgetting decreases. This is illustrated in Figure 2. By understanding the nature of forgetting, we can better organize a recycling program which will be more efficient. The forgetting curve in Figure 2 indicates that it is critical to have a review session soon after the learning session, but less essential as time goes on. The principle of *expanding rehearsal* was derived from this insight, which suggests that learners review new material soon after the initial meeting and then at gradually increasing intervals (Pimsleur, 1967; Baddeley, 1990, pp. 156–158). One explicit memory schedule proposes reviews 5–10 minutes after the end of the study period, 24 hours later, 1 week later, 1 month later, and finally 6 months later (Russell, 1979, p. 149). In this way, the forgetting is minimized (Figure 3). Students can use the principle of expanding rehearsal to individualize their learning. They should test themselves on new words they have studied. If they can remember them, they should increase the interval before the next review, but if they cannot, they should shorten the interval.

Landauer and Bjork (1978) combined the principle of expanding practice with research results demonstrating that the greater the interval between presentations of a target item, the greater the chances it would be subsequently recalled. From this, they suggest that the ideal practice interval is the longest period that a learner can go without forgetting a word. Research by Schouten-van Parreren (1991, pp. 10–11) shows that some easier words may be overlearned (in the sense that more time is devoted to them than nec-

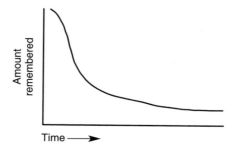

Figure 2   Typical pattern of forgetting.

essary), whereas more difficult abstract words are often underlearned. A practice schedule based on the expanding rehearsal principle may help in avoiding this problem.

Memory comes in two basic types: *short-term memory* (also known as *working memory*) and *long-term memory*. Long-term memory retains information for use in anything but the immediate future. Short-term memory is used to store or hold information while it is being processed. It normally can hold information for only a matter of seconds. However, this can be extended by rehearsal, for example, by constantly repeating a phone number so that it is not forgotten. Short-term memory is fast and adaptive but has a small storage capacity. Long-term memory has an almost unlimited storage capacity but is relatively slow. The object of vocabulary learning is to transfer the lexical information from the short-term memory, where it resides during the process of manipulating language, to the more permanent long-term memory.

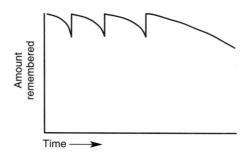

Figure 3   Pattern of forgetting with expanded rehearsal.

The main way of doing this is by finding some preexisting information in the long-term memory to "attach" the new information to. In the case of vocabulary, it means finding some element already in the mental lexicon to relate the new lexical information to. This can be done in various ways. One is through imaging techniques such as the Keyword Approach. Another is through grouping the new word with already-known words that are similar in some respect. The new word can be placed with words with a similar meaning (*prank→trick, joke, jest*), a similar sound structure (*prank→tank, sank, rank*), the same beginning letters (*prank→pray, pretty, prod*), the same word class *(prank→cow, greed, distance),* or other grouping parameter, although by far the most common must be meaning similarity. Because the "old" words are already fixed in the mind, relating the new words to them provides a "hook" to remember them by so they will not be forgotten. New words that do not have this connection are much more prone to forgetting.

Vocabulary learning strategies

One approach of facilitating vocabulary learning that has attracted increasing attention is *vocabulary learning strategies* (VLS). Interest in VLS has paralleled a movement away from a predominantly teaching-oriented perspective to one that includes interest in how the actions of learners might affect their acquisition of language. It seems that many learners do use strategies for learning vocabulary, especially when compared to language tasks that integrate several linguistic skills (e.g., oral presentation that involves composing the speech content, producing comprehensible pronunciation, fielding questions, etc.). This might be due to the relatively discrete nature of vocabulary learning compared to more integrated language activities, making it easier to apply strategies effectively. It may also be due to the fact that classrooms tend to emphasize discrete activities over integrative ones, or that students particularly value vocabulary learning.

Commonly used VLS seem to be simple memorization, repetition, and taking notes on vocabulary. These more mechanical strategies are often favored over more complex ones requiring significant active manipulation of information (imagery, inferencing, Keyword Method). If we follow the depth of processing perspective, it would seem that learners often favor relatively "shallow" strategies, even though they may be less effective than "deeper" ones. Indeed, research into some "deeper" vocabulary learning strategies, such as forming associations (Cohen & Aphek, 1981) and using the Keyword Method (Hulstijn, 1997), have been shown to enhance retention better than rote memorization. However, even rote repetition can be effective if students are accustomed to using it (O'Malley & Chamot, 1990). If a generalization can be made, shallower activities may be more suitable for beginners, because they contain less material that may only distract a novice, whereas intermediate or advanced learners can benefit from the context usually included in deeper activities (Cohen & Aphek, 1981).

Rather than being used individually, multiple VLS are often used concurrently. This means that active management of strategy use is important. Good learners do things such as use a variety of strategies, structure their vocabulary learning, review and practice target words, and they are aware of the semantic relationships between new and previously learned L2 words; that is, they are conscious of their learning and take steps to regulate it. Poor learners generally lacked this awareness and control (Ahmed, 1989; Sanaoui, 1995).

When considering which vocabulary learning strategies to recommend to our students, we need to consider the overall learning context. The effectiveness with which learning strategies can be both taught and used will depend on a number of variables, including the proficiency level, L1 and culture of students, their motivation and purposes for learning the L2, the task and text being used, and the nature of the L2 itself. It is important to gain cooperation of the learners, because a study has shown that students who resisted strategy training learned worse than those who relied on their familiar rote repetition approach (O'Malley & Chamot, 1990). We thus have to take learning culture into consideration, because learners from different culture groups sometimes have quite different opinions about the usefulness of various vocabulary learning strategies (Schmitt, Bird, Tseng, & Yang, 1997). Proficiency level has also been shown to be quite important, with one study showing word lists better for beginning students, and contextualized words better for more advanced students (Cohen & Aphek, 1981). In addition, the frequency of the target words is relevant. High-frequency words should probably be taught, so they mainly require strategies for review and consolidation, whereas low-frequency words will mostly be met incidentally while reading or listening, and so initially require strategies for determining their meanings, such as guessing from context and using word parts (Nation, 1990, Chapter 9).

Examples of vocabulary learning strategies

There are numerous different VLS, with one list containing fifty-eight different strategies (Schmitt, 1997). To give you some impression of the range of possibilities, some of the strategies from that list follow.

Strategy group	*Strategy*

Strategies for the discovery of a new word's meaning

DET	Analyze part of speech
DET	Analyze affixes and roots
DET	Check for L1 cognate
DET	Analyze any available pictures or gestures
DET	Guess meaning from textual context
DET	Use a dictionary (bilingual or monolingual)
SOC	Ask teacher for a synonym, paraphrase, or L1 translation of new word
SOC	Ask classmates for meaning

Strategies for consolidating a word once it has been encountered

SOC	Study and practice meaning in a group
SOC	Interact with native speakers
MEM	Connect word to a previous personal experience
MEM	Associate the word with its coordinates
MEM	Connect the word to its synonyms and antonyms
MEM	Use semantic maps
MEM	Image word form
MEM	Image word's meaning
MEM	Use Keyword Method
MEM	Group words together to study them
MEM	Study the spelling of a word
MEM	Say new word aloud when studying
MEM	Use physical action when learning a word
COG	Verbal repetition
COG	Written repetition
COG	Word lists
COG	Put English labels on physical objects
COG	Keep a vocabulary notebook
MET	Use English-language media (songs, movies, newscasts, etc.)
MET	Use spaced word practice (expanding rehearsal)
MET	Test oneself with word tests
MET	Skip or pass new word
MET	Continue to study word over time

Source: Schmitt, 1997.

Such a long list becomes unwieldy unless it is organized in some way, so it is categorized in two ways. First, the list is divided into two major classes: (1) strategies that are useful for the initial discovery of a word's meaning, and (2) those useful for remembering that word once it has been introduced. This reflects the different processes necessary for working out a new word's meaning and usage, and for consolidating it in memory for future use. Second, the strategies are further classified into five groupings. The first contains strategies used by an individual when faced with discovering a new word's meaning without recourse to another person's expertise (*Determination strategies* [DET]). This can be done through guessing from one's structural knowledge of a language, guessing from an L1 cognate, guessing from context, or using reference materials.

Social strategies (SOC) use interaction with other people to improve language learning. One can ask teachers or classmates for information about a new word and they can answer in a number of ways (synonyms, translations, etc.). One can also study and consolidate vocabulary knowledge with other people, although my research shows that most learners (at least my Japanese subjects) preferred to study vocabulary individually.

Memory strategies (MEM) (traditionally known as *mnemonics*) involve relating the word to be retained with some previously learned knowledge, using some form of imagery, or grouping. A new word can be integrated into many kinds of existing knowledge (e.g., previous experiences or known words) or images can be custom-made for retrieval (e.g., images of the word's form or meaning attributes). Groupings is an important way to aid recall, and people seem to organize words into groups naturally without prompting. If words are organized in some way before memorization, recall is improved (Cofer, Bruce, & Reicher, 1966; Craik & Tulving, 1975). Another kind of mnemonic strategy involves focusing on the target word's orthographic or phonological form to facilitate recall. The use of physical action when learning has been shown to facilitate language recall (Saltz & Donnenwerth-Nolan, 1981). Asher (1977) has made it the basis for a whole methodology, the Total Physical Response Method (TPR), which seems to be especially amenable to the teaching of beginners.

It is worth noting that memory strategies generally involve the kind of elaborative mental processing that facilitates long-term retention. This takes time, but the time expended will be well spent if used on important words that really need to be learned, such as high-frequency vocabulary and technical words essential in a particular learner's field of study. A learner may not have time to "deeply process" every word encountered, but it is certainly worth attempting for key lexical items.

Cognitive strategies (COG) exhibit the common function of "manipulation or transformation of the target language by the learner" (Oxford, 1990, p. 43). They are similar to memory strategies, but are not focused so specifically on manipulative mental processing; they include repetition and using mechanical means to study vocabulary, including the keeping of vocabulary notebooks.

Finally, *Metacognitive strategies* (MET) involve a conscious overview of the learning process and making decisions about planning, monitoring, or evaluating the best ways to study. This includes improving access to input, deciding on the most efficient methods of study/review, and testing oneself to gauge improvement. It also includes deciding which words are worth studying and which are not, as well as persevering with the words one chooses to learn.

Utilizing the full version of the strategy list above, I asked six hundred Japanese respondents which strategies they used and which they felt were useful. Bilingual dictionaries, written and spoken repetition, and strategies that focused on form were the most favored strategies, although the percentage of respondents who used these depended on whether they were junior high school, high school, university, or adult learners. This supports other research that has indicated that patterns of strategy use can change over time as a learner either matures or becomes more proficient in the target language. Of course, these are purely Japanese results; learners from other cultures will produce somewhat different patterns (Schmitt et al., 1997).

So it seems that learners do use strategies and find them helpful. This suggests that we should incorporate strategy training in our classes, but raises the question of how effective such training is. Research is inconclusive on this point: some studies report a reasonable degree of success, whereas others report only limited success, or even student resistance. It seems that much depends on the proficiency of the learners (Kern, 1989) and the knowledge and acceptance of the teachers involved (Chamot, 1987). McDonough (1995) reviews strategy training research and, among other things, concludes that improvement caused by strategy training is relatively weak and only shows up on certain measures, is culture-specific, and may be better for beginning students. An earlier summary by Skehan (1989) had also suggested that strategies may be performance-based, and that the only strategies that can be taught are those that affect the immediate task being done. Strategy training can also depend on outside factors, such as support from the school administration. In sum, I would suggest that VLS have a great deal of potential, but that we must be very sensitive to our learners and their needs when we incorporate strategy instruction into our curriculum.

Implications for teachers

Vocabulary is learned incrementally and this obviously means that lexical acquisition requires multiple exposures to a word. This is certainly true for incidental learning, as the chances of learning and retaining a word from one exposure when reading are only about 5%–14% (Nagy, 1997, p. 74). Other studies suggest that it requires five to sixteen or more repetitions for a word to be learned (Nation, 1990, p. 44). If recycling is neglected, many partially known words will be forgotten, wasting all the effort already put into learning them (ibid., p. 45). Fortunately, this recycling occurs naturally as more frequent words appear repeatedly in texts and conversations. This repetition does not happen to nearly as great an extent for less frequent words, so teachers should look for ways to bolster learner input to offset this. Extensive reading seems to be one effective method.

For explicit learning, however, recycling has to be consciously built into any study program. Teachers must guard against presenting a word once and then forgetting about it, or else their students will do the same. This implies developing a more structured way of presenting vocabulary that reintroduces words repeatedly in classroom activities. Learning activities themselves need to be designed to require multiple manipulations of a word, such as in vocabulary notebooks in which students have to go back and add additional information about the words (Schmitt & Schmitt, 1995). Understanding how memory behaves can help us design programs that give maximum benefit from revision time spent.

L2 learners benefit from a complementary combination of explicit teaching and incidental learning. Explicit teaching can supply valuable first introductions to a word, but of course not all lexical aspects can be covered during these encounters. The varied contexts in which learners encounter the word during later incidental meetings can lead to broader understanding of its collocations, additional meaning senses, and other higher-level knowledge. In addition, repeated exposure will help to consolidate the lexical aspects first learned.

Additionally, explicit teaching is probably essential for the most frequent words of any L2, because they are prerequisites for language use. The learning of these basic words cannot be left to chance, but should be taught as quickly as possible, because they open to the door to further learning. Less frequent words, on the other hand, may be best learned by reading extensively, because there is just not enough time to learn them all through conscious study. Thus, explicit teaching and incidental learning complement each other well, with each being necessary for an effective vocabulary program.

It is probably worth considering adding a vocabulary learning strategies component to your vocabulary program. You will not be able to teach all the words students will need, and even the input generated by extensive reading has its limitations. Students will eventually need to effectively control their own vocabulary learning. The list in this chapter gives some idea of the range possible, but research has shown that to be effective training must be tailored to your particular situation, taking into account the age, motivation, proficiency, and desires of your students. Also, it appears that learners naturally mature into using different strategies at different times of their life, so it seems reasonable to introduce them to a variety of strategies and let them decide which ones are right for them.

Summary

Understanding key notions of how vocabulary is acquired can help us deliver more realistic and effective vocabulary teaching. Words can be learned from explicit teaching, or they can be learned incidentally while students' attention is on the meaning of the discourse. In either case, words are learned incrementally. This means that they need to be met numerous times before they are acquired, and so repetition needs to be built into vocabulary learning. Expanding rehearsal is the most time-effective way to manage the review of partially known vocabulary that has been explicitly considered. Students need to take some responsibility for their own vocabulary learning, making it necessary to introduce them to vocabulary learning strategies so that they can do this more effectively.

Exercises for expansion

1. Here are some words along with their approximate frequency level as taken from Kučera and Francis (1967). Take any extended written text, or transcript of oral communication, and check if and how often these words occur. What do the results tell you about the likelihood of learning words of different frequencies incidentally from exposure? Is there enough repetition to learn the words from a single passage? What is the likelihood of meeting the words in a different passage? At what frequency point do you think the benefit of learning these words is outweighed by the cost of spending time explicitly teaching them? As a side issue, you might wish to consider the list itself. It came from a corpus of (only) one million words. Do you think using a larger corpus would have made any difference in the frequency of these words?

1	the
500	book
1,000	scene
1,500	master
2,000	spite
2,500	confusion
3,000	swimming
4,000	staring
5,000	attract
10,000	abbey
20,000	studs
30,000	bunny
>30,000	lesion
>30,000	ornithology

2. Here are the ten most used vocabulary learning strategies from the survey of Japanese learners (Schmitt, 1997). How much mental manipulation does each strategy seem to require? To what extent do these highly used strategies entail the depth of cognitive processing that we believe facilitates retention?

Strategies	% of respondents who reported using strategy
Bilingual dictionary	85
Verbal repetition	76
Written repetition	76
Study the spelling of target word	74
Guess word's meaning from textual context	74
Ask classmates for meaning of word	73
Say new word aloud when studying	69
Take notes in class about vocabulary	64
Study the sound of target word	60
Use word lists to study words	54

3. Choose a text that you have recently read for pleasure that contained some words new to you. Assuming that you did not stop and explicitly try to learn them, this should be an indication of incidental learning for you. Can you remember what some of these words were without looking at the text? If so, you have some productive knowledge, but how much – what can you remember about these words? If not, glance at the text to remind yourself of the words without rereading the surrounding context. Now what can you remember? Finally, try reading the word again within the surrounding context. What can you say about the words now? What kinds of word knowledge do you have about these words,

and to what degree? Where are they in terms of receptive/productive mastery?

4. Below are two lists of twenty Thai words each, with their English equivalents. Study List A for 10 minutes and List B for 16 minutes. After 1 hour review List A for 2 minutes, then tomorrow for 2 minutes, then in 1 week for 2 minutes. Cover up the list you are not studying so that you do not accidentally see it. In two weeks' time, test yourself on both lists by carefully covering the Thai words and trying to remember them from the English equivalents. Was there a difference between the two lists in terms of what you could remember? What does this tell you about revision methodology? Would it have made any difference if you had covered the English equivalents and tried to remember them from seeing the Thai words?

List A

advertisement	kho-sa-naa	international	naa-naa-chart
bank	tha-na-khaan	contented	phaw-jai
bird	nok	estimate	ka
ceremony	phi-thee	conversation	son-tha-naa
cry	rong-hai	necessary	jam-pen
absolute	som-boon	eyesight	sye-taa
cooked	suk	government	rat-tha-baan
immediately	than-thee	expensive	phaeng
hot	phet	cost	raa-khaa
human being	ma-nut	opportunity	o-khart

List B

association	sa-ma-khom	fashionable	than-sa-mai
bread	kha-nom-pang	gratitude	ka-tan-you
egg	khai	fish	plaa
blanket	pha-hom	behavior	ki-ri-yaa
doubt	song-sai	amusing	ta-lok
bright	sa-waang	language	phaa-saa
enough	phor	nobody	mai-mee-khrai
important	sam-khan	fluently	khlong
heavy	nak	guarantee	pra-kan
husband	saa-mee	minute	naa-thee

Further reading

For more on explicit versus incidental approaches to vocabulary acquisition: Huckin, Haynes, and Coady (1993) and Coady and Huckin (1997).

For more on attrition: Weltens and Grendel (1993) and *Studies in Second Language Acquisition 11*(2) (1989), special issue on attrition.

For more details on memory: Baddeley (1990), Gathercole and Baddeley (1993), and Searleman and Herrmann (1994).

For more information on vocabulary learning strategies: Schmitt (1997), Sanaoui (1995), and Stoffer (1995).

8 Teaching and learning vocabulary

It should be said at the beginning of this chapter that there is no "right" or "best" way to teach vocabulary. The best practice in any situation will depend on the type of student, the words that are targeted, the school system and curriculum, and many other factors. Thus, this chapter cannot prescribe a regimen of vocabulary teaching that is optimal for all teaching situations. Rather, it will draw together points from the previous chapters and outline a number of guiding principles that should be considered when developing a vocabulary component to a language course.

How many and which words to teach

To get some idea of how many words we need to teach, let us examine what some goals for vocabulary size might be. If a learner only wished to survive a short vacation in a foreign country, perhaps he or she would be best advised to invest in a good phrase book and to only bother learning the most basic lexis of the L2, such as numbers from 1 to 10 and WH question words (*what, where, when, why,* and *how*). A slightly larger "survival list" of 120 items also includes vocabulary for everyday activities such as buying and bargaining, reading signs, and ordering food (Nation & Crabbe, 1991). But most students have higher aspirations than mere survival, and would wish to be able to express themselves, however simply, in their chosen second language. For this, a vocabulary of about 2,000 words would be a realistic goal, as Schonell, Meddleton, and Shaw (1956) found that people (Australians in their study) regularly use about this many different words in their daily conversations. Of course, this will not enable a conversation on every topic, and certainly not an in-depth conversation on most topics, but it should still allow satisfying interactions with native speakers on topics focusing on everyday events and activities. In fact, 2,000 words seems to be the most commonly cited initial goal for second language learners. In addition to allowing basic conversation, this number of words is seen as providing a solid basis for moving into more advanced study.

As a learner becomes more proficient and having the vocabulary to communicate on everyday subjects becomes less of a problem, the next step is acquiring enough vocabulary to begin to read authentic texts. There is no magic vocabulary size threshold that allows this, but the consensus seems to be that 3,000–5,000 word families is enough to provide initial access to this kind of written material (Nation & Waring, 1997). If the material is challenging, as in university textbooks, the figure may be closer to 10,000 word families (Hazenberg & Hulstijn, 1996). If a learner wishes to communicate in a particular subject area, then a foundation of higher-frequency vocabulary plus the specialized vocabulary for that area can be a useful target. If a learner's goal is to develop a vocabulary similar in size to that of a native speaker, then a vocabulary size of 15,000–20,000 word families is necessary (Nation & Waring, 1997).

These figures imply that a viably-sized vocabulary cannot realistically be taught exclusively through explicit study. But certainly some of it can be taught, and the question becomes which words to focus upon. Of course, many teachers are constrained by mandatory lists of words dictated by school authorities. But many teachers do have a choice, and it makes sense to have some principles guiding those choices. Nation (1995) proposes a cost-benefit perspective for deciding which words to teach. He suggests that the most frequent 2,000 words are essential for any real language use, and so are worth the effort required to teach and learn them explicitly. The General Service List (GSL) (West, 1953) is a good source for these key words (see page 84). Most of these extremely frequent words are polysemous, and the GSL has the advantage of giving information about the frequency of each meaning sense. This has obvious application in helping teachers to sequence the order in which the different senses are presented.

The first 2,000 words of a language are so important that Meara (1995) wonders whether it might not be better to concentrate on teaching them right at the beginning of a language course. This might not be as radical as it seems. If a student could learn fifty words per week (a figure certainly attainable if students were not concentrating on other language aspects such as grammar), then in 40 weeks of school this basic vocabulary could be introduced. Although the students would not know a lot about grammar at the end of this vocabulary-based period, I suspect that they would quickly make up this shortfall, and would soon overtake students who were taught by more traditional methodologies.

The main reason for believing that vocabulary knowledge can help grammar acquisition is that knowing the words in a text or conversation permits learners to understand the meaning of the discourse, which in turn allows the grammatical patterning to become more transparent (Ellis, 1997).

Learners can see for themselves how certain grammatical structures and sequences of words lead to certain meanings. In addition, "knowing" the first 2,000 words should increase comprehensible language input, as students would be able to understand more of the speech they are exposed to and also more of the written texts that they read.

The 2,000 level is only a beginning, and teaching words explicitly beyond this level can still supply sufficient benefits that warrant the time expended. But Nation (1990) believes that there comes a point where words occur so infrequently that it is better to use teaching time (which is always limited) to help students acquire the strategies necessary to learn these words on their own. Guessing from context, learning word roots and affixes, and applying mnemonic techniques are three strategies that he believes are especially useful. The students can then independently learn the less frequent words through a combination of extensive reading and explicit self-study. In this way, vocabulary-learning strategies can take learners beyond the level of word lists.

Frequency is not the only criterion for choosing words to teach explicitly. Another is words particularly useful in a specific topic area (e.g., technical vocabulary). Once a solid foundation of 5,000 or so words have been mastered, technical vocabulary can be the logical next step in vocabulary building. Vocabulary beyond this frequency level is mostly used in limited and rather specific situations in any case, so it makes sense to concentrate on the lower-frequency vocabulary most likely to occur in your field of interest.

A third category of words to focus on explicitly is those that students want to learn. The learner-centered movement was built on the premise that taking student wishes into account can be motivating to their learning. If students choose some of the words they study, they may well be more dedicated in trying to learn them.

A fourth category, especially important at the beginning of a course, is the vocabulary necessary for classroom management. Although words such as *pen, pencil, book,* and *page* are not especially frequent in general English, it makes sense to teach them at the beginning of a course so that basic commands such as "Please open your books to page 30" can be transacted in the target language as soon as possible.

So far, I have discussed general vocabulary size goals, and which words make obvious targets for teaching. This leaves the question of how many words to teach per class period. Numbers in the area of ten new words per 1-hour session are sometimes cited, and this does not seem unreasonable. However, it is useful to remember that teachers can improve their students' vocabulary by deepening their quality of knowledge about words already partially known, even if no new words are introduced. In fact, teaching new words in class may not be the most efficient way of handling vocabulary. It is probably more productive to assign students homework that introduces them to new words, such as word lists or reading, and then elaborate, expand, and consolidate these words in the classroom. Looking back at the vocabulary learning strategy list (page 134), we find that most "Discover New Word's Meaning" activities can be done well enough individually, whereas many "Consolidation" activities are amenable to classroom work.

This does not mean that all elaboration work needs to be done in formal classes; many elaboration exercises, such as semantic mapping, can be done in study groups. My research in Japan (Schmitt, 1997) indicates that most people tend to think of vocabulary learning as an individual pursuit, unaware of the advantages many researchers have attributed to cooperative group learning: It promotes active processing of information and cross-modeling/imitation, the social context enhances motivation of the participants, cooperative learning can prepare the participants for "team activities" outside the classroom, and, because there is less instructor intervention, students have more time to actually use and manipulate language in class (Dansereau, 1988). Newton (in Nation & Newton, 1997) found that about half of the words required by the classroom tasks he gave were known by at least one, though not all, of the members in his student groups. Furthermore, he found that the students were generally able to negotiate unknown vocabulary successfully, indicating that students can be a useful vocabulary resource for one another. Thus teachers may well find it useful to set up vocabulary learning groups in which members work together and encourage each other.

Of course, learners can also take individual responsibility for their own learning, by using such strategies as keeping a vocabulary notebook. Research has shown that learning thirty words per hour is possible (at least in the sense of gaining some initial partial knowledge) by using techniques such as word lists or the keyword method, so how much vocabulary one learns seems to be limited only by personal ambition.

Teaching vocabulary

In any well-structured vocabulary program there needs to be the proper mix of explicit teaching and activities from which incidental learning can occur. With rank beginners, it is probably necessary to explicitly teach all words until students have enough vocabulary to start making use of the unknown words they meet in context. But beyond this most basic level, incidental learning should be structured into the program in a principled way. It is important for at least two reasons: meeting a word in different contexts expands what is known about it (improving quality of knowledge), and the additional exposures help consolidate it in memory. Taking an incremental view of vocabulary acquisition, such elaboration and consolidation are both crucial. Explicit approaches to vocabulary learning, whether teacher-led in a classroom or through self-study, can only provide some elements of lexical knowledge. Even lexical information amenable to conscious study, such as meaning, cannot be totally mastered by explicit study, because it is impossible to present and practice all of the creative uses of a word that a student might come across. We have also seen that some kinds of word knowledge, such as collocation, register constraints, and frequency, can only be fully grasped through numerous exposures. Therefore, explicit and incidental approaches are both necessary in the course of learning vocabulary, each with its own strengths and weaknesses.

Explicit approach

Traditional approaches to vocabulary teaching have unsurprisingly focused on activities for the explicit study of vocabulary. There are numerous sources that illustrate a wide variety of vocabulary exercises, including teachers' reference books such as *Techniques in Teaching Vocabulary* (Allen, 1983), *Vocabulary* (Morgan & Rinvolucri, 1986), *Working with Words* (Gairns & Redman, 1986), *Teaching and Learning Vocabulary* (Nation, 1990), and *Implementing the Lexical Approach* (Lewis, 1997). Vocabulary textbooks also contain numerous different exercises, with a few examples being *Ways with Words* (Kirn, 1984), *Meaning by All Means* (Mason, 1986), *Common Threads* (Sökmen, 1992), and *English Vocabulary in Use* (McCarthy & O'Dell, 1994, 1999). Computer-Aided Language Learning (CALL) has begun to address vocabulary learning as well, with *Oxford Interactive Word Magic* (1998) giving us a taste of what will undoubtedly become an increasingly important element of vocabulary instruction. Now that most computers include multimedia capability (they have sound as well as pictures), they are ideal for language practice that requires a variety of written and spoken contexts. They are also very patient about repetition and recycling. These traits fit very well with the requirements of vocabulary learning.

Sökmen (1997) surveys explicit vocabulary teaching and highlights a number of key principles:

- build a large sight vocabulary
- integrate new words with old

- provide a number of encounters with a word
- promote a deep level of processing
- facilitate imaging
- make new words "real" by connecting them to the student's world in some way
- use a variety of techniques
- encourage independent learning strategies

Most of these principles should be familiar from earlier chapters in this book, and are indeed based on our most recent understanding of how words are acquired and remembered. A number of other principles are also worth being aware of. Sökmen mentions integrating new words with old, which is often done by some form of grouping similar words together. However, if two or more similar words are initially taught together, it might actually make them more difficult to learn. This is because students learn the word forms and learn the meanings, but confuse which goes with which (*cross-association*). As a beginning teacher I often confused my students in this way by teaching *left* and *right* together in the same class. After extensive drilling, I would ask the students at the end of the class to raise their left hands. To my consternation, a large number always raised their right hand. The problem was that the words were too similar, with all the semantic features being the same except for "direction." Research shows that cross-association is a genuine problem for learners (Higa, 1963; Tinkham, 1993; Waring, 1997), with Nation (1990, p. 47) suggesting that about 25% of similar words taught together are typically cross-associated. Antonyms are particularly prone to cross-association, because they tend to come in pairs like *deep/shallow* or *rich/poor,* but synonyms and other words from closely related semantic groupings (e.g., days of the week, numbers, foods, clothing) are also at risk. Nation (1990) suggests that the way to avoid cross-association is to teach the most frequent or useful word of a pair first (e.g., *deep*), and only after it is well established introducing its partner(s) (e.g., *shallow*).

Another principle is teaching the underlying meaning concept of a word. Many words are polysemous in English, and often some of their different meaning senses have a common underlying trait. Let us take the word *fork* as an example. It can mean a *fork* to eat with, a *fork* in a road or river, a *tuning fork* for use with music, a *pitchfork,* which farmers use to throw hay, or several other things. The GSL indicates that the meaning sense of "implement used for eating or in gardening" makes up 86% of the occurrences, while "anything so shaped," like *a fork in the road,* makes up 12%. This would suggest that "eating fork" is the most important meaning sense, but in this case, we can capture all of the meaning senses by defining the word with a drawing like this:⅄. By defining the underlying meaning concept, we maximize the effect of the teaching, by enabling students to understand the word in a much wider variety of contexts. Similarly, Nation (1990, pp. 72–73) suggests that defining *run* with a definition such as "go quickly, smoothly, or continuously" is best, because it covers meaning senses like *the girl ran, the road runs up the hill,* and *run a business.*

We can also maximize vocabulary learning by teaching word families instead of individual word forms. Teachers can make it a habit when introducing a new word to mention the other members of its word family. In this way, learners form the habit of considering a word's derivations as a matter of course. To reinforce this habit, teachers may eventually ask students to guess a new word's derivatives at the time of introduction. Including a derivation section as part of assessment also promotes the idea that learning the complete word family is important.

When teaching vocabulary, it is quite useful to have some idea of what makes words relatively easy or difficult to learn. Factors can be related to the word itself (*intralexical factors*), or they can involve how well the learner's L1 matches the L2 (*crosslinguistic factors*). Laufer (1997) summarizes the various intralexical factors as follows, but note that the first one involves the degree of matching with the L1 sound system.

Intralexical factors which affect vocabulary learning

Facilitating factors	Difficulty-inducing factors	Factors with no clear effect
familiar phonemes	presence of foreign phonemes	
familiar letter combinations (sland)	unfamiliar letter combinations (ndasl)	
stress always on same syllable	variable stress	
consistency of sound-script relationship	incongruency in sound-script relationship	
		word length
inflexional regularity	inflexional complexity	
derivational regularity	derivational complexity	
transparency of word parts (preview = look before)	deceptive transparency (outline ≠ out of line)	
	similarity of word forms (affect/effect)	
		part of speech
		concreteness/ abstractness

Facilitating factors	Difficulty-inducing factors	Factors with no clear effect
general words with neutral register	specific words with register constraints	
	idiomaticity	
one form for one meaning	one form with several meanings	

(Adapted from Laufer, 1997, p. 154)

In general, we find that the more regular the behavior of a language's vocabulary, the easier it is to learn; it is the exceptions that cause problems. But an even more important influence on difficulty is likely to be crosslinguistic factors. Swan (1997, p. 166) suggests that learners typically use a form of "equivalence hypothesis" when learning new L2 words, expressing a strategy something like "Regard everything [words in the L2 and L1] as the same unless you have a good reason not to." Learners do seem to assume that the core meaning senses of translation equivalents are the same across languages, but that more peripheral, irregular, or idiomatic uses are not (Kellerman, 1978, 1986). This is probably generally correct, and shows that learners have intuitions about the relationships between L2 and L1 words. Swan argues that these intuitions can be sharpened by making learners more aware of the similarities and differences between the native language and the target language: "Informed teaching can help students to formulate realistic hypotheses about the nature and limits of crosslinguistic correspondences, and to become more attentive to important categories in the second language which have no mother-tongue counterpart" (p. 179). In other words, contrasting key aspects of the L2 and the L1 can help students make better guesses about when it is appropriate to transfer knowledge about L1 words over to their L2 counterparts.

Incidental learning approach

In contrast to explicit approaches to vocabulary teaching and learning, the key to an incidental learning approach is to make sure that learners get maximum exposure to language. Undoubtedly, the most effective way to do this is to transplant the learner into a country or situation where the L2 is the primary language. Milton and Meara (1995) estimate that the European exchange students they studied learned an average of 275 English words per half year at home, whereas their vocabulary increase during 6 months at a British university averaged 1,325 words, a growth rate about five times larger in magnitude. These students were studying in an English-medium environment, but were not taking English-language courses (their courses included management science and literature). There was a great deal of variation in the students' vocabulary improvement, but most of them did benefit from immersion into the L2, with the weaker students making the largest gains. These were advanced students, but there is no reason to believe that lower-level students would not also benefit.

Unfortunately, this desirable approach is not widely available to students around the world. Teachers must find ways of increasing their students' exposure to the L2 without their getting onto an airplane. The consensus on how to do this is to have the students read more. The book-flood studies showed that additional reading led to a tangible increase in learners' vocabularies, even though the classroom discussions about the books read focused on meaning and the students' enjoyment of the texts. As with the Milton and Meara study, it seems that just using a language can be a potent way to learn it, even without explicit focus on linguistic forms. Because reading is considered such a key means to vocabulary improvement, I will give priority to it in my discussion of vocabulary and the four skills.

Vocabulary and reading

Reading is an important part of all but the most elementary of vocabulary programs. For intermediate and advanced learners with vocabularies above 3,000 or so words, reading offers a portal of exposure to all remaining words. Even beginning students with a limited vocabulary can benefit from reading, by accessing *graded readers* (books written with a controlled vocabulary and limited range of grammatical structures). Of course, many words can be learned incidentally through verbal exposure, but considering that spoken discourse is associated with more frequent words and lower type–token ratios than written discourse (only about 2,000 words made up the majority of speech in the Schonell, Meddleton, and Shaw [1956] study), it would be optimistic to expect to learn a wide vocabulary from only spoken discourse. Written discourse, on the other hand, tends to use a wide variety of vocabulary, making it a better resource for acquiring a broader range of words.

There is plenty of evidence that learners can acquire vocabulary from reading only. In one of the classic studies, learners read *A Clockwork Orange,* a English novel that uses Russian slang words called *nadsat.* Since the nadsat glossaries were removed from the novels before being given to the learners, and they did not speak Russian, the only way of learning these words was from context. The researchers found that, on average, 75% of the ninety nadsat words tested were known receptively even though the vocabulary test was unexpected (Sarangi, Nation, & Meister, 1978). However, most other studies show that the vocabulary uptake from reading is really rather small, and it is only through numerous repeated exposures from a great deal of reading that any significant number of words are learned.

This means that the odd reading session may not have much of an effect on vocabulary learning. Vocabulary learning can be somewhat enhanced by making certain words salient, such as by glossing them clearly in book margins (Hulstijn, 1992). But what is really needed is extensive reading, as in the book-flood studies, where reading is both consistent and takes place over a period of time. Advanced students can take advantage of a wide variety of authentic texts, but for beginning students, graded readers probably give the best access to this amount of input. These readers are typically graded into a number of levels. Below are the vocabulary guidelines for the *Oxford Bookworms* series.

Level	New words	Cumulative words
1	400	400
2	300	700
3	300	1,000
4	400	1,400
5	400	1,800
6	700	2,500

(Nation, 1999)

These guidelines ensure that vocabulary is systematically recycled and added to as the reader works through the series. Nation believes that graded readers are an effective resource that should not be ignored, especially as they provide the following benefits: they are an important means of vocabulary expansion, they provide opportunities to practice guessing from context and dictionary skills in a supportive environment in which most words are already known, and partially known words are repeatedly met so that they can be consolidated.

For intermediate students just on the threshold of reading authentic texts, *narrow reading* may be appropriate. The idea is to read numerous authentic texts, but all on the same topic. Reading on one subject means that much of the topic-specific vocabulary will be repeated throughout the course of reading, which both makes the reading easier and gives the reader a better chance of learning this recurring vocabulary. One example of this approach is reading daily newspaper accounts of an ongoing story. Two studies (Hwang & Nation, 1989; Schmitt & Carter, under review) showed that the vocabulary load in a series of running stories was substantially lower than in an equivalent amount of unrelated stories. This is good news, because newspapers are often a convenient source of authentic L2 material, especially if English is the target language. Also, running stories seem to be easy to find in newspapers; Hwang and Nation (1989) report that 19% of stories in international, domestic, and sports sections of the newspapers they looked at were on a recurring topic.

Narrow reading can accelerate access into authentic materials, but of course most of the words in any text need to be known before it can be read. The exact percentage has not been established, and almost certainly depends on factors such as familiarity with topic and whether the unknown words are essential to the gist of the text. A figure of 95% known words (Laufer, 1988) crops up in the literature frequently, and at the moment this seems to be a reasonable estimate.

The percentage of known and unknown vocabulary is one of the most important factors that determine the difficulty of a text. Thus, one way to determine students' reading levels is to gauge their vocabulary knowledge. One can do this by using *cloze tests*. The following is an example of how this can be done. First, take passages at a variety of levels of difficulty. Then prepare the cloze tests by deleting 25 words from each passage and replacing them with blanks (deleting every 7th word is common technique). Students are instructed to fill in the blanks with the word they think was deleted. Scoring can be either on an *exact word* (only exact matches are marked as correct) or an *appropriate word* (any suitable word is marked as correct) basis. If you already know the reading levels of some students, their scores can be used to set scoring bands that indicate ability to handle the various difficulty levels. For example, if students who have been reading comfortably at a certain level are all able to answer between 15 and 25 blanks, then one would expect other students with a similar score to be able to cope with this reading level (Nuttall, 1982, p. 184). If you do not have any students with known reading levels to calibrate the cloze passages, Mikulecky (1990) suggests the following bands. If a student can fill in 15 to 25 blanks with an appropriate answer, then he or she has enough vocabulary to read that level of passage independently. If the score is 10 to 14, that level may be a challenge, but the student should be able to manage it with some support from the teacher. But if the score is 9 or less, the student will only become frustrated, and needs to drop to an easier level of readings.

The percentage of text known also affects the ability to guess an unknown word's meaning from context (also called *inferencing* from context).

Guessing a new word's meaning from context is a key vocabulary learning skill, and Nation (1990) identifies it as one of the three principal strategies for handling low-frequency vocabulary. However, we now know that inferencing is a complicated process, and we cannot assume that learners will automatically be successful. In addition to needing to know enough of the words in a text, extensive research has highlighted a number of other factors that affect the likelihood of inferencing success, some of which are listed below. (See Huckin, Haynes, & Coady, 1993, for a book-length treatment of inferencing.)

1. *The context must be rich enough to offer adequate clues to guess a word's meaning.* Although many contexts offer multiple clues to a new word's meaning, the undeniable fact is that many contexts simply do not offer enough. This means that inferencing is not a strategy that can be used in every situation. For example, readers would have a very difficult time inferencing the meaning of *intractable* from the following context, other than getting a vague negative impression:

It is the purpose of many presidential trips abroad to raise vague hopes and obscure intractable local realities, so it should come as no surprise if Clinton has made a vow that he cannot fulfill. (*Atlantic Monthly,* September 1998, p. 30)

Even if enough clues are present, a single context is rarely sufficient for a reader to guess the full meaning of a word; repeated encounters in diverse contexts is necessary for this (Parry, 1993).

2. *Readers are better able to use local clues in proximity to an unknown word than more global clues that are located further away.*

3. *Learners may mistake an unknown word for one they already know with a similar orthographic or phonological form.* Once this happens, learners may continue with this interpretation even if it does not make sense in the context. In other words, learners may interpret the surrounding context in a way that is congruent with their erroneous reading of the unknown word, rather than letting the context help define the word (Haynes, 1993).

4. *Cognates can help guessing from context if they are used prudently.* Especially for speakers of Romance languages, awareness of cognates can help increase the number of English words that are known in a text, which increases the chances for inferencing success.

5. *Background knowledge about the topic and the culture being discussed aids inferencing.*

6. *Learners need to be skilled in guessing.* Learners need to know what clues to look for and where to find them. With the almost unlimited variety of clues possible, a systematic approach to guessing from context may be advisable. Clarke and Nation (1980) propose the following method:

Step 1. Look at the unknown word and decide its part of speech. Is it a noun, a verb, an adjective, or an adverb?

Step 2. Look at the clause or sentence containing the unknown word. If the unknown word is a noun, what adjectives describe it? What verb is it near? That is, what does this noun do, and what is done to it?

If the unknown word is a verb, what nouns does it go with? Is it modified by an adverb?

If it is an adjective, what noun does it go with?

If it is an adverb, what verb is it modifying?

Step 3. Look at the relationship between the clause or sentence containing the unknown word and other sentences or paragraphs. Sometimes this relationship will be signaled by a conjunction such as *but, because, if, when,* or by an adverb such as *however, as a result.* Often there will be no signal. The possible types of relationship include cause and effect, contrast, inclusion, time, exemplification, and summary. (See Nation, 1990 [Appendix 6], and Halliday & Hasan, 1976, for a fuller list.) Punctuation may also serve as a clue. Semicolons often signal a list of inclusion relationships; dashes may signal restatement. Reference words such as *this, that,* and *such* also provide useful information.

Step 4. Use the knowledge you have gained from Steps 1–3 to guess the meaning of the word.

Step 5. Check that your guess is correct.
   a. See that the part of speech of your guess is the same as the part of speech of the unknown word. If it is not the same, then something is wrong with your guess.
   b. Replace the unknown word with your guess. If the sentence makes sense, your guess is probably correct.
   c. Break the unknown word into its prefix, root, and suffix, if possible. If the meanings of the prefix and root correspond to your guess, good. If not, look at your guess again, but do not change anything if you feel reasonably certain about your guess using the context.

(Clarke & Nation, 1980; also in Nation, 1990)

Many people would look at the word parts first, but Clarke and Nation suggest that this is not a very reliable process. They feel that it is better as a confirmation procedure, in which a mistaken reading of the root and affixes will not lead the learner astray from the beginning of the process. Notice how in this system the context is paramount, taking precedence over the other sources of information. This is because the context is least likely to lead to incorrect guesses.

It must be admitted that this guessing procedure is elaborate and may initially be time-consuming. But, as learners become more proficient with it, they will learn to quickly skip steps that are not pertinent to a particular context, and the other steps will become much more automatic. This means that the whole process can be accelerated to the point where it is a viable thing to do while reading.

7. *Guessing a word from context does not mean that it will be remembered.* If a word is easy to guess, then a learner will inference it quickly with the minimum amount of mental processing in order to carry on with reading. This shallow processing may not ensure that the word is retained. Also, the text may be so rich with clues that it can be comprehended without the unknown word. On the other hand, if the clues are sparser and the guessing process requires more cognitive effort, then the word is more likely to be remembered. Thus guessability and retainability may have an inverse relationship (Mondria & Wit-de-Boer, 1991). This does not mean that inferencing is unimportant, but it might facilitate fluent reading more than vocabulary acquisition.

Vocabulary and writing, listening, and speaking

Vocabulary research has tended to focus on reading, but vocabulary is obviously necessary for the other three skills as well. In the teaching of writing, many teachers focus on the grammatical well-formedness of a composition. However, it seems that lexis may be the element requiring more attention. Research has shown that lexical errors tend to impede comprehension more than grammatical errors, and native-speaking judges tend to rate lexical errors as more serious than grammatical errors (Ellis, 1994). In addition, lexical errors tend to be relatively frequent; Dušková (1969) analyzed the compositions of Czech learners of English and found that about 23% of the errors identified were lexical in nature, the highest category with the exception of articles.

A typical problem is that learners often use basic vocabulary where a good native-speaking writer would use more precise lower-frequency words. Improving learners' vocabulary size is the best answer to this problem, as well as recycling and elaborating receptive vocabulary until it becomes productive. A more immediate answer is to encourage use of "productive" learner dictionaries, such as the *Longman Language Activator* (1993) or the *Oxford Learner's Wordfinder Dictionary* (Trappes-Lomax, 1997). These allow students to look up basic words that they are likely to know *(listen)* in order to be directed to more precise lexical choices *(eavesdrop):*

• LISTEN

1 to listen to someone or something
2 to listen to a radio programme or radio station
3 to deliberately listen to other people's conversations when they do not know you are listening
4 ways of telling someone to listen to something
5 someone who listens to a speech or performance or to what someone is saying
6 someone who regularly listens to a particular radio programme or radio station

↓

3 to deliberately listen to other people's conversations when they do not know you are listening

listen in	**tap**
eavesdrop	**monitor**
bug	

↓

eavesdrop / iːvz ‖ -draːp/ to listen secretly to someone's private conversation, especially when you are hidden behind a door, wall, etc [vI]

(*Longman Language Activator,* 1993)

We should also be careful not to take regular dictionary skills for granted. Scholfield (1997) shows that there are a number of things a learner must be able to do to find the correct entry and meaning sense for a word: (1) the word's spelling must be guessed, even if it has only been heard; (2) alphabetical order must be known to locate the word; (3) the learner must decide the proper word form under which to look up the word or phrase (e.g., to find *scruffier,* you must look under *scruffy;* to find *to put your nose to the grindstone,* you must look under *nose*); and (4) in the plentiful case of polysemous words, multiple meaning senses must be examined before deciding upon the appropriate one. This complexity suggests that learners should be given some practice in dictionary use at the beginning of a course, or at the very least, made to read and understand the front matter in their dictionaries. Unless this is made a requirement, all too many learners neglect this informative source of dictionary knowledge.

When it comes to verbal skills, lexis is somewhat easier because much less is required for listening and speaking than for reading and writing. Nation (1990) recommends reading stories aloud, glossing new words when they occur, and dictation exercises as ways of improving listening vocabulary. For speaking, a number of possibilities exist. Pair-work activities that have an information gap are often used to stimulate oral communicative practice. These can be made more effective by giving key vocabulary to one of the partners, which then has to be negotiated with the other. Practice with paraphrasing can help learners when they do not know a word, by making full use of the words they do know. Joe, Nation, and Newton (1996) give a number of ways of adapting speaking tasks for vocabulary learning. For a variety of other listening and speaking activities that have a lexical focus, see Nation (1994).

Conclusion

To close this chapter, let us again highlight the incremental nature of vocabulary learning. The implication of this is that, except for totally new words, learners will be adding to some existing knowledge of the L2 words. When attempting to enhance this partial knowledge, vocabulary learning will depend on what the learner already knows, and how well the learner wishes to know the word. Graves (1987) highlights the multiplicity of vocabulary learning, distinguishing six types: (1) learning to read known words, (2) learning new meaning senses for known words, (3) learning new words representing known concepts, (4) learning new words representing new concepts, (5) clarifying and enriching the meanings of known words, and (6) moving words from receptive to productive vocabularies. One can see that Graves's list emphasizes the ongoing learning of a word, as all of these except (4) involve prior knowledge of either the word or the associated concept. Although Graves is referring to L1 vocabulary, the list should apply equally to an L2 context. The important lesson to be taken from this is that vocabulary teaching means more than just introducing new words, it also includes nurturing partially known vocabulary along to the point where learners can use it at will.

Summary

This chapter summarizes and adds to the "Applications to teaching" sections in previous chapters. The number of words a student needs depends largely on the eventual goal: 2,000 words for conversational speaking, 3,000 word families to begin reading authentic texts, perhaps as many as 10,000 for challenging academic texts, and 15,000 to 20,000 to equal an educated native speaker.

Vocabulary can be acquired through explicit study or incidentally through exposure to words in context. The most frequent 2,000 words are essential enough to warrant explicit attention, but less frequent words may have to be largely acquired incidentally. When explicitly teaching vocabulary, it is beneficial to avoid cross-association, to teach underlying meanings and complete word families when possible, and to be aware of the intralexical and cross-linguistic factors that may make certain words difficult for our learners.

Reading can provide a good context for incidental learning, although only large amounts of it are likely to lead to any significant vocabulary improvement. Thus extensive and narrow reading programs may be the most beneficial for students. Guessing from context is an important way to access vocabulary, but has limitations and may be more of a reading skill than a vocabulary acquisition one.

Vocabulary acquisition is an incremental process, and teachers must concentrate not only on introducing new words, but also on enhancing learners' knowledge of previously presented words.

Exercises for expansion

1. A number of language goals given in this chapter were related to a certain-sized vocabulary. The first is enough vocabulary to simply survive in a foreign country during a short trip; the second is to be able to communicate verbally in everyday situations; the third is to start to read authentic materials. The last is to have a nativelike vocabulary. List a number of other language goals and the vocabulary size that you think might allow them. How could you go about validating your guess in a vocabulary research study?

2. Do you agree with the suggestion by Meara (1995) and myself that it might make sense to prime the language-learning pump by teaching a large amount of vocabulary at the beginning of a course of study? Why or why not? Do you think such an idea might work in the teaching situation you are most familiar with?

3. Choose some vocabulary exercises or activities and analyze them from a word-knowledge perspective. Which types of word knowledge do they address and hopefully enhance? Which types of word knowledge are not addressed? Does it matter that some word-knowledge types are not addressed?

4. It has been suggested that vocabulary learning strategies are important because they enable students to learn the words that cannot be explicitly taught because of time constraints. Look at the list of vocabulary learning strategies on page 134. Which of these strategies do you think it might be most useful to teach to the students you are most familiar with?

5. The following three passages have been taken from different editions of the same magazine, so they should have a similar style and level. They have been modified to simulate varying percentages of unknown words, by replacing words with blanks. In the first passage, 5 of every 100 words have been replaced (5% unknown), the second passage 10 out of 100 (10% unknown), and the third 15 out of 100 (15%). Because the rarest words are the ones most likely to be unknown, the least frequent content words were the ones chosen for deletion, with the exception of names and titles. How much more difficult does both guessing word meanings from context and comprehending the meaning of the text become as the percentage of unknown words becomes higher? Is there a point where either breaks down? The missing words are in Appendix E.

Passage 1: **Pain**

Pain – like death and taxes – seems to be one of life's eternal and _____ _____. But in fact the concept of pain is anything but eternal: It has changed radically over the course of history, and it also differs from one culture to another, even from one individual to another. Moreover, an increasing number of experts say that pain need not be _____. The fact that it still is for many people may be the fault of current medical practices – and of our _____ attitudes.

In *The Wilson Quarterly,* David B. Morris recently suggested that for the past three centuries Western society has relied on a _____, _____ idea of pain's origins and significance. During the Middle Ages and _____, he writes, human suffering seemed an expression of God's will, to be _____ with faith and _____. Pain was considered as much a psychological or religious phenomenon as a medical one.

In the 17th century, European thinkers began to develop what Morris calls "the medical model of pain." In his *Treatise of Man* (1662), René Descartes _____ the modern understanding of _____ and _____, describing pain as a mechanism that informed the brain when a particular part of the body required attention: If a person put his foot in a fire, the pain was what told him to pull his foot back from the flames.

That seems logical enough. And it's the explanation that most people, physicians and _____ alike, continue to accept. Morris argues, however, that it is wrong to suppose that the pain itself, once its "message" arrives at the brain, is essentially meaningless. An increasing body of evidence, he writes, indicates that "meaning is often fundamental to the experience of pain. . . . Pain is never entirely a matter of nerves and _____ but taps into our emotional, psychological, and cultural experience."

For example, low-back pain, the most common form of _____

_____ pain, often cannot be blamed on any specific physical cause. In one study Morris _____, most adults who complained of back pain turned out to have _____ disk disease – as did 70 percent of those who reported *no* back pain. In fact, Morris suggests, "the strongest signs predicting that a [person] will develop _____ back pain are job dissatisfaction and unsatisfactory social relations in the workplace." The old _____ model may be partially right after all: Pain's roots lie deeply buried in human psychology.

(*Civilization,* January/February 1995, p. 16)

Passage 2: **Dinosaurs**

With Steven Spielberg's computer-generated dinosaurs just finishing their second _____ across America, _____ dinosaurs – and all sorts of other _____ – are becoming hot collector's items. Even Sotheby's is getting in on the action, with plans to _____ the largest and most complete *Tyrannosaurus rex* ever found. (It's expected to go for as much as $5 million.) Private collectors and dealers are bone hunting like mad and, as Wendy Marston reports in *The Sciences,* many _____ aren't at all pleased.

At a recent _____-collectors' _____ in Tucson, Marston found dealers _____ cave bear _____, dinosaur eggs and "about fifty _____, _____-size birds from the _____ period called *Confuciusornis sanctus,* which have _____ on the ends of their wings. The *Confuciusornis* [sold] _____, most for under $5,000 _____."

But collecting such _____ is a far less _____ _____ than trading _____ cards or stamps, critics say. "Every _____ has a story to tell, and if one isn't collected right, it loses its context, its story, and essentially becomes an art object," says David W. Krause, a former president of the Society of _____ _____. Scientists also worry that private owners of _____ restrict public and scientific access to them. If a collector buys the *T. rex* at Sotheby's, _____ may never learn whether, as they suspect, the dinosaur suffered from _____.

The scientific community is particularly concerned about a new push to open up federal lands – currently the exclusive _____ of academic _____ – to private _____ hunters. Collectors claim that, just as _____ and mining companies have a right to extract raw materials from public lands, so they should be allowed to dig up the _____ _____. And some aren't waiting for official permission: The federal government has had to set up a _____ operation to catch illegal _____ in the act of _____ federal lands.

Even on private land, _____ have _____ trouble when forced to share access with for-profit _____ hunters. One scientist was driven off his dig on the Blackfeet Indian Reservation in Montana when a commercial _____ company, following a standard industry practice, offered the property owners money to dig on the land. When one owner, in turn, asked the scientist to pay, he couldn't – so he had to abandon the dig.

(*Civilization,* October/November 1997, pp. 36–37)

Passage 3: **Wine**

Americans have been making wine ever since the first European settlers found wild _____ _____ on the East Coast. But until recently the results of their efforts often came closer to _____ than they did to _____ _____, writes Paul Lukacs in *American Heritage.* _____ American _____ _____ make good eating but disappointing wine, so _____ Colonial _____, including Thomas Jefferson, Lord Baltimore and William Penn, experimented with _____ _____ European _____ _____. The _____ failed – not only because of the extremes of the East Coast _____ but also because of the _____ _____ that attacked the _____. The _____ did not exist in the more _____ West, however, and by the 1850s Californians were planting _____ widely. At the end of the century, California was producing wines that could rival Europe's. "_____," writes Lukacs, "they were better known in London than in New York."

The _____ movement at the beginning of the 20th century did not prevent farmers from growing _____ and making their own wine, writes Lukacs; "what died was any _____ for its_____." When _____ of _____ came in 1933, the country was in the depths of the _____. Wine was regarded simply as _____ _____, and was usually sweetened or _____. It was not until the '60s that Americans began experimenting with new tastes and ideas. American _____ _____ in two ways: Ernest and Julio Gallo tried to figure out what _____ wanted and to provide it; Robert Mondavi set out to produce wines that "belong in the company of the truly fine wines of the world."

The very lack of _____ _____, writes Lukacs, has helped to give American wines today a _____ and character of their own. _____ with science and _____, Californians were able to _____ in a short time what had taken centuries of _____ and _____ in Europe. And, _____, Europeans began to realize that there was more than _____ _____ behind the popularity of American _____. In 1976, a _____ tasting of international wines before _____ French judges signaled the _____ of a new _____. The two winners – a _____ and a _____ – were both produced in the Napa Valley.

(*Civilization,* February/March 1997, pp. 27–28)

Further reading

Several key references for vocabulary teaching appear on page 146 of this chapter. Additional sources include: Beck, McKeown, and Omanson (1987), Graves (1987), Nation (1994), Nation and Newton (1997), and Sökmen (1997).

9 Assessing vocabulary knowledge

- I am familiar with multiple-choice tests. What other kinds of tests are there to measure vocabulary?
- I would like to know how well my students know selected words. How can I measure this?
- What words should I test?

There are a number of reasons why vocabulary testing should be regarded as a useful element in a well-run language-teaching program. Most obviously, if vocabulary is considered to be an important component of language knowledge, then it naturally needs to be assessed in some way. For some learners, particularly beginners, vocabulary may be about the only aspect of language they know well enough to be tested on. If a language program focuses on the skill of reading, vocabulary measurement is appropriate because vocabulary knowledge is one of the most important factors in reading ability.

Another reason has to do with learner attitudes. Testing researchers have found that tests have consequences far beyond providing estimates of examinees' abilities. They also shape the way learners view the content of a course. Most teachers are aware that learners partially judge the importance of classroom material by whether it appears on subsequent tests or not. This effect is called *backwash* (or *washback*), and can be positive or negative. If a teacher thinks vocabulary is important, then it is worth including a vocabulary component in an assessment scheme to build positive attitudes toward vocabulary study. On the other hand, if vocabulary is stressed in classes, but never addressed during assessment, students might come away with the negative conclusion that vocabulary does not really matter.

For whatever reason, most teachers will wish to gauge their learners' vocabulary progress and knowledge. Unfortunately, few teachers feel confident in their knowledge of testing theory and methodology. This chapter aims to provide you with enough background to be able to better evaluate existing vocabulary tests, and with a framework to write your own tests, if you so wish. It will do this by focusing on four key questions for vocabulary test development. (These questions are also discussed in Schmitt, 1994.)

Why do you want to test?

This question could be rephrased as "What use will you make of the resulting test scores?" There are several possible purposes for giving a vocabulary test. Perhaps the most common one is to find out if students have learned the words that were taught, or that they were expected to learn (*achievement test*). Alternatively, a teacher may want to find where students' vocabularies have gaps, so that specific attention can be given to those areas (*diagnostic test*). Vocabulary tests can also be used to help place students in the proper class level (*placement test*). Vocabulary items that are part of commercial *proficiency tests,* such as the TOEFL (1998a, 1998b) provide some indication of a learner's vocabulary size, which is related to overall language proficiency. Other possibilities include utilizing tests as a means to motivate students to study, to show students their progress in learning new words, and to make selected words more salient by including them on a test.

On a more general basis, a test's purpose is related to the kind of lexical information desired. A typical purpose for testing is to obtain an estimate of the size of learners' vocabularies, that is, *how many* words or word families they know. This is sometimes referred to as *breadth of knowledge.* Another possibility is to measure *how well* target words or word families are known (*depth* or *quality of knowledge*). Almost all of the widely used vocabulary tests to date have been of the "size" variety, returning an estimate of the number of words known from frequency lists or other word samples. Even everyday vocabulary tests made by classroom teachers might be considered breadth tests in the sense that they estimate how many words are known from a pool of those studied. But there is a growing awareness that these tests have their limitations, and that measuring quality of knowledge is also desirable. This distinction will be a recurring theme throughout this chapter.

Having a clear idea of a test's purpose(s) should lead to more principled answers in the following steps.

What words do you want to test?

If the teacher wants to test students' class achievement, then the words tested should obviously be drawn from the ones covered in the course. It is better to avoid standardized tests in this case, because, unless an instructor teaches solely from a single book, any general-purpose test is unlikely to be as suitable to a particular classroom and set of students as one the instructor could custom-make (Heaton, 1988). The teacher is in the best position to know her students and which words they should have mastered. The exception to this is when the syllabus is designed around a particular word list, as some ministries of education prescribe. In cases like this, prepared tests based on that word list may be suitable, particularly toward the end of the course.

Vocabulary tests used for placement or diagnostic purposes may need to sample from a more general range of words. If the students to be tested all come from the same school, or have been taught from similar syllabi, then it is possible to draw words from those taught in their courses. However, if students come from different schools with different syllabi and language-teaching methodologies, as may be the case in a university placement situation, then the selection must be more broadly based. In these cases, words are often taken from word-frequency lists. Because students can generally be expected to know more frequent words best regardless of their previous schooling, use of these lists allows the principled selection of target words that can be adjusted for students' anticipated language level. (The exception is cognates, which can be relatively easy even if they are infrequent in the L2.) The results from tests based on these lists can supply information not only about how many words are known, but also at what frequency level.

Vocabulary tests that are part of proficiency tests need to include the broadest range of words of all. Many universities rely on commercial proficiency tests to control admissions. Therefore, the tests must include a range of words that will provide a fair evaluation of people of different nationalities, native languages, and cultures, as well as proficiency levels. Some of the words on these tests must be uncommon enough to allow the highest-level test takers to demonstrate their superior knowledge.

If the purpose of a test is to give an estimate of a learner's total vocabulary size, then some method is needed to sample from all of the words the learner might know. For lower-level learners, frequency lists up to the 10,000-word level are suitable, because such students are unlikely to know many words beyond this. In fact, sampling from the most frequent 1,000 and 2,000 levels is often sufficient, especially for beginners. But, for very advanced learners (and native speakers) it is necessary to sample from all the words in a language. In this case, the *dictionary method* is often used. This involves systematically choosing words from a large dictionary, for example, the 5th word from every 10th page. These words are then fixed on a test. The percentage of correct answers is then multiplied by the number of words in the dictionary to arrive at an estimate of vocabulary size. Unfortunately, this method has several problems, the main one being that the resulting total size estimate will depend on the size of the dictionary used. Also, direct sampling, as mentioned above, will result in skewed results, so some adjustments in the sampling procedure need to be made (see Nation, 1993, for details on how to do this).

Another problem is that the number of words finding their way onto the test compared to the total number of possible words is very low. This issue of *sample rate* is an important one in vocabulary testing. Let us say that the purpose of a test is to measure knowledge of the most frequent 1,000 words of English, and it includes a sample of 100 of those words. The 1 in 10 sample rate is probably sufficient for us to infer the degree of knowledge of the whole 1,000 word set. But if the test included only 20 words (1 in 50), we would be much less confident that these accurately reflected knowledge of the set. In general, higher sample rates and greater numbers of words make for a better vocabulary test.

Sample rate has direct effects on the three major criteria in language testing: *validity, reliability,* and *practicality. Validity* is a complex issue, but for our purposes here, it refers to how well a test measures what it is supposed to measure. In other words, do learners' responses to the test items represent their actual knowledge of the target words, both those on the test and the others in the set that did not make it onto the test? (See Read, in press, for much more on the three testing criteria). For example, a vocabulary test in which a target word is embedded in a sentence or paragraph is supposed to measure knowledge of that word. But in order to answer that item, a learner must also know the other words in the context, as well as be able to read. So the test item is tapping other knowledge in addition to knowledge of the target word. Many test types wish to capture this integrated interaction of multiple linguistic aspects, but if a test purports to measure mainly vocabulary knowledge, these other aspects can affect the vocabulary scores in ways that are difficult to determine. This can compromise validity. Of the many things that influence the validity of a vocabulary test, sample rate is important in that higher rates obviously allow a more representative sample of the total target word pool.

Reliability concerns the stability or consistency of a test's behavior over time. If an examinee took a test several times, without his or her ability changing, the test would ideally produce the same score on each administration (perfect reliability). In the real world, the test scores would vary to a certain degree, because of such factors as examinee alertness or fatigue, motivation, the testing environment, and the test itself. If the test scores varied wildly, we would have no idea which particular score most closely corresponded with the examinee's true ability. In general, the more *items* (questions) a test contains (which means a higher sampling rate), the more reliable the test is.

Therefore, in terms of validity and reliability, longer tests are better. But unreasonably extensive tests often fail in terms of *practicality;* for example, tests with hundreds of words are unlikely to be of much use in the classroom. Thus, there is always tension between having a test long enough to be valid and reliable, yet short enough to be administered. A useful rule of thumb is that the more important the consequences of a test, the longer and more carefully constructed it should be. High-stakes tests that greatly affect the lives of examinees (such as whether they gain entrance to a high school or university) obviously need to be more comprehensive than tests that have a relatively minor effect (e.g., a quiz that counts for only a small percentage of a course grade).

The bottom line is that we are often dealing with large sets of words when assessing learners' total vocabulary size, and the larger the vocabulary set we wish to measure, the lower the sampling rate is likely to be. Thus, it is an advantage if an item format can be answered quickly, allowing the maximum number of items to be placed on a test.

What aspects of these words do you want to test?

After the target words have been chosen, the next step is to decide which aspects of those words will be tested. We have seen that lexical knowledge is complex, composed of a number of different components. In addition, vocabulary learning is incremental, and so mastery of these aspects will tend to vary on a continuum stretching from "no knowledge" at one end to "complete knowledge and control" at the other. Thus, there is a great deal of latitude in what we might try to measure about the knowledge of a word, although in practical terms we will never be able to capture everything. Different responses to the first question ("Why do you want to test?) will suggest different answers to the question being discussed in this section. Henrickson's (1999) three dimensions of vocabulary development provide a tool with which to consider the possible lexical aspects:

1. the degree of mastery that the test attempts to measure (partial–precise)
2. the degree to which the various word-knowledge aspects are captured
3. a focus on receptive or productive knowledge

As previously mentioned, vocabulary tests are normally used as achievement, placement, or diagnostic tests, as well as components of proficiency tests. I will first use Henrickson's model to discuss which aspects are normally captured in such "size" tests, and then look at the situation for depth of knowledge tests. (See Chapelle, 1994, for an alternative model of vocabulary ability.)

Lexical aspects and vocabulary size tests

Below are four types of items commonly used on size tests.
1. *firm*
   a. deep
   b. hard
   c. warm
   d. clean
2. The writing on the page was *illegible.*
   a. handwritten in ink
   b. written in large letters
   c. difficult to read
   d. written in many colors
3. serious _____ (Give L1 translation)
4. A _____ is a large cat with stripes that lives in the jungle.

Upon contemplation, it becomes obvious that all of these items are only capturing partial knowledge of the target words. Example 1 requires knowing that a synonym for *firm* is *hard,* but this only addresses one meaning sense, and does not tap other senses such as "a company" (a business firm) or "unyielding" (a firm commitment to something). Example 2 measures recognition of *illegible* in this sentence context, but does not show whether test takers can recognize the word in other contexts. Example 3 asks for an L1 translation of the L2 word *serious,* which does not demonstrate the ability to use it in English discourse. Examinees need to know the concrete meaning sense of *tiger* to fill in Example 4, but may not know the figurative meaning sense of "a person who is aggressive in his or her actions."

Not only are these items limited in the lexical aspects they address, but they only describe the degree of knowledge in terms of *correct/not correct.* This means that learners may know something about a target word, but still get no score because the degree of their knowledge was below the threshold necessary to answer the item correctly. Such dichotomously scored items will never be able to give a very precise indication of what a learner knows about a word.

These comments should indicate the difficulty of devising an item format that captures precisely all of a learner's lexical knowledge; in fact, such an item is probably impossible. But it is also clear that all of these example items are capturing only a partial amount of a learner's potential knowledge.

If we consider how well these items capture the various types of word knowledge, we see that they are limited in this respect as well. The main focus is on meaning, and the test taker must also be able to read the written words in order to answer the items. But, as already noted, these items measure only a single meaning sense, whereas words in English are very often polysemous. Beyond this, the items do not seem to address the other word-knowledge types to any great extent. The ability to understand the target words in spoken discourse is not measured, nor are intuitions of how frequently they occur. Grammatical knowledge about word class is not elicited in Examples 1 and 2, because the options are all the same class, and so the examinees do not have to choose between different parts of speech. This factor does come into play in Example 4, where an appropriate answer must be a noun, although in Example 3 the translation equivalent is likely to be the same word class as the target word. But in none of these examples is morphological knowledge of the other word-family derivatives required. Likewise, register is not involved, in this case because *illegible* and *tiger* do not seem to have any strong connotative loading in these particular sentence contexts. (*Illegible* could have a very negative connotation in a sentence such as "She died because of a mistake caused by the doctor's *illegible* handwriting.") Collocation may be involved to a slight degree in contextualized sentences 2 and 4, but nothing like the degree it would be in a productive composition task.

The first two examples are clearly receptive items, and the second two are productive. But Examples 3 and 4 are productive only to a degree. From the prompts, examinees have to produce the appropriate word form, but this does not guarantee that they could use the word in their speech or writing. Only if a test taker produces a word appropriately of his or her own accord can we say that productive mastery has been demonstrated, and then only in that particular context.

So we can see that the amount of information obtainable from such items is surprisingly limited. Meaning and word form are the main types of word knowledge captured with all these items, and the measurement of these is in the form of a crude *knows/does not know* evaluation. The items are relatively quick to take, which helps the sampling rate, but they provide only a partial picture of the total underlying lexical knowledge about the word. Nevertheless, though a close analysis exposes these items' weaknesses, we should not be overly negative. If we are primarily interested in obtaining an estimate of vocabulary size, then such items probably address a sufficient number of lexical aspects to allow inferences to be made about *how many* words are known. But we do have to be cautious in interpreting the results of such tests. They are usually based on measurement of single meaning senses, and so should probably be seen as estimates of how many words are known *to some partial extent.* It would be a mistake to assume that all words marked as "correct" on such tests were at the learner's immediate command.

Lexical aspects and depth of knowledge tests

Teachers wishing to know about *how well* target words are known will clearly need a different type of item format than that illustrated above. Here is one example of a depth item that ideally taps a greater number of lexical aspects.

5. Rate your knowledge of the target word. If you choose (d), please compose a sentence using that word.

   expand
   a. I don't know this word.
   b. I have seen this word before but am not sure of the meaning.
   c. I understand the word when I see or hear it in a sentence, but I don't know how to use it in my own speaking or writing.
   d. I can use the word in a sentence.

                                                    (Scarcella & Zimmerman, 1996)

In this item format, test takers rate their own knowledge of the target words, and at the highest level (d) demonstrate their knowledge by producing a sentence. An item like this clearly addresses more lexical aspects than the examples given in the "size" section. In Henrickson's terms, it is written to give a fuller and more precise description of the learner's lexical knowledge and, at the highest level, addresses various word-knowledge types. In order to write an appropriate and descriptive sentence, test takers must use their knowledge of the word's meaning, its word class, and possibly its collocations and register marking. Perhaps this item's greatest strength is that it captures degrees of mastery between "no knowledge" and "full knowledge." However, it is more difficult to analyze in terms of receptive and productive knowledge. At the highest level, the nature of the knowledge is clearly productive if an appropriate sentence is generated, although it stems from receptive recognition of the target word, so the test taker does not have to actually produce the word form from memory. The task at Levels (a), (b), and (c) is self-rating, and this is not exactly the same thing as recognizing and comprehending a word in an authentic context. In testing, as in acquisition, we find that the distinction between receptive and productive mastery of a word is not always clear-cut.

Although this item provides a clearer picture of a learner's lexical knowledge, it is obvious that it will take longer to complete than the "size" formats discussed earlier. This means that fewer words can be tested, limiting the practicality of such tests to some extent. This format is also prone to students' overestimating their mastery, because only the final level is verified by a demonstration of knowledge. The challenge for vocabulary-testing specialists is to devise item formats that give quality of knowledge information in a time-efficient and verifiable manner. Some experimental formats produced for research purposes will be illustrated later.

The depth of knowledge discussion so far has concentrated on quality measures of a learner's sum knowledge of a word. There are times, however, that teachers may wish to measure specific components of lexical knowledge. This might occur if students of a particular L1 have consistent problems with a particular lexical aspect. Ryan (1997) found that many of her Middle Eastern students had serious problems reading and spelling English words because of interference from Arabic. She designed a specific lexical instrument to test for this (see also page 66).

6. Underline any word which is wrong, and write the correct word above it.

  1. Have you met my aren't? She's my mother's sister.
  2. The cat is under the table.
  3. The torn came into the railway station.
  4. Oh dear! You've cut your finger – look at the build.

(Ryan, 1997, p. 196)

In this test, a particular lexical feature is addressed, namely, discriminating between words with a similar form: *aren't–aunt, torn–train, build–blood* (item 2 has no mistake). The purpose of this test has nothing to do with size or depth; rather it was designed to diagnose a specific learning problem. The different lexical aspects that could be focused upon in this way are numerous, with the following two examples illustrating how collocational and morphological knowledge can be isolated and tested, perhaps for diagnostic purposes.

7. Fill in the grid.   + = collocates   ? = questionable   x = does not collocate

	problem	*amount*	*shame*	*man*
large				
great				
big				
major				

(McCarthy, 1990, p. 12)

8. Fill in the blank with the appropriate word.
   He has an _____ mind. (analyze, analysis, analytical, analytically)

Other considerations

A last aspect that teachers should consider in vocabulary testing is mode of the test. Although the vast majority of vocabulary tests are in the written mode, tests in the verbal mode are also possible; dictation and interviews are just two examples. Mode is related to another factor – whether the test will be a discrete measure of only vocabulary knowledge or whether it will measure how well vocabulary can be used when it is embedded in other language skills, such as reading and writing. This is important because many test formats require the testee to rely heavily on other language skills to answer the item correctly. Consider this example:

9. Write a sentence illustrating the meaning of *gather.*

A student may know the meaning of *gather* but might not be a proficient enough writer to produce a sentence expressing that knowledge. If teachers want to test vocabulary, they should try to minimize the difficulty of the reading, writing, speaking, and listening involved in the test items so that limitations in these language skills do not restrict students' ability to demonstrate their vocabulary knowledge. An example of how to achieve this is to always use words of a higher frequency in the definitions and sentence/discourse context than the target words being tested.

How will you elicit students' knowledge of these words?

All of the points raised above lead to the writing of a testing instrument that elicits output from students indicating their vocabulary knowledge. This involves key issues such as word choice, item format, and length of test. These issues have already been touched upon, so let us look at vocabulary tests more globally. Read (in press) has proposed three dimensions that determine the nature of vocabulary tests. Consideration of these dimensions can help us judge the type of vocabulary test most suited to our purposes. Note that the term *construct* refers to the theoretical understanding of some aspect of language.

Discrete ◄─────────► *Embedded*

A measure of vocabulary knowledge or use as an independent
construct

A measure of vocabulary that forms
part of the assessment of some
other, larger construct

Selective ◄─────────► *Comprehensive*

A measure in which specific
vocabulary items are the
focus of the assessment

A measure that takes account of the
whole vocabulary content
of the input material (reading/
listening tasks) or the test taker's
response (writing/speaking tasks)

Context-independent ◄─────────► *Context-dependent*

A vocabulary measure in which
the test taker can produce
the expected response
without referring to any
context

A vocabulary measure that assesses
the test taker's ability to take
account of contextual information
in order to produce the expected
response

If the teacher is interested in measuring vocabulary knowledge as separate
from other language skills, then tests tending toward the discrete end of the
Discrete/Embedded continuum will be most appropriate. Examples are the
Vocabulary Levels and Checklist tests in the next section. Similarly, tests
measuring vocabulary size are likely to have the same tendency. Measures
that look into how well a word can be used in language, such as in writing,
will often be embedded in a test of the four skills, for example, in an essay
examination. If we wish to test knowledge of specific words, then we select
them and put them on a test. This is a standard practice with which we are
all familiar. But this does not give us any indication of how well the words
can be spontaneously used by the test taker. One way around this is to ask
the learner to produce language and then analyze the vocabulary content of
all that is produced. This gives a better idea of the mastery of these words,
but it is very difficult to constrain the task enough to elicit any particular
words. The Lexical Frequency Profile and type – token ratios discussed in
the next section are examples of such comprehensive measures.

There is an ongoing debate about whether vocabulary should be tested
in context. In principle, it is a good idea, but it often leads to test items that
are expensive in terms of time. Also, many context-dependent formats really only provide a generic context that means little at all. For example,
many multiple-choice context sentences have very little content, simply because test writers do not want to give away the meaning of the target word.

It is difficult to design formats that truly require engagement with context, which is why words still tend to be presented in isolation or in single sentence contexts.

In practice, items set on traditional tests have mainly been selective and context-independent, while the tests themselves have tended to be discrete. But the more test writers wish to measure learners' ability to actually use words in real-world situations, the further the tests need to move toward the embedded, comprehensive, and context-dependent ends of the continuums. Once again, teachers need to be clear about the purposes of the test before they can decide upon the most appropriate type.

Examples of current vocabulary test development

There is no commonly accepted standardized test of English vocabulary. The closest thing we have is the *Vocabulary Levels Test,* first devised by Paul Nation (1990). Rather than giving a single estimate of total vocabulary size, it measures knowledge of words at four frequency levels: 2,000, 3,000, 5,000, and 10,000. It also has a special level for academic English words. It uses the following item format:

1. bitter
2. independent   _____ small
3. lovely   _____ beautiful
4. merry   _____ liked by many people
5. popular
6. slight

The test is designed to require minimal reading, and so is fairly quick to take. The option words all have different meaning senses, so learners who have even a vague idea of a target word's meaning sense should be able to make the correct match. As such, it measures threshold meaning knowledge of the target words. Because the test gives estimates of vocabulary size at 5 levels, it is useful for placement purposes, and diagnosing vocabulary gaps. I have written two new and equivalent versions of the Vocabulary Levels Test, with Version 1 being presented in Appendix F. (See Schmitt, Schmitt, and Clapham, under review, and Schmitt and Schmitt, under review, for more on these new versions.)

Checklist tests utilize a format that allows large numbers of words to be tested. Target words are presented on a list and learners are merely required to check (✓) if they know them or not. The obvious problem is that many subjects might overestimate their vocabulary knowledge and check words they really do not know. To compensate for this, nonwords that look like real words but are not, such as *flinder* or *trebron,* are put onto the test along with the real words. If some of these nonwords are "checked," that indicates that the student is overestimating his or her vocabulary knowledge. A formula compensates for this overestimation to give more accurate scores. The compensation formula works well if students are careful and mark only a few nonwords, but if they mark very many, then their scores are severely penalized and the test becomes unreliable. Paul Meara is most closely associated with this format, having developed a book of pencil-and-paper checklist tests called the *EFL Vocabulary Tests* (Meara, 1992), a commercial computerized version called the *Eurocentres Vocabulary Size Test* (EVST) (Meara & Jones, 1990), as well as a series of single-level computerized tests called the LLEX tests (Meara, 1994). (See also Meara & Buxton, 1987.) As with the Vocabulary Levels Test, these tests focus on meaning, and are particularly suitable as placement tests.

As for depth of knowledge tests, two approaches can be taken. The first attempts to measure how vocabulary develops over time (developmental approach), and the other measures which word-knowledge types are known (dimensions approach) (Read, 1997). Test item No. 5 in this chapter illustrates the developmental approach. A similar, but more elaborate, self-assessment scale that is becoming increasingly used in vocabulary research is the *Vocabulary Knowledge Scale* (VKS) (Paribakht & Wesche, 1993).

1. I don't remember having seen this word before.
2. I have seen this word before, but I don't know what it means.
3. I have seen this word before, and I think it means _____ (synonym or translation)
4. I know this word. It means _____. (synonym or translation)
5. I can use this word in a sentence: _____.
   (If you do this section, please also do Section 4.)

This test format combines student self-report with production to ensure that students do know the words. This kind of test can give a teacher some indication of where along the acquisition continuum a word exists in a student's lexicon. In addition, because it emphasizes what students know, rather than what they do not know, by allowing them to show their partial knowledge of a word, it may be more motivating than other types of tests. But scales such as this have several weaknesses that need to be addressed. The first is that the lower-level judgments are not verified. Second, the scale mixes receptive and productive measures, which makes it difficult to interpret. Third, it is not clear in principle how many levels such a scale should have, and so the number usually has more to do with convenience than theory. Also, the increments between each stage are unlikely to be equivalent in magnitude. Fourth, test takers often write sentences that do not really illustrate whether a word is mastered or not, although this scale at least controls for this eventuality by asking for a synonym or translation.

The dimensions approach can be exemplified by tests focusing on word associations. Although this is a new direction, there is some evidence indicating that there is a gradual progression in the development of the associations of words taught in class, suggesting that association tests may be valuable in capturing this incremental aspect of vocabulary learning (Beck, 1981). The Word Associates Test (Read, 1993, 1998) was one of the first attempts to use associations to measure associative and collocational word knowledge, in addition to conceptual knowledge. In it, the target word is followed by a eight options, four of which have some relationship with the target word and four of which do not. The words in the left box have a paradigmatic relationship (*sudden – quick, surprising*) with the target word, and the ones in the right box have a syntagmatic relationship (*sudden change, sudden noise*). Learners are told that there are four associates and are asked to find them.

sudden

beautiful quick surprising thirsty	change doctor noise school

Read (1998) concludes that the test composed of these items gives a good overall view of the test taker's vocabulary knowledge, but that individual items are not very reliable indicators of the quality of knowledge of each target word, mainly because the effects of guessing are difficult to compensate for. If the four associates are chosen, the learner can be assumed to have good knowledge of the target word; if none are chosen, the word is not known. But it is very difficult to interpret "split" scores in which some associates are chosen, but also some of the nonassociated words. In these cases, it is difficult to know whether the associates chosen were really known or just guessed.

The Association Vocabulary Test developed by Vives Boix (1995) does not seem to have such a problem with guessing. In her format, learners are presented with three-word clusters in which two words are associated and the other is not. Learners then choose the unrelated word. (Note: *creciente* = growing, *veneno* = poison, *pócima* = nasty drink.)

[ ] creciente   [ ] veneno   [ ] pócima

She asked a number of learners to think aloud while completing the test and found that the percentage of successful guessing with this format was very low.

Vives Boix suggests that this format measures the degree of lexical organization rather than the number of words known well. Thus, she believes that it might be a good supplement to the type of size tests that are normally given. This highlights an interesting direction in vocabulary testing: trying to describe a learner's overall lexicon in addition to the individual words within it. As the state of vocabulary testing advances, we may well use vocabulary tests that include a number of different formats, each giving information about a different facet of vocabulary knowledge. Three facets in particular would be important in such a global measure: the number of words known, the degree of organization of the lexicon, and the degree to which words within the lexicon can be used automatically.

The last type of vocabulary measure we will examine resides on the embedded, comprehensive, context-dependent sides of the testing continuum. It involves analyzing the vocabulary produced in a written composition through statistical analysis. Lexical density (total number of content words divided by total number of words in the composition) gives some indication of the "content load" of a composition, with a higher figure indicating a higher density of content words (see page 75). Lexical variation or type–token ratio (number of different words in a text divided by total number of words in a text) shows the range of words used in a text. A higher figure means that the writer has used more variety of words with less repetition. *Lexical sophistication* (number of sophisticated word families in a text divided by total number of word families in a text) shows the proportion of relatively advanced words occurring in a text. The definition of what is advanced has to be defined for a particular group of students with their particular background and proficiency, but lower frequency of occurrence is one obvious criterion.

Laufer and Nation (1995) used the 1,000 and 2,000 frequency lists, along with the University Word List (UWL) to create the *Lexical Frequency Profile* (LFP). They use a computer program to sort all of the words in a composition into a four-category profile. For example, the profile for a learner producing 200 1,000-level word families, 50 2,000-level, 20 UWL, and 10 others not on these lists (280 in total) would be 71%–18%–7%–4%. Further research by Laufer (1994) suggested that taking the percentage of words beyond the 2,000 level gave a better indication of the vocabulary progress with her students. All of these methods have the advantage that the students produce the words of their own accord in the composition, and that they are used in context. The downside is that these statistical procedures will need to be researched further before their classroom applications are clear.

Implications for teachers

Perhaps the greatest lesson to be drawn from this testing review is that the purpose of a test needs to be established before any evaluation of a particular test format can be made. For most teachers, the purpose will usually be achievement, placement, or diagnostic in nature, and so you may well continue to rely on traditional test formats. Still, using the frameworks suggested in this chapter can help to analyze these tests in a much more rigorous way, which should facilitate achieving a better match between purpose and realization. If you wish to write vocabulary tests, the questions should give you a basis to go through the development process in a principled manner. Another key point is that proper test development is recursive, and involves getting feedback on draft test versions from piloting or from colleagues, and revising the tests on the basis of that feedback.

We have seen that no test format gives a complete specification of how well a word is known. This means that vocabulary tests give incomplete information about an examinee's lexical knowledge. Thus, you need to be careful about how you interpret test results. Analyzing the test items to see what they require of the test takers will give you a better idea about what inferences can be made about the underlying lexical knowledge.

Summary

Testing vocabulary is a more complicated business than might at first be assumed. A number of important factors need to be considered in the development of a well-designed vocabulary test. This chapter offered a systematic way of considering these factors. It also suggested one framework for evaluating which lexical aspects to consider focusing on in vocabulary tests, and another for analyzing the general attributes of a test. Several tests which are currently being used in vocabulary research were illustrated to show present thinking in the area of vocabulary test development.

Exercises for expansion

1. Look at the following test items. Analyze what they require of the test takers and what we can confidently infer about their lexical knowledge if they answer the items correctly. Or incorrectly?

   i. Write your native-language translation for the word.
       support _____
       experience _____
       difficult _____

   ii. Fill in the missing words.
       I think that was t _____ happiest summer of my l _____. There
       was no trouble i _____ our valley. Fletcher was a _____ on a
       business trip most of t _____ summer. He was trying t _____ get
       a contract to s _____ large amounts of beef t _____ an Indian
       Reservation some d _____ away.

       (Wallace, 1982, p. 115)

   iii. Choose the *best* pair of words to fill in the two blanks in the sentence.
        Though the *Oxford English Dictionary* is undoubtedly the greatest dictionary ever _____, it is designed for scholars and research workers rather than the _____ dictionary user.
        a. assembled, assiduous
        b. demonstrated, amateur
        c. compiled, casual
        d. published, professional
        e. projected, omniscient

        (Nurnberg & Rosenblum, 1977, p. 301)

   iv. Circle the entry that does not fit with the rest of the group.

       a. editorial   b. court
          business section   lawyer
          cartoons   jail
          weather   author
          research paper   judge
          advertisements   jury

       (Paul Nation, personal communication)

2. There have been ongoing attempts to make the lexical items on the TOEFL more context-dependent. The current computerized version presents a passage on the left side of the screen. For a vocabulary item, part of the passage is highlighted in bold font. The test taker is directed to the target word in the passage, and then must find a synonym for it within the highlighted excerpt:

(Text highlighted in bold)

The Southwest has always been a dry country, where water is scarce, but the Hopi and Zuni were able to bring water from streams to their fields and gardens through irrigation ditches. Because it is so rare, yet so important, water played a major role in their religion.

(Item)
Look at the word **rare** in the passage.
Click on the word in **bold** text that has the same meaning.

(TOEFL, 1998a, 1998b)

How much must test takers engage with the passage context in order to answer this type of item? Is there a way to make vocabulary items completely context-dependent?

3. Develop your own test of academic vocabulary using the procedures outlined in this chapter. Use the Academic Word List in Appendix B to sample from. Issues you will have to consider include purpose of the test, which words to sample from the list, how many words to sample, and which item format to adopt.

Further reading

For more on vocabulary testing: Nation (1990), Read (1997), and Read (2000).

For details on testing in general: Hughes (1989), Bachman (1990), Cohen (1994), and Bachman and Palmer (1996).

For an accessible how-to-do-it handbook that includes vocabulary testing: Heaton (1988).

Appendixes

Appendix A   Word associations for *illuminate*

One hundred British university students gave three associations each to form this list. The top three responses are indicated in bold.

aglow
attention
Blackpool 10
bright 22
brighten 10
brightness 2
bulb 8
candle 2
Christmas 6
clarify 6
clarity 3
clear 5
clothes
colorful
colors 4
darkness
dazzling
dim
discover
display
educate
electric
electricity 2

enhance
enknowledge
enlighten 8
excited
explain
expose
expressive
fair
fire 2
flood
floodlight
florescent
glass
glow 4
golden
grasp
green
highlight 8
idea 4
inspire
knowledge 2
lamp 5
lazer

learn
light 78
lighten 8
light up 6
lit
make clear
manuscript
meaning
medieval
monks
moon
night
noticeable
open
physics
picture 2
point out
precise
present
question
raise
realization 2
red

reveal 3
rocket
room
see 3
shine 12
show 5
sign 2
stars
sun 3
switch
tacky
thought
torch
tree
ultraviolet
understand 5
unpack
wonder
write
yellow

(Personal files)

Appendix B   The Academic Word List (AWL)

The AWL was compiled by Averil Coxhead (1998) from a corpus of written academic English, which contains approximately 3.5 million words. The corpus included texts from twenty-eight subject areas, including seven each from four faculty sections: Arts, Commerce, Law, and Science. Thus the AWL contains words that occur in a wide variety of academic contexts. The words on the list were selected according to three criteria: range, frequency, and uniformity. As such, AWL words should be seen as essential support vocabulary that is necessary to read academic topics, regardless of the discipline. The list is divided into ten sublists, with 1 being the most frequent and 10 being the least frequent.

abandon	8	analyse	1	benefit	1
abstract	6	annual	4	bias	8
academy	5	anticipate	9	bond	6
access	4	apparent	4	brief	6
accommodate	9	append	8	bulk	9
accompany	8	appreciate	8	capable	6
accumulate	8	approach	1	capacity	5
accurate	6	appropriate	2	category	2
achieve	2	approximate	4	cease	9
acknowledge	6	arbitrary	8	challenge	5
acquire	2	area	1	channel	7
adapt	7	aspect	2	chapter	2
adequate	4	assemble	10	chart	8
adjacent	10	assess	1	chemical	7
adjust	5	assign	6	circumstance	3
administrate	2	assist	2	cite	6
adult	7	assume	1	civil	4
advocate	7	assure	9	clarify	8
affect	2	attach	6	classic	7
aggregate	6	attain	9	clause	5
aid	7	attitude	4	code	4
albeit	10	attribute	4	coherent	9
allocate	6	author	6	coincide	9
alter	5	authority	1	collapse	10
alternative	3	automate	8	colleague	10
ambiguous	8	available	1	commence	9
amend	5	aware	5	comment	3
analogy	9	behalf	9	commission	2

commit	4	contrast	4	discrete	5
commodity	8	contribute	3	discriminate	6
communicate	4	controversy	9	displace	8
community	2	convene	3	display	6
compatible	9	converse	9	dispose	7
compensate	3	convert	7	distinct	2
compile	10	convince	10	distort	9
complement	8	cooperate	6	distribute	1
complex	2	coordinate	3	diverse	6
component	3	core	3	document	3
compound	5	corporate	3	domain	6
comprehensive	7	correspond	3	domestic	4
comprise	7	couple	7	dominate	3
compute	2	create	1	draft	5
conceive	10	credit	2	drama	8
concentrate	4	criteria	3	duration	9
concept	1	crucial	8	dynamic	7
conclude	2	culture	2	economy	1
concurrent	9	currency	8	edit	6
conduct	2	cycle	4	element	2
confer	4	data	1	eliminate	7
confine	9	debate	4	emerge	4
confirm	7	decade	7	emphasis	3
conflict	5	decline	5	empirical	7
conform	8	deduce	3	enable	5
consent	3	define	1	encounter	10
consequent	2	definite	7	energy	5
considerable	3	demonstrate	3	enforce	5
consist	1	denote	8	enhance	6
constant	3	deny	7	enormous	10
constitute	1	depress	10	ensure	3
constrain	3	derive	1	entity	5
construct	2	design	2	environment	1
consult	5	despite	4	equate	2
consume	2	detect	8	equip	7
contact	5	deviate	8	equivalent	5
contemporary	8	device	9	erode	9
context	1	devote	9	error	4
contract	1	differentiate	7	establish	1
contradict	8	dimension	4	estate	6
contrary	7	diminish	9	estimate	1

ethic	9	generation	5	innovate	7
ethnic	4	globe	7	input	6
evaluate	2	goal	4	insert	7
eventual	8	grade	7	insight	9
evident	1	grant	4	inspect	8
evolve	5	guarantee	7	instance	3
exceed	6	guideline	8	institute	2
exclude	3	hence	4	instruct	6
exhibit	8	hierarchy	7	integral	9
expand	5	highlight	8	integrate	4
expert	6	hypothesis	4	integrity	10
explicit	6	identical	7	intelligence	6
exploit	8	identify	1	intense	8
export	1	ideology	7	interact	3
expose	5	ignorant	6	intermediate	9
external	5	illustrate	3	internal	4
extract	7	image	5	interpret	1
facilitate	5	immigrate	3	interval	6
factor	1	impact	2	intervene	7
feature	2	implement	4	intrinsic	10
federal	6	implicate	4	invest	2
fee	6	implicit	8	investigate	4
file	7	imply	3	invoke	10
final	2	impose	4	involve	1
finance	1	incentive	6	isolate	7
finite	7	incidence	6	issue	1
flexible	6	incline	10	item	2
fluctuate	8	income	1	job	4
focus	2	incorporate	6	journal	2
format	9	index	6	justify	3
formula	1	indicate	1	label	4
forthcoming	10	individual	1	labor	1
found	9	induce	8	layer	3
foundation	7	inevitable	8	lecture	6
framework	3	infer	7	legal	1
function	1	infrastructure	8	legislate	1
fund	3	inherent	9	levy	10
fundamental	5	inhibit	6	liberal	5
furthermore	6	initial	3	licence	5
gender	6	initiate	6	likewise	10
generate	5	injure	2	link	3

locate	3	occupy	4	presume	6
logic	5	occur	1	previous	2
maintain	2	odd	10	primary	2
major	1	offset	8	prime	5
manipulate	8	ongoing	10	principal	4
manual	9	option	4	principle	1
margin	5	orient	5	prior	4
mature	9	outcome	3	priority	7
maximise	3	output	4	proceed	1
mechanism	4	overall	4	process	1
media	7	overlap	9	professional	4
mediate	9	overseas	6	prohibit	7
medical	5	panel	10	project	4
medium	9	paradigm	7	promote	4
mental	5	paragraph	8	proportion	3
method	1	parallel	4	prospect	8
migrate	6	parameter	4	protocol	9
military	9	participate	2	psychology	5
minimal	9	partner	3	publication	7
minimize	8	passive	9	publish	3
minimum	6	perceive	2	purchase	2
ministry	6	percent	1	pursue	5
minor	3	period	1	qualitative	9
mode	7	persist	10	quote	7
modify	5	perspective	5	radical	8
monitor	5	phase	4	random	8
motive	6	phenomenon	7	range	2
mutual	9	philosophy	3	ratio	5
negate	3	physical	3	rational	6
network	5	plus	8	react	3
neutral	6	policy	1	recover	6
nevertheless	6	portion	9	refine	9
nonetheless	10	pose	10	regime	4
norm	9	positive	2	region	2
normal	2	potential	2	register	3
notion	5	practitioner	8	regulate	2
notwithstanding	10	precede	6	reinforce	8
nuclear	8	precise	5	reject	5
objective	5	predict	4	relax	9
obtain	2	predominant	8	release	7
obvious	4	preliminary	9	relevant	2

reluctance	10	sole	7	text	2
rely	3	somewhat	7	theme	8
remove	3	source	1	theory	1
require	1	specific	1	thereby	8
research	1	specify	3	thesis	7
reside	2	sphere	9	topic	7
resolve	4	stable	5	trace	6
resource	2	statistic	4	tradition	2
respond	1	status	4	transfer	2
restore	8	straightforward	10	transform	6
restrain	9	strategy	2	transit	5
restrict	2	stress	4	transmit	7
retain	4	structure	1	transport	6
reveal	6	style	5	trend	5
revenue	5	submit	7	trigger	9
reverse	7	subordinate	9	ultimate	7
revise	8	subsequent	4	undergo	10
revolution	9	subsidy	6	underlie	6
rigid	9	substitute	5	undertake	4
role	1	successor	7	uniform	8
route	9	sufficient	3	unify	9
scenario	9	sum	4	unique	7
schedule	8	summary	4	utilise	6
scheme	3	supplement	9	valid	3
scope	6	survey	2	vary	1
section	1	survive	7	vehicle	8
sector	1	suspend	9	version	5
secure	2	sustain	5	via	8
seek	2	symbol	5	violate	9
select	2	tape	6	virtual	8
sequence	3	target	5	visible	7
series	4	task	3	vision	9
sex	3	team	9	visual	8
shift	3	technical	3	volume	3
significant	1	technique	3	voluntary	7
similar	1	technology	3	welfare	5
simulate	7	temporary	9	whereas	5
site	2	tense	8	whereby	10
so-called	10	terminate	8	widespread	8

Appendix C Frequency of selected words in CIC/BNC corpora

Word	Frequency compared to *disaster*	Number of occurrences per one million words
1. and	732.82	25516.91
2. age	6.08	211.88
3. effort	3.02	114.21
4. wine	1.84	63.94
5. device	1.58	54.93
6. disaster	1.00	34.82
7. complication	.38	13.14
8. emblem	.09	3.11
9. vanquish	.03	.95
10. brainy	.01	.44

Appendix D   Concordance for *made it plain*

	made it plain	
Benny Polymer, the Titford manager,	**made it plain**	at the start of the season that promotion was
"He	**made it plain**	enough," I said.
quality of his stance, his expression,	**made it plain**	he had overheard.
about six months, since Stephen had	**made it plain**	how much he objected even to a friendship
right hon. Friend the Prime Minister	**made it plain**	in his statement that we shall explore further
Boswell had by now	**made it plain**	over a number of years that he wished to write
Fourthly, the 1966 White Paper	**made it plain**	that at that time it was the government's
come to power, Napoleon III had	**made it plain**	that for him the problem of Paris was not simply
What it does mean is that he had	**made it plain**	that he intended a legal relationship to exist
He	**made it plain**	that he now wants to forgive and forget Mr
Innocent had also	**made it plain**	that he was the final authority in matrimonial
again (though Edward VIII	**made it plain**	that he would only comply if the Liberal
Yet The Stock Exchange has	**made it plain**	that it does not intend to require compliance with
The British Shippers" Council has	**made it plain**	that it welcomes foreign competition as a means
Iran has	**made it plain**	that it would take it amiss if it were left out of any
and their allies have always	**made it plain**	that January 15th was merely the point after which
by families, but Mrs Thatcher has	**made it plain**	that she expects families to take on extra
inner cities, the Prime Minister	**made it plain**	that she was to spearhead the inner city campaign
at the foot of the stairs the dog	**made it plain**	that stairs were an innovation he'd not
Mr Li has	**made it plain**	that there will be no more special economic zones
v. Atack whether the police had	**made it plain**	that they did not want the defendant's "help," and
However, the Government	**made it plain**	that they intended to go back into the ERM when
for the Republicans have already	**made it plain**	that they plan to use New York to frighten voters
where the manager and staff	**made it plain**	to me that if staff were concerned about their safety
She	**made it plain**	to them that she was upset by his tactless gesture.
Before I took that stand, I	**made it plain**	what I was going to do.

Suggested answers for Chapter 6 Expansion Exercises

1. Upon examining the 59 cases of *made it plain* occurring in the BNC (of which 26 are given here), I found that in 37 cases (63%) the person or entity making something plain is in a position of importance or authority (manager, Prime Minister, official report). Thus, we find an element of authority implied with this construction. It is also interesting to note that the agent is often inanimate (the Stock Exchange, Iran, the Government). On the right side of the node phrase, there is a sense of something as yet unfulfilled. This sense is realized linguistically by future modals ("we shall explore"), indicators of future potential ("would take it amiss," "only comply if"), and verbs incorporating a future tense ("wished to," "intended to"). By far the most frequent pattern is *made it plain that*. The main variable expression for *made it plain* can thus be represented as:

   SOMEONE/SOMETHING   *made it plain that*   SOMETHING AS YET UNREALIZED
   (OFTEN WITH AUTHORITY)   WAS INTENDED OR DESIRED

2.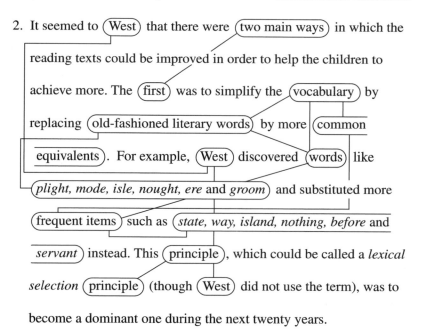

   It seemed to (West) that there were (two main ways) in which the reading texts could be improved in order to help the children to achieve more. The (first) was to simplify the (vocabulary) by replacing (old-fashioned literary words) by more (common equivalents). For example, (West) discovered (words) like (*plight, mode, isle, nought, ere* and *groom*) and substituted more (frequent items) such as (*state, way, island, nothing, before* and *servant*) instead. This (principle), which could be called a *lexical selection* (principle) (though (West) did not use the term), was to become a dominant one during the next twenty years.

3.

determiner	numerative	adjective (evaluative)	adjective (objective)	classifier	thing
those	two	splendid	old	electric	trains
that		big noisy	brown	cuckoo	clock

Sinclair (1972) suggests that modifiers are generally ordered according to the categories above, although the order can be changed to highlight particular elements. Can you think of any examples that contradict this pattern? How generalizable is it?

Appendix E Missing Words from the Chapter 8 Reading Passages

Passage 1: **Pain**

inescapable	burdens	inescapable	contemporary	flawed
inadequate	Renaissance	endured	stoicism	prefigured
neurons	neurotransmitters	laymen	neurotransmitters	nonmalignant
chronic	cites	lumbar	chronic	medieval

Passage 2: **Dinosaurs**

rampage	genuine	fossils	auction	paleontologists
fossil	convention	hawking	skeletons	fossilized
magpie	Jurassic	claws	briskly	apiece
relics	innocent	pastime	baseball	fossil
Vertebrate	Paleontology	fossils	paleontologists	gout
domain	paleontologists	fossil	lumber	bony
bounty	surveillance	looters	pillaging	paleontologists
encountered	fossil	fossil		

Passage 3: **Wine**

grapes	flourishing	vinegar	premier	cru
Indigenous	labrusca	grapes	prominent	planters
cultivating	traditional	vinifera	grapes	vines
climate	phylloxera	aphid	roots	aphid
temperate	vinifera	Ironically	temperance	grapes
culture	appreciation	repeal	Prohibition	Depression
cheap	hooch	fortified	entrepreneurs	reacted
consumers	winemaking	tradition	style	Armed
technology	accomplish	trial	error	eventually
sheer	entrepreneurship	vintages	blind	professional
dawn	era	Cabernet	Chardonnay	

Appendix F   Vocabulary Levels Test: Version 1

This is one of two versions of the Vocabulary Levels Test that are available. See Schmitt, Schmitt, & Clapham for details on the procedures used to validate this test, and Schmitt and Schmitt (under review) for Version 2.

This is a vocabulary test. You must choose the right word to go with each meaning. Write the number of that word next to its meaning. Here is an example.

1. business
2. clock   _____ part of a house
3. horse   _____ animal with four legs
4. pencil   _____ something used for writing
5. shoe
6. wall

You answer it in the following way.

1. business
2. clock   ___*6*___ part of a house
3. horse   ___*3*___ animal with four legs
4. pencil   ___*4*___ something used for writing
5. shoe
6. wall

Some words are in the test to make it more difficult. You do not have to find a meaning for these words. In the example above, these words are *business, clock,* and *shoe.*

If you have no idea about the meaning of a word, do not guess. But if you think you might know the meaning, then you should try to find the answer.

Version 1: The 2,000-word level

1. birth
2. dust   _____ game
3. operation   _____ winning
4. row   _____ being born
5. sport
6. victory

1. choice
2. crop   _____ heat
3. flesh   _____ meat
4. salary   _____ money paid regularly for doing a job
5. secret
6. temperature

1. cap
2. education   _____ teaching and learning
3. journey   _____ numbers to measure with
4. parent   _____ going to a far place
5. scale
6. trick

1. attack
2. charm   _____ gold and silver
3. lack   _____ pleasing quality
4. pen   _____ not having something
5. shadow
6. treasure

1. cream
2. factory   _____ part of milk
3. nail   _____ a lot of money
4. pupil   _____ person who is studying
5. sacrifice
6. wealth

1. adopt
2. climb   _____ go up
3. examine   _____ look at closely
4. pour   _____ be on every side
5. satisfy
6. surround

1. bake
2. connect   _____ join together
3. inquire   _____ walk without purpose
4. limit   _____ keep within a certain size
5. recognize
6. wander

1. burst
2. concern   _____ break open
3. deliver   _____ make better
4. fold   _____ take something to someone
5. improve
6. urge

1. original
2. private   _____ first
3. royal   _____ not public
4. slow   _____ all added together
5. sorry
6. total

1. brave
2. electric   _____ commonly done
3. firm   _____ wanting food
4. hungry   _____ having no fear
5. local
6. usual

Version 1: The 3,000-word level

1. belt
2. climate   _____ idea
3. executive   _____ inner surface of your hand
4. notion   _____ strip of leather worn around the waist
5. palm
6. victim

1. acid
2. bishop   _____ cold feeling
3. chill   _____ farm animal
4. ox   _____ organization or framework
5. ridge
6. structure

1. bench
2. charity   _____ long seat
3. jar   _____ help to the poor
4. mate   _____ part of a country
5. mirror
6. province

1. boot
2. device   _____ army officer
3. lieutenant   _____ a kind of stone
4. marble   _____ tube through which blood flows
5. phrase
6. vein

1. apartment
2. candle   _____ a place to live
3. draft   _____ chance of something happening
4. horror   _____ first rough form of something written
5. prospect
6. timber

1. betray
2. dispose   _____ frighten
3. embrace   _____ say publicly
4. injure   _____ hurt seriously
5. proclaim
6. scare

1. encounter
2. illustrate   _____ meet
3. inspire   _____ beg for help
4. plead   _____ close completely
5. seal
6. shift

1. assist
2. bother   _____ help
3. condemn   _____ cut neatly
4. erect   _____ spin around quickly
5. trim
6. whirl

1. annual
2. concealed   _____ wild
3. definite   _____ clear and certain
4. mental   _____ happening once a year
5. previous
6. savage

1. dim
2. junior   _____ strange
3. magnificent   _____ wonderful
4. maternal   _____ not clearly lit
5. odd
6. weary

Version 1: The 5,000-word level

1. balloon
2. federation   _____ bucket
3. novelty   _____ unusual interesting thing
4. pail   _____ rubber bag that is filled with air
5. veteran
6. ward

1. alcohol
2. apron   _____ stage of development
3. hip   _____ state of untidiness or dirtiness
4. lure   _____ cloth worn in front to protect your clothes
5. mess
6. phase

1. apparatus
2. compliment   _____ expression of admiration
3. ledge   _____ set of instruments or machinery
4. revenue   _____ money received by the government
5. scrap
6. tile

1. bulb
2. document   _____ female horse
3. legion   _____ large group of soldiers or people
4. mare   _____ a paper that provides information
5. pulse
6. tub

1. concrete
2. era   _____ circular shape
3. fiber   _____ top of a mountain
4. loop   _____ a long period of time
5. plank
6. summit

1. blend
2. devise   _____ mix together
3. hug   _____ plan or invent
4. lease   _____ hold tightly in your arms
5. plague
6. reject

1. abolish
2. drip   _____ bring to an end by law
3. insert   _____ guess about the future
4. predict   _____ calm or comfort someone
5. soothe
6. thrive

1. bleed
2. collapse   _____ come before
3. precede   _____ fall down suddenly
4. reject   _____ move with quick steps and jumps
5. skip
6. tease

1. casual
2. desolate   _____ sweet-smelling
3. fragrant   _____ only one of its kind
4. radical   _____ good for your health
5. unique
6. wholesome

1. gloomy
2. gross   _____ empty
3. infinite   _____ dark or sad
4. limp   _____ without end
5. slim
6. vacant

Version 1: The 10,000-word level

1. antics
2. batch   _____ foolish behavior
3. connoisseur   _____ a group of things
4. foreboding   _____ person with a good knowledge of art or music
5. haunch
6. scaffold

1. auspices
2. dregs   _____ confused mixture
3. hostage   _____ natural liquid present in the mouth
4. jumble   _____ worst and most useless parts of anything
5. saliva
6. truce

1. casualty
2. flurry   _____ someone killed or injured
3. froth   _____ being away from other people
4. revelry   _____ noisy and happy celebration
5. rut
6. seclusion

1. apparition
2. botany   _____ ghost
3. expulsion   _____ study of plants
4. insolence   _____ small pool of water
5. leash
6. puddle

1. arsenal
2. barracks   _____ happiness
3. deacon   _____ difficult situation
4. felicity   _____ minister in a church
5. predicament
6. spore

1. acquiesce
2. bask   _____ to accept without protest
3. crease   _____ sit or lie enjoying warmth
4. demolish   _____ make a fold on cloth or paper
5. overhaul
6. rape

1. blaspheme
2. endorse   _____ slip or slide
3. nurture   _____ give care and food to
4. skid   _____ speak badly about God
5. squint
6. straggle

1. clinch
2. jot   _____ move very fast
3. mutilate   _____ injure or damage
4. smolder   _____ burn slowly without flame
5. topple
6. whiz

1. auxiliary
2. candid   ___ bad-tempered
3. luscious   ___ full of self-importance
4. morose   ___ helping, adding support
5. pallid
6. pompous

1. dubious
2. impudent   _____ rude
3. languid   _____ very ancient
4. motley   _____ of many different kinds
5. opaque
6. primeval

Version 1: Academic vocabulary

1. benefit
2. labor   _____ work
3. percent   _____ part of 100
4. principle   _____ general idea used to guide one's actions
5. source
6. survey

1. element
2. fund   _____ money for a special purpose
3. layer   _____ skilled way of doing something
4. philosophy   _____ study of the meaning of life
5. proportion
6. technique

1. consent
2. enforcement   _____ total
3. investigation   _____ agreement or permission
4. parameter   _____ trying to find information about something
5. sum
6. trend

1. decade
2. fee   _____ 10 years
3. file   _____ subject of a discussion
4. incidence   _____ money paid for services
5. perspective
6. topic

1. colleague
2. erosion   _____ action against the law
3. format   _____ wearing away gradually
4. inclination   _____ shape or size of something
5. panel
6. violation

1. achieve
2. conceive   _____ change
3. grant   _____ connect together
4. link   _____ finish successfully
5. modify
6. offset

1. convert
2. design   _____ keep out
3. exclude   _____ stay alive
4. facilitate   _____ change from one thing into another
5. indicate
6. survive

1. anticipate
2. compile   _____ control something skillfully
3. convince   _____ expect something will happen
4. denote   _____ produce books and newspapers
5. manipulate
6. publish

1. equivalent
2. financial   _____ most important
3. forthcoming   _____ concerning sight
4. primary   _____ concerning money
5. random
6. visual

1. alternative
2. ambiguous   _____ last or most important
3. empirical   _____ something different that can be chosen
4. ethnic   _____ concerning people from a certain nation
5. mutual
6. ultimate

References

Adams, W. R. (1969). *Increasing reading speed.* London: Macmillan.

Ahmed, M. O. (1989). Vocabulary learning strategies. In P. Meara (Ed.), *Beyond words* (pp. 3–14). London: CILT.

Aitchison, J. (1987; 2nd ed. 1994). *Words in the mind: An introduction to the mental lexicon.* Oxford: Blackwell.

Alderson, J. C., Clapham, C. M., & Steel, D. (1997). Metalinguistic knowledge, language aptitude, and language proficiency. *Language Teaching Research 1,* 93–121.

Alexander, R. J. (1984). Fixed expressions in English: Reference books and the teacher. *English Language Teaching Journal 38,*(2) 127–134.

Allen, V. F. (1983). *Techniques in teaching vocabulary.* Oxford: Oxford University Press.

Allerton, D. J. (1984). Three (or four) levels of word cooccurrence restriction. *Lingua 63,* 17–40.

Alper, T. G. (1942). A diagnostic spelling scale for the college level: Its construction and use. *Journal of Educational Psychology 33,* 273–290.

Anderson, R. C., & Nagy, W. E. (1989). Word meanings. In *Handbook of reading research,* 2nd ed. London: Longman.

Anderson, R. C., & Pearson, P. D. (1988). A schema-theoretic view of basic processes in reading comprehension. In P. L. Carrell, J. Devine, & D. E. Eskey (Eds.), *Interactive approaches to second language reading* (pp. 37–55). Cambridge: Cambridge University Press.

Armstrong, S. L., Gleitman, L. R., & Gleitman, H. (1983). What some concepts might not be. *Cognition 13,* 263–308.

Arnaud, P. J. L. (1989). Estimations subjectives des fréquences des mots. *Cahiers de Lexicologie 54,*(1), 69–81.

Arnaud, P. J. L. (1990). Subjective word frequency estimates in L1 and L2. Paper presented at the Ninth World Congress of Applied Linguistics. Thessalonki. April. ERIC Document ED329120.

Asher, J. J. (1977). *Learning another language through actions.* Los Gatos, CA: Sky Oaks.

Aston, G., & Burnard, L. (1998). *The BNC handbook.* Edinburgh: Edinburgh University Press.

Bachman, L. F. (1990). *Fundamental considerations in language testing*. Oxford: Oxford University Press.

Bachman, L. F., & Palmer, A. S. (1996). *Language testing in practice*. Oxford: Oxford University Press.

Baddeley, A. (1990). *Human memory: Theory and practice*. Needham Heights, MA: Allyn and Bacon.

Bahns, J., & Eldaw, M. (1993). Should we teach EFL students collocations? *System 21*(1), 101–114.

Bahns, J. (1993). Lexical collocations: A contrastive view. *ELT Journal 47*(1), 56–63.

Balota, D. A. (1994). Visual word recognition. In M. A. Gernsbacher (Ed.), *Handbook of psycholinguistics* (pp. 303–357). San Diego: Academic Press.

Barnbrook, G. (1996). *Language and computers*. Edinburgh: Edinburgh University Press.

Barron, R. W. (1980). Visual and phonological strategies in reading and spelling. In U. Frith (Ed.), *Cognitive processes in spelling* (pp. 195–213). London: Academic Press.

Bauer, L., & Nation, I. S. P. (1993). Word families. *International Journal of Lexicography 6*(3), 1–27.

Beck, J. (1981). New vocabulary and the associations it provokes. *Polyglot 3*(3), C7:F14.

Beck, I. L., McKeown, M. G., & Omanson, R. C. (1987). The effects and uses of diverse vocabulary instructional techniques. In M. G. McKeown & M. E. Curtis (Eds.), *The nature of vocabulary acquisition* (pp. 147–163). Hillsdale, NJ: Lawrence Erlbaum.

Benson, M. (1985). Collocations and idioms. In R. Ilson (Ed.), *Dictionaries, lexicography and language learning* (pp. 61–68). Oxford: Pergamon.

Benson, J. D., & Greaves, W. S. (1981). Field of discourse: Theory and application. *Applied Linguistics 2*(1), 45–55.

Benson, M., Benson, E., & Ilson, R. (1986). *The BBI combinatory dictionary of English: A guide to word combinations*. Amsterdam/Philadelphia: John Benjamins.

Bensoussan, M., & Laufer, B. (1984). Lexical guessing in context in EFL reading comprehension. *Journal of Research in Reading 7*, 15–32.

Berko, J. (1958). The child's learning of English morphology. *Word 14*, 150–177.

Besner, D., & Johnston, J. C. (1989). Reading and the mental lexicon: On the uptake of visual information. In W. D. Marslen-Wilson (Ed.), *Lexical representation and process* (pp. 291–316). Cambridge, MA: Bradford.

Biskup, D. (1992). L1 influences on learners' renderings of English collocations: A Polish/German empirical study. In P. J. L. Arnaud & Béjoint H. (Eds.), *Vocabulary and applied linguistics* (pp. 85–93). London: Macmillan.

Bolinger, D. (1976). Meaning and memory. *Forum Linguisticum 1*, 1–14.

Bowen, J. D., Madsen, H., & Hilferty, A. (1985). *TESOL: Techniques and procedures.* New York: Newbury House.

Brazil, D. (1995). *A grammar of speech.* Oxford: Oxford University Press.

Brown, R., & Berko, J. (1960). Word association and the acquisition of grammar. *Child Development 31*, 1–14.

Brown, R., & McNeill, D. (1966). The "tip of the tongue" phenomenon. *Journal of Verbal Learning and Verbal Behavior 5*, 325–337.

Bryant, P. E., & Bradley, L. (1980). Why children sometimes write words which they do not read. In U. Frith (Ed.), *Cognitive processes in spelling* (pp. 355–370). London: Academic Press.

Bryson, B. (1990). *The mother tongue.* New York: Avon.

Cambridge international dictionary of English. (1995). Cambridge: Cambridge University Press.

Cambridge international dictionary of phrasal verbs. (1997). Cambridge: Cambridge University Press.

Carey, S. (1978). The child as word learner. In M. Halle, J. Bresnan, & G. A. Miller (Eds.), *Linguistic theory and psychological reality* (pp. 264–293). Cambridge: MIT Press.

Carney, E. (1997). *English spelling.* London: Routledge.

Carrell, P. L., & Eisterhold, J. C. (1988). Schema theory and ESL reading pedagogy. In P. L. Carrell, J. Devine, & D. E. Eskey (Eds.), *Interactive approaches to second language reading* (pp. 73–92). Cambridge: Cambridge University Press.

Carroll, J. B. (1964). Words, meanings, and concepts. *Harvard Educational Review 34*(2), 178–202.

Carroll, L. (1971). *Alice's Adventures in Wonderland and Through the Looking Glass.* London: Oxford University Press.

Carter, R. (1982). A note on core vocabulary. *Nottingham Linguistic Circular 11*(2), 39–51.

Carter, R. (1998). *Vocabulary: Applied linguistic perspectives* (2nd ed.). London: Routledge.

Carter, R., Goddard, A., Reah, D., Sanger, K., & Bowring, M. (1997). *Working with texts.* London: Routledge.

Carter, R., & McCarthy, M. (1988). *Vocabulary and language teaching.* London: Longman.

Carter, R., & McCarthy, M. (1997). *Exploring spoken English.* Cambridge: Cambridge University Press.

Carter, R., & McCarthy, M. (In press). *Cambridge advanced grammar of English.* Cambridge: Cambridge University Press.

Cattell, J. M., & Bryant, S. (1889). Mental association investigated by experiment. *Mind 14*, 230–250.

Celce-Murcia, M. (1991). Language teaching approaches: An overview. In

M. Celce-Murcia (Ed.), *Teaching English as a second or foreign language* (pp. 3–11). Boston, MA.: Newbury House.

Chafe, W., & Danielewicz, J. (1987). Properties of spoken and written language. In R. Horowitz & S. J. Samuels (Eds.), *Comprehending oral and written language* (pp. 83–113). New York: Academic Press.

Chamot, A. U. (1987). The learning strategies of ESL students. In A. Wenden & J. Rubin (Eds.), *Learner strategies in language learning* (pp. 71–83). New York: Prentice Hall.

Chapelle, C. A. (1994). Are C-tests valid measures for L2 vocabulary research? *Second Language Research 10*(2), 157–187.

Chui, R. K. (1972). Measuring register characteristics: A prerequisite for preparing advanced level TESOL programmes. *TESOL Quarterly 6*(2), 129–141.

Claiborne, R. (1983). *Our marvelous native tongue.* New York: Times Books.

Clarke D. F., & Nation, I. S. P. (1980). Guessing the meanings of words from context: Strategy and techniques. *System 8*(3), 211–220.

Coady, J. (1993). Research on ESL/EFL vocabulary acquisition: Putting it in context. In T. Huckin, M. Haynes, & J. Coady (Eds.), *Second language reading and vocabulary learning* (pp. 3–23). Norwood, NJ: Ablex.

Coady, J., & Huckin, T. (Eds.). (1997). *Second language vocabulary acquisition.* Cambridge: Cambridge University Press.

Cofer, C. N., Bruce, D. R., & Reicher, G. M. (1966). Clustering in free recall as a function of certain methodological variations. *Journal of Experimental Psychology 71,* 858–866.

Cohen, A. D. (1989). Attrition in the productive lexicon of two Portuguese third language speakers. *Studies in Second Language Acquisition 11*(2), 135–149.

Cohen, A. D. (1994). *Assessing language ability in the classroom.* Boston, MA: Heinle and Heinle.

Cohen, A. D., & Aphek, E. (1981). Easifying second language learning. *Studies in Second Language Acquisition 3*(2), 221–326.

Collins COBUILD English dictionary. (1989). London: HarperCollins.

Collins COBUILD dictionary of idioms. (1995). London: HarperCollins.

Collins COBUILD English dictionary. (1995). 2nd ed. London: HarperCollins.

Collins COBUILD grammar patterns I: Verbs. (1996). London: HarperCollins.

Collins COBUILD grammar patterns II: Nouns and adjectives. (1998). London: HarperCollins.

Collinson, W. E. (1939). Comparative synonymics: Some principles and illustrations. *Transactions of the Philological Society,* 54–77.

Cook, G. (1998). The uses of reality: A reply to Ronald Carter. *English Language Teaching Journal 52*(1), 57–63.

Corder, S. (1973). *Introducing applied linguistics.* Baltimore: Penguin Books.

Coulmas, F. (1979). On the sociolinguistic relevance of routine formulae. *Journal of Pragmatics 3,* 238–266.

Coulthard, M. (1985). *An introduction to discourse analysis.* London: Longman.

Cowie, A. P. (1978). Vocabulary exercises within an individualized study programme. *ELT Documents 103,* 37–44.

Cowie, T., & Howarth, P. (1995). Phraseological competence and written proficiency. Paper read at the British Association of Applied Linguistics (BAAL) Conference, Southampton, England, September.

Coxhead, A. (1998). *An academic word list.* English Language Institute Occasional Publication No. 18. Wellington, NZ: School of Linguistics and Applied Language Studies, Victoria University of Wellington.

Craik, F. I. M., & Tulving, E. (1975). Depth of processing and the retention of words in episodic memory. *Journal of Experimental Psychology 104,* 268–284.

Crowdy, S. (1993). Spoken corpus design. *Literary and Linguistic Computing 8*(2), 259–265.

Cruse, D. A. (1977). The pragmatics of lexical specificity. *Journal of Linguistics 13,* 153–164.

Cruse, D. A. (1986). *Lexical semantics.* Cambridge: Cambridge University Press.

Crystal, D. (1987). *The Cambridge encyclopedia of language.* Cambridge: Cambridge University Press.

Crystal, D. (1988). *The English language.* London: Penguin.

Crystal, D., & Davy, D. (1975). *Advanced conversational English.* London: Longman.

Cutler, A., & Butterfield, S. (1992). Rhythmic cues to speech segmentation: Evidence from juncture misperception. *Journal of Memory and Language 31,* 218–236.

Cutler, A., & Carter, D. M. (1987). The predominance of strong initial syllables in the English vocabulary. *Computer Speech and Language 2,* 133–142.

Cutler, A., & Clifton, C. E. (1984). The use of prosodic information in word recognition. In H. Bouma & D. G. Bouwhuis, *Attention and performance X: Control of language processes* (pp. 183–196). Hillsdale, NJ: Lawrence Erlbaum.

D'Anna, C. A., Zechmeister, E. B., & Hall, J. W. (1991). Toward a meaningful definition of vocabulary size. *Journal of Reading Behavior 23,* 109–122.

Dagut, M., & Laufer, B. (1985). Avoidance of phrasal verbs – a case for contrastive analysis. *Studies in Second Language Acquisition 7,* 73–80.

Dansereau, D. F. (1988). Cooperative learning strategies. In C. E. Weinstein, E. T. Goetz, & P. A. Alexander (Eds.), *Learning and study strategies: Issues in assessment, instruction, and evaluation* (pp. 103–120). New York: Academic Press.

DeRocher, J. E., Miron, M. S., Patten, S. M., & Pratt, C. C. (1973). *The Counting of words: A review of the history, techniques and theory of word counts with annotated bibliography.* Syracuse, NY: Syracuse University Research Corp. ERIC document ED098814.

deVilliers, & deVilliers, (1978). *Language acquisition.* Cambridge: Harvard University Press.

Drum, P. A., & Konopak, B. C. (1987). Learning word meanings from written context. In M. G. McKeown & M. E. Curtis (Eds.), *The nature of vocabulary acquisition* (pp. 73–87). Hillsdale, NJ: Lawrence Erlbaum.

Dulay, H., & Burt, M. (1973). Should we teach children syntax? *Language Learning 23,* 245–258.

Dulay, H., & Burt, M. (1974). Natural sequences in child second language acquisition. *Language Learning 24,* 37–53.

Dušková, L. (1969). On sources of error in foreign language teaching. *International Review of Applied Linguistics 7,* 11–36.

Ebbinghaus, H. (1885). *Über das Gedächtnis.* Leipzig, Duncker. Translated by H. Ruger & C. E. Bussenius (1913). Cited in R. S. Woodworth & H. Schlosberg (1955), *Experimental psychology.* London: Methuen.

Edinburgh Associative Thesaurus. Internet Address: http://www.itd.clrc.ac.uk/activity/psych+267 Background information available in G. R. Kiss, C. Armstrong, R. Milroy, J. Piper (1973), An associative thesaurus of English and its computer analysis, in A. J. Aitkin, R. W. Bailey, & N. Hamilton-Smith, (Eds.), *The computer and literary studies* (pp. 153–165). Edinburgh: Edinburgh University Press.

Ehri, L. C. (1980). The development of orthographic images. In U. Frith (Ed.), *Cognitive processes in spelling.* London: Academic Press.

Elley, W. B. (1991). Acquiring literacy in a second language: The effect of book-based programs. *Language Learning 41*(3), 375–411.

Ellis, N. C. (1996). Sequencing in SLA. *Studies in Second Language Acquisition 18,* 91–126.

Ellis, N. C. (1997). Vocabulary acquisition: Word structure, collocation, word-class, and meaning. In N. Schmitt & M. McCarthy (Eds.), *Vocabulary: Description, acquisition, and pedagogy* (pp. 122–139). Cambridge: Cambridge University Press.

Ellis, N. C., & Beaton, A. (1995). Psycholinguistic determinants of foreign language vocabulary learning. In B. Harley (Ed.), *Lexical issues in language learning (pp. 107–165). Ann Arbor: John Benjamins.*

Ellis, R. (1992). Second language acquisition and language pedagogy. Clevedon: Multilingual Matters.

Ellis, R. (1994). The study of second language acquisition. *Oxford: Oxford University Press.*

Entwisle, D. R. (1966). *Word associations of young children.* Baltimore: Johns Hopkins University Press.

Entwisle, D. R., Forsyth, D. F., & Muuss, R. (1964). The syntactic-paradigmatic shift in children's word associations. *Journal of Verbal Learning and Verbal Behavior 3,* 19–29.

Ervin, S. M. (1961). Changes with age in the verbal determinants of word association. *American Journal of Psychology, 74,* 361–372.

Eskey, D. E., & Grabe, W. (1988). Interactive models for second language reading: Perspectives on instruction. In P. L. Carrell, J. Devine, & D. E. Eskey (Eds.), *Interactive approaches to second language reading* (pp. 223–238). Cambridge: Cambridge University Press.

Feigenbaum, L. H. (1958). For a bigger better alphabet. *High Points 40,* 34–36.

Firth, J. R. (1957). *Papers in linguistics 1934–1951.* London: Oxford University Press.

Flower, J. (1993). *Phrasal verb organizer.* Hove, England: LTP.

Forster, K. (1976). Accessing the mental lexicon. In R. J. Wales & E. Walker (Eds.), *New Approaches to Language Mechanisms.* Amsterdam: New Holland.

Freyd, P., & Baron, J. (1982). Individual differences in acquisition of derivational morphology. *Journal of Verbal Learning and Verbal Behavior 21,* 282–295.

Frith, U. (Ed.) (1980). *Cognitive processes in spelling.* London: Academic Press.

Frost, R., Katz, L., & Bentin, S. (1987). Strategies for visual word recognition and orthographical depth: A multilingual comparison. *Journal of Experimental Psychology: Human Perception and Performance 13*(1), 104–115.

Gairns, R., & Redman, S. (1986). *Working with words.* Cambridge: Cambridge University Press.

Galton, F. (1879–1880). Psychometric experiments. *Brain 2,* 149–162.

Garnham, A. (1985). *Psycholinguistics: Central topics.* London: Routledge.

Gathercole, S. E., & Baddeley, A. D. (1993). *Working memory and language.* Hove, England: Lawrence Erlbaum.

Goldstein, H. (1983). Word recognition in a foreign language: A study of speech perception. *Journal of Psycholinguistic Research, 12*(4), 417–427.

Goodglass, H., & Baker, E. (1976). Semantic field, naming and auditory comprehension in aphasia. *Brain and Language 3,* 359–374.

Goulden, R., Nation, P., & Read, J. (1990). How large can a receptive vocabulary be? *Applied Linguistics 11,* 341–363.

Granger, S. (1998). Prefabricated patterns in advanced EFL writing: Collocations and lexical phrases. In A. P. Cowrie (Ed.), *Phraseology: Theory, analysis and applications.* Oxford: Clarendon Press/Oxford University Press.

Graves, M. F. (1987). The roles of instruction in fostering vocabulary development. In M. G. McKeown & Curtis M. E. (Eds.), *The nature of vocabulary acquisition* (pp. 165–184). Hillsdale, NJ: Lawrence Erlbaum.

Gregory, M. (1967). Aspects of varieties differentiation. *Journal of Linguistics 3*(2), 177–198.

Grosjean, F. (1985). The recognition of words after their acoustic offset: Evidence and implications. *Perception and Psychophysics 38,* 299–310.

Hakuta, K. (1974). Prefabricated patterns and the emergence of structure in second language acquisition. *Language Learning 24,* 287–298.

Halliday, M. A. K. (1978). *Language as social semiotic.* London: Edward Arnold.

Halliday, M. A. K., & Hasan, R. (1976). *Cohesion in English.* London: Longman.

Hammerly, H. (1979). Conveying lexical meanings in second-language teaching. *Canadian Modern Languages Review 35,* 567–580.

Hatch, E., & Brown, C. (1995). *Vocabulary, semantics, and language education.* Cambridge: Cambridge University Press.

Haynes, M. (1993). Patterns and perils of guessing in second language reading. In T. Huckin, M. Haynes, & J. Coady (Eds.), *Second language reading and vocabulary learning* (pp. 46–65). Norwood, NJ: Ablex.

Hazenberg, S., & Hulstijn, J. H. (1996). Defining a minimal receptive second-language vocabulary for non-native university students: An empirical investigation. *Applied Linguistics 17*(2), 145–163.

Heaton, J. B. (1988). *Writing English language tests.* Harlow, England: Longman.

Henricksen, B. (1999). Three dimensions on vocabulary development. *Studies in Second Language Acquisition 21*(2), 303–317.

Higa, Masanori. (1963). Interference effects of intralist word relationships in verbal learning. *Journal of Verbal Learning and Verbal Behavior 2,* 170–175.

Hill, J., & Lewis, M. (1997). *LTP dictionary of selected collocations.* Hove, England: LTP.

Hirtle, W. (1994). Meaning and referent: For a linguistic approach. *Word 45*(2), 103–117.

Hoey, M. (1991). *Patterns of lexis in text.* Oxford: Oxford University Press.

Hofland, K., & Johansson, S. (1982). *Word frequencies in British and American English.* Bergen: Norwegian Computing Centre for the Humanities.

Howard, D. V., McAndrews, M. P., & Lasaga, M. I. (1981). Semantic priming of lexical decisions in young and old adults. *Journal of Gerontology 36,* 707–714.

Howarth, P. (1998). Phraseology and second language proficiency. *Applied Linguistics 19*(1), 24–44.

Howatt, A. P. R. (1984). *A history of English language teaching.* Oxford: Oxford University Press.

Howes, D. H. (1966). A word count of spoken English. *Journal of Verbal Learning and Verbal Behaviour 5,* 572–606.

Huckin, T., & Bloch, J. (1993). Strategies for inferring word-meanings in context: A cognitive model. In T. Huckin, M. Haynes, & J. Coady (Eds.), *Second language reading and vocabulary learning* (pp. 153–178). Norwood, NJ: Ablex.

Huckin, T., Haynes, M., & Coady, J. (Eds.). (1993). *Second language reading and vocabulary learning*. Norwood, NJ: Ablex.

Hudson, T. (1988). The effects of induced schemata on the "short circuit" in L2 reading: Non-decoding factors in L2 reading performance. In P. L. Carrell, J. Devine, & D. E. Eskey (Eds.), *Interactive approaches to second language reading* (pp. 183–205). Cambridge: Cambridge University Press.

Hughes, A. (1989). *Testing for language teachers*. Cambridge: Cambridge University Press.

Hulstijn, J. H. (1992). Retention of inferred and given word meanings: Experiments in incidental vocabulary learning. In P. Arnaud & H. Béjoint (Eds.), *Vocabulary and applied linguistics* (pp. 113–125). London: Macmillan.

Hulstijn, J. H. (1997). Mnemonic methods in foreign language vocabulary learning. In J. Coady & T. Huckin (Eds.), *Second language vocabulary acquisition* (pp. 203–224). Cambridge: Cambridge University Press.

Hunston, S., Francis, G., & Manning, E. (1997). Grammar and vocabulary: Showing the connections. *English Language Teaching Journal 51*(3), 208–216.

Hwang K., & Nation, P. (1989). Reducing the vocabulary load and encouraging vocabulary learning through reading newspapers. *Reading in a Foreign Language 6*(1), 323–335.

Hymes, D. (1972). On communicative competence. In J. B. Pride & J. Holmes (Eds.), *Sociolinguistics* (pp. 269–293). New York: Penguin.

Ijaz, I. H. (1986). Linguistic and cognitive determinants of lexical acquisition in a second language. *Language Learning 36*(4), 401–451.

Imai, M., Gentner, D., & Uchida, N. (1994). Children's theories of word meaning: The role of shape similarity in early acquisition. *Cognitive Development 9*, 45–75.

Jenkins, J. J. (1970). The 1952 Minnesota word association norms. In L. Postman & G. Keppel, *Norms of word associations* (pp. 1–38). New York: Academic Press.

Jenkins, J. J., & Russell, W. A. (1960). Systematic changes in word association norms: 1910–1952. *Journal of Abnormal and Social Psychology 60*(3), 293–304.

Joe, A., Nation, P., & Newton, J. (1996). Vocabulary learning and speaking activities. *English Teaching Forum 34*(1), 2–7.

Johansson, S. (1978). *Some aspects of the vocabulary of learned and scientific English*. Gothenburg: Acta Universitatis Gothoburgensis.

Johansson, S., & Hofland, K. (1989). *Frequency analysis of English vocabulary and grammar: Based on the LOB Corpus*. 2 vols. Oxford: Clarendon Press.

Johnston, M. H. (1974). Word associations of schizophrenic children. *Psychological Reports 35*, 663–674.

Katz, J. J., & Fodor, J. A. (1963). The structure of a semantic theory. *Language 39*, 170–210.

Keller, R. (1979). Gambits: Conversational strategy signals. *Journal of Pragmatics 3*, 219–237.

Kellerman, E. (1978). Giving learners a break: Native language intuitions as a source of predictions about transferability. *Working Papers in Bilingualism 15*, 309–315.

Kellerman, E. (1986). An eye for an eye: Crosslinguistic constraints on the development of the L2 lexicon. In E. Kellerman & M. Sharwood-Smith (Eds.), *Crosslinguistic influence in second language acquisition* (pp. 35–48). Oxford: Pergamon.

Kelly, L. G. (1969). *Twenty-five centuries of language teaching.* Rowley, MA: Newbury House.

Kent, G. H., & Rosanoff, A. J. (1910). A study of association in insanity. *American Journal of Insanity 67*, 37–96, 317–390.

Kern, R. G. (1989). Second language reading instruction: Its effects on comprehension and word inference ability. *Modern Language Journal 73*(2), 135–149.

Kirn, E. (1984). *Ways with words.* New York: Holt, Rinehart and Winston.

Kiss, G. R. (1973). Grammatical word classes: A learning process and its simulation. In G. H. Bower (Ed.), *The psychology of learning and motivation: Advances in research and theory* (vol. 7; pp. 1–41). New York: Academic Press.

Koda, K. (1997). Orthographic knowledge in L2 lexical processing. In J. Coady & T. Huckin (Eds.), *Second language vocabulary acquisition* (pp. 35–52). Cambridge: Cambridge University Press.

Krashen, S. (1977). Some issues relating to the Monitor Model. In H. Brown, C. Yorio, & R. Crymes (Eds.), *On TESOL '77*. Washington, DC: TESOL.

Kučera, H., & Francis, W. N. (1967). *Computational analysis of present-day American English.* Providence, RI: Brown University Press.

Lambert, W. E., & Moore, N. (1966). Word association responses: Comparisons of American and French monolinguals with Canadian monolinguals and bilinguals. *Journal of Personality and Social Psychology 3*(3), 313–320.

Landau, S. (1989). *The art and craft of lexicography.* Cambridge: Cambridge University Press.

Landauer, T. K., & Bjork, R. A. (1978). Optimum rehearsal patterns and name learning. In M. M. Gruneberg, P. E. Morris, & R. N. Sykes (Eds.), *Practical aspects of memory* (pp. 625–632. London: Academic Press.

Larsen-Freeman, D. (1975). The acquisition of grammatical morphemes by adult ESL students. *TESOL Quarterly 9*, 409–430.

Larsen-Freeman, D. (1986). *Techniques and principles in language teaching.* New York: Oxford University Press.

Larsen-Freeman, D., & M. H. Long (1991). *An introduction to second language acquisition research.* London: Longman.

Laufer, B. (1988). What percentage of text-lexis is essential for comprehension? In C. Laurén & M. Nordmann (Eds.), *Special language: From humans to thinking machines* (pp. 316–323). Clevedon: Multilingual Matters.

Laufer, B. (1989). A factor of difficulty in vocabulary learning: Deceptive transparency. *AILA Review 6,* 10–20.

Laufer, B. (1992). Reading in a foreign language: How does L2 lexical knowledge interact with the reader's general academic ability? *Journal of Research in Reading 15*(2), 95–103.

Laufer, B. (1994). The lexical profile of second language writing: Does it change over time? *RELC Journal 25*(2), 21–33.

Laufer, B. (1997). What's in a word that makes it hard or easy: Some intralexical factors that affect the learning of words. In N. Schmitt & M. McCarthy (Eds.), *Vocabulary: Description, acquisition, and pedagogy* (pp. 140–155). Cambridge: Cambridge University Press.

Laufer, B., & Bensoussan, M. (1982). Meaning is in the eye of the beholder. *English Teaching Forum 20*(2), 10–14.

Laufer, B., & Nation, P. (1995). Vocabulary size and use: Lexical richness in L2 written production. *Applied Linguistics 16*(3), 307–322.

Laufer, B., & Paribakht, T. S. (1998). The relationship between passive and active vocabularies: Effects of language learning context. *Language Learning 48*(3), 365–391.

Levenston, E. The acquisition of polysemic words with both literal and metaphorical meaning. Unpublished manuscript.

Lewis, M. (1993). *The lexical approach.* Hove, England: LTP.

Lewis, M. (1997). *Implementing the lexical approach.* Hove, England: LTP.

Long, M., & Sato, C. (1984). Methodological issues in interlanguage studies: An interactionist perspective. In A. Davies, C. Criper, & A. Howatt (Eds.), *Interlanguage* (pp. 253–279). Edinburgh: Edinburgh University Press.

Longman dictionary of contemporary English. (1995). 3rd ed. London: Longman.

Longman dictionary of English language and culture. (1992). Harlow, England: Longman.

Longman language activator. (1993). Harlow, England: Longman.

Lovell, G. D. (1941). Interrelations of vocabulary skills: Commonest versus multiple meanings. *Journal of Educational Psychology 32,* 67–72.

Lyons, J. (1977). *Semantics* (Vols. 1 & 2). New York: Cambridge University Press.

Malvern, D., & Richards, B. (1997). A new measure of lexical diversity. In

A. Ryan & A. Wray (Eds.), *Evolving models of language* (pp. 58–71). Clevedon: Multilingual Matters.

Marsh, G., Friedman, M., Welch, V., & Desberg, P. (1980). The development of strategies in spelling. In U. Frith (Ed.), *Cognitive processes in spelling* (pp. 339–353). London: Academic Press.

Marslen-Wilson, W. D., & Tyler, L. K. (1980). The temporal structure of spoken language understanding. *Cognition 8*(1), 1–71.

Mason, C. (1986). *Meaning by all means.* Englewood Cliffs, NJ: Prentice Hall Regents.

Matthews, P. H. (1991). *Morphology: Introduction to the theory of word structure.* Cambridge: Cambridge University Press.

McCarthy, M. (1984). A new look at vocabulary in EFL. *Applied Linguistics 5*(1), 12–22.

McCarthy, M. (1990). *Vocabulary.* Oxford: Oxford University Press.

McCarthy, M. (1991). *Discourse analysis for language teachers.* Cambridge: Cambridge University Press.

McCarthy, M. (1998). *Spoken language and applied linguistics.* Cambridge: Cambridge University Press.

McCarthy, M., & Carter, R. (1997). Written and spoken vocabulary. In N. Schmitt & M. McCarthy (Eds.), *Vocabulary: Description, acquisition, and pedagogy* (pp. 20–39). Cambridge: Cambridge University Press.

McCarthy, M., & O'Dell, F. (1994). *English vocabulary in use: Upper intermediate.* Cambridge: Cambridge University Press.

McCarthy, M., & O'Dell, F. (1999). *English vocabulary in use: Elementary.* Cambridge: Cambridge University Press.

McDonough, S. H. (1995). *Strategy and skill in learning a foreign language.* London: Edward Arnold.

McEnery, T., & Wilson, A. (1996). *Corpus linguistics.* Edinburgh: Edinburgh University Press.

Meara, P. (1980). Vocabulary acquisition: A neglected aspect of language learning. *Language Teaching and Linguistics: Abstracts 13*(4), 221–246.

Meara, P. (1983). *Vocabulary in a second language* (Vol. 1). London: Centre for Information on Language Teaching and Research (CILT).

Meara, P. (1983). Word associations in a foreign language. *Nottingham Linguistic Circular 11*(2), 29–38.

Meara, P. (1986). The DIGAME project. In V. J. Cook (Ed.), *Experimental approaches to second language learning* (pp. 101–110). Oxford: Pergamon Press.

Meara, P. (1987). *Vocabulary in a second language.* (Vol. 2). London: Centre for Information on Language Teaching and Research (CILT).

Meara, P. (1990). A note on passive vocabulary. *Second Language Research 6*(2), 150–154.

Meara, P. (1992). *EFL vocabulary tests.* University of Wales, Swansea: Centre for Applied Language Studies.

Meara, P. (1992). Vocabulary in a second language (Vol. 3). *Reading in a Foreign Language 9,* 1. (Complete issue)

Meara, P. (1994). LLEX: Threshold level vocabulary tests. University of Wales, Swansea: Centre for Applied Language Studies.

Meara, P. (1995). The importance of an early emphasis on L2 vocabulary. *The Language Teacher 19*(2), 8–10.

Meara, P. (1997). Towards a new approach to modelling vocabulary acquisition. In N. Schmitt & M. McCarthy (Eds.), *Vocabulary: Description, acquisition, and pedagogy* (pp. 109–121). Cambridge: Cambridge University Press.

Meara, P., & Buxton, B. (1987). An alternative to multiple choice vocabulary tests. *Language Testing 4*(2), 142–154.

Meara, P., & Jones, G. (1990). *Eurocentres vocabulary size tests 10KA.* Zurich: Eurocentres Learning Service.

Melka, F. (1997). Receptive vs. productive aspects of vocabulary. In N. Schmitt & M. McCarthy (Eds.), *Vocabulary: Description, acquisition and pedagogy* (pp. 84–102). Cambridge: Cambridge University Press.

Mikulecky, B. S. (1990). *A short course in teaching reading skills.* Reading, MA: Addison-Wesley.

Miller, G. A., & Fellbaum, C. (1991). Semantic networks in English. *Cognition 41,* 197–229.

Miller, G. A., & Gildea, P. M. (1987). How children learn words. *Scientific American 257,* 94–99.

Milton, J., & Hales, T. (1997). Applying a lexical profiling system to technical English. In A. Ryan & A. Wray (Eds.), *Evolving models of language* (pp. 72–83). Clevedon: Multilingual Matters.

Milton, J., & Meara, P. (1995). How periods abroad affect vocabulary growth in a foreign language. *ITL Review of Applied Linguistics 107–108,* 17–34.

Miyazaki, H. (1992). *My neighborhood Totoro.* Bellevue, WA: Tokuma Shoten.

Mondria, J. A., & Wit-de-Boer, M. (1991). The effects of contextual richness on the guessability and the retention of words in a foreign language. *Applied Linguistics 12*(3), 249–267.

Moon, R. (1997). Vocabulary connections: Multi-word items in English. In N. Schmitt & M. McCarthy (Eds.), *Vocabulary: Description, acquisition, and pedagogy* (pp. 40–63). Cambridge: Cambridge University Press.

Morgan, C. L., & Bonham, D. N. (1944). Difficulty of vocabulary learning as affected by parts of speech. *Journal of Educational Psychology 35*(5), 369–377.

Morgan, J., & Rinvolucri, M. (1986). *Vocabulary.* Oxford: Oxford University Press.

Morton, J. (1979). Word recognition. In J. Morton and J. C. Marshall (Eds.). *Psycholinguistics 2: Structure and processes* (pp. 107–156). London: Elek.

Nagy, W. (1997). On the role of context in first- and second-language vocabulary learning. In N. Schmitt & M. McCarthy (Eds.), *Vocabulary: Description, acquisition, and pedagogy* (pp. 64–83). Cambridge: Cambridge University Press.

Nagy, W., & Anderson, R. C. (1984). How many words are there in printed school English? *Reading Research Quarterly 19,* 304–330.

Nagy, W., Anderson, R. C., Schommer, M., Scott, J. A., & Stallmann, A. C. (1989). Morphological families in the internal lexicon. *Reading Research Quarterly 24*(3), 262–282.

Nagy, W. E., Diakidoy, I. N., & Anderson, R. C. (1993). The acquisition of morphology: Learning the contribution of suffixes to the meanings of derivatives. *Journal of Reading Behavior 25*(2), 155–170.

Nation, I. S. P. (1983). *Teaching and learning vocabulary.* Victoria University of Wellington: English Language Institute.

Nation, I. S. P. (1990). *Teaching and learning vocabulary.* New York: Newbury House.

Nation, I. S. P. (1999). *Learning vocabulary in another language.* Victoria University of Wellington: English Language Institute Occasional Publication No. 19.

Nation, P. (1993). Using dictionaries to estimate vocabulary size: Essential, but rarely followed procedures. *Language Testing 10*(1), 27–40.

Nation, P. (Ed.). (1994). *New ways in teaching vocabulary.* Alexandria, VA: TESOL.

Nation, P. (1995). The word on words: An interview with Paul Nation. Interviewed by N. Schmitt. *The Language Teacher 19*(2), 5–7.

Nation, P., and Crabbe, D. (1991). A survival language learning syllabus for foreign travel. *System 19*(3), 191–201.

Nation, P., & Newton, J. (1997). Teaching vocabulary. In J. Coady & T. Huckin, (Eds.), *Second language vocabulary acquisition* (pp. 238–254). Cambridge: Cambridge University Press.

Nation, P., & Waring, R. (1997). Vocabulary size, text coverage and word lists. In Schmitt, N., & McCarthy, M. (Eds.), *Vocabulary: Description, acquisition, and pedagogy* (pp. 6–19). Cambridge: Cambridge University Press.

Nattinger, J. R., & DeCarrico, J. S. (1992). *Lexical phrases and language teaching.* Oxford: Oxford University Press.

Nurnberg, M., & Rosenblum, M. (1977). *How to build a better vocabulary.* New York: Warner Books.

Nuttall, C. (1982). *Teaching reading skills in a foreign language.* Oxford: Heinemann.

Odlin, T., & Natalicio, D. (1982). Some characteristics of word classification in a second language. *Modern Language Journal 66,* 34–38.

Olshtain, E. (1989). Is second language attrition the reversal of second language acquisition? *Studies in Second Language Acquisition 11*(2), 151–165.

O'Malley, J. M., & Chamot, A. U. (1990). *Learning strategies in second language acquisition.* Cambridge: Cambridge University Press.

Oxford advanced learner's dictionary. (1995). 5th ed. Oxford: Oxford University Press.

Oxford interactive word magic. (1998). Oxford: Oxford University Press.

Oxford, R. L. (1990). *Language learning strategies: What every teacher should know.* Boston: Newbury House.

Palmer, H. E., West, M. P., & Faucett, L. (1936). *Interim report on vocabulary selection for the teaching of English as a foreign language.* Report of the Carnegie Conference, New York 1934, and London 1935. London: P. S. King and Son.

Papagno, C., Valentine, T., & Baddeley, A. (1991). Phonological short-term memory and foreign-language vocabulary learning. *Journal of Memory and Language 30,* 331–347.

Paribakht, T. S., & Wesche, M. B. (1993). Reading comprehension and second language development in a comprehension-based ESL program. *TESL Canada Journal 11*(1), 9–29.

Parry, K. (1993). Too many words: Learning the vocabulary of an academic subject. In T. Huckin, M. Haynes, & J. Coady (Eds.), *Second language reading and vocabulary learning* (pp. 109–129). Norwood, NJ: Ablex.

Pawley, A., & Syder, F. H. (1983). Two puzzles for linguistic theory: Nativelike selection and nativelike fluency. In J. Richards & R. Schmidt (Eds.), *Language and communication* (pp. 191–226). London: Longman.

Peters, A. (1983). *The units of language acquisition.* Cambridge: Cambridge University Press.

Phillips, T. A. (1981). Difficulties in foreign language vocabulary learning and a study of some of the factors thought to be influential. M.A. project, Birkbeck College, University of London.

Pienemann, M. (1984). Psychological constraints on the teachability of languages. *Studies in Second Language Acquisition 6*(2), 186–214.

Pimsleur, P. (1967). A memory schedule. *Modern Language Journal 51*(2), 73–75.

Postman, L., & Keppel, G. (1970). *Norms of word association.* New York: Academic Press.

Rayner, K., & Balota, D. A. (1989). Parafoveal preview and lexical access during eye fixations in reading. In W. D. Marslen-Wilson (Ed.), *Lexical representation and process* (pp. 261–290). Cambridge, MA: Bradford.

Rayner, K., & Hagelberg, E. M. (1975). Word recognition cues for beginning and skilled readers. *Journal of Experimental Child Psychology 20*, 444–455.

Redman, S., & Ellis, R. (1989). *A way with words. Book 1.* Cambridge: Cambridge University Press.

Read, J. (1993). The development of a new measure of L2 vocabulary knowledge. *Language Testing 10*(3), 355–371.

Read, J. (1997). Vocabulary and testing. In N. Schmitt & M. McCarthy (Eds.), *Vocabulary: Description, acquisition, and pedagogy* (pp. 303–320). Cambridge: Cambridge University Press.

Read, J. (1998). Validating a test to measure depth of vocabulary knowledge. In A. Kunnan (Ed.), *Validation in language assessment* (pp. 41–60). Mahwah, NJ: Lawrence Erlbaum.

Read, J. (2000). *Assessing vocabulary.* Cambridge: Cambridge University Press.

Richards, J. C. (1976). The role of vocabulary teaching. *TESOL Quarterly 10*(1), 77–89.

Riegel, K. F., & Zivian, I. W. M. (1972). A study of inter- and intralingual associations in English and German. *Language Learning 22*(1), 51–63.

Robinson, P. J. (1988). A Hallidayan framework for vocabulary teaching – An approach to organizing the lexical content of an EFL syllabus. *IRAL 26*(3), 229–238.

Rodgers, T. S. (1969). On measuring vocabulary difficulty: An analysis of item variables in learning Russian-English vocabulary pairs. *International Review of Applied Linguistics,* 327–343.

Rosch, E. (1975). Cognitive representations of semantic categories. *Journal of Experimental Psychology 104,* 192–233.

Rosenzweig, M. R. (1961). Comparisons among word-association responses in English, French, German, and Italian. *American Journal of Psychology 74,* 347–360.

Rosenzweig, M. R. (1964). Word associations of French workmen: Comparisons with associations of French students and American workmen and students. *Journal of Verbal Behavior and Verbal Learning 3,* 57–69.

Russell, P. (1979). *The brain book.* London: Routledge and Kegan Paul.

Russell, W. A., & Jenkins, J. J. (1954). *The complete Minnesota norms for responses to 100 words from the Kent-Rosanoff word association test.* Tech. Rep. No. 11, Contract No. N8-onr-66216, Office of Naval Research and University of Minnesota.

Ryan, A. (1994). "Vowel blindness" in Arabic learners of English. Unpublished Ph.D. thesis. University of Wales, Swansea.

Ryan, A. (1997). Learning the orthographic form of L2 vocabulary – a receptive and productive process. In N. Schmitt & M. McCarthy (Eds.), *Vocabulary: Description, acquisition, and pedagogy* (pp. 181–198). Cambridge: Cambridge University Press.

Saltz, E., & Donnenwerth-Nolan, S. (1981). Does motoric imagery facilitate memory for sentences? A selective interference test. *Journal of Verbal Behavior and Verbal Learning 20,* 322–332.

Sanaoui, R. (1995). Adult learners' approaches to learning vocabulary in second languages. *Modern Language Journal 79,* 15–28.

Sandra, D. (1988). Is morphology used to encode derivations when learning a foreign language? *ITL Review of Applied Linguistics 79/80,* 1–23.

Sandra, D. (1993). The use of lexical morphology as a natural aid in learning foreign language vocabulary. In J. Chapelle & M. T. Claes (Eds.), *Memory and memorization in acquiring and learning languages.* Centre de Langues à Louvain-la-neuve et en Woluwe.

Sandra, D. (1994). The morphology of the mental lexicon: Internal word structure viewed from a psycholinguistic perspective. *Language and Cognitive Processes 9*(3), 227–269.

Sarangi, T., Nation, I. S. P., & Meister, G. F. (1978). Vocabulary learning and reading. *System 6*(2), 72–78.

Scarcella, R., & Zimmerman, C. (1996). Academic words and gender: ESL student performance on a test of academic lexicon. *Studies in Second Language Acquisition 20,* 27–49.

Schmitt, N. (1994). Vocabulary testing: Questions for test development with six examples of tests of vocabulary size and depth. *Thai TESOL Bulletin 6*(2), 9–16.

Schmitt, N. (1995a). A fresh approach to vocabulary using a word knowledge framework. *RELC Journal 26*(1), 86–94.

Schmitt, N. (1995b). Verbal suffix and word association knowledge of Japanese students. Unpublished M. Phil. Thesis, University of Wales, Swansea.

Schmitt, N. (1997). Vocabulary learning strategies. In N. Schmitt & M. McCarthy (Eds.), *Vocabulary: Description, acquisition, and pedagogy* (pp. 199–227). Cambridge: Cambridge University Press.

Schmitt, N. (1998a). Quantifying word association responses: What is nativelike? *System 26*(3), 389–401.

Schmitt, N. (1998b). Tracking the incremental acquisition of second language vocabulary: A longitudinal study. *Language Learning 48*(2), 281–317.

Schmitt, N. (1999). The relationship between TOEFL vocabulary items and meaning, association, collocation, and word class knowledge. *Language Testing 16,* 189–216.

Schmitt, N., Bird, R., Tseng, A. -C., & Yang, Y. -C. (1997). Vocabulary learning strategies: Student perspectives and cultural considerations. *Independence* (Spring), 4–6.

Schmitt, N., & Carter, R. (under review). The lexical advantages of narrow reading for second language learners.

Schmitt, N., & Dunham, B. (1999). Word frequency intuitions of native and nonnative speakers. *Second Language Research 15*(3), 389–411.

Schmitt, N., & McCarthy, M. (Eds.). (1997). *Vocabulary: Description, acquisition, and pedagogy.* Cambridge: Cambridge University Press.

Schmitt, N., & Meara, P. (1997). Researching vocabulary through a word knowledge framework: Word associations and verbal suffixes. *Studies in Second Language Acquisition 19*(1), 17–36.

Schmitt, N., & Schmitt, D. (1995). Vocabulary notebooks: Theoretical underpinnings and practical suggestions. *English Language Teaching Journal 49*(2), 133–143.

Schmitt, N., & Schmitt, D. (under review). *The Vocabulary Levels Test* – Versions 1 and 2.

Schmitt, N., Schmitt, D., & Clapham, C. (under review). *Validating the Vocabulary Levels Test.*

Scholfield, P. (1994). *New light on English vocabulary from corpora.* Proceedings of the annual meeting of the English Language and Literature Association of Korea. Seoul: Ellak.

Scholfield, P. (1997). Vocabulary reference works in foreign language learning. In N. Schmitt & M. McCarthy (Eds.), *Vocabulary: Description, acquisition, and pedagogy* (pp. 279–302). Cambridge: Cambridge University Press.

Schonell, F. J., Meddleton, I. G., & Shaw, B. A. (1956). *A study of the oral vocabulary of adults.* Brisbane: University of Queensland Press.

Schonell, F., Meddleton, I., Shaw, B., Routh, M., Popham, D., Gill, G., Mackrell, G., & Stephens, C. (1956). *A study of the oral vocabulary of adults.* Brisbane and London: University of Queensland Press/University of London Press.

Schouten-van Parreren, C. (1991). Psychological aspects of vocabulary learning in a foreign language. Paper presented at the Vocabulary Acquisition in L2 Symposium, Málaga, Spain. December.

Scott, M. (1997). *Wordsmith tools.* Oxford: Oxford University Press.

Searleman, A., & Herrmann, D. (1994). *Memory from a broader perspective.* Singapore: McGraw-Hill.

Shapiro, B. J. (1969). The subjective estimation of relative word frequency. *Journal of Verbal Learning and Verbal Behavior 8*, 248–251.

Sharp, D., & Cole, M. (1972). Patterns of responding in the word associations of West African children. *Child Development 43*, 55–65.

Shemesh, R., & Waller, S. (1999). *Teaching English spelling.* Cambridge: Cambridge University Press.

Simpson, J. (1988). The vocabulary of English. In E. G. Stanley & T. F. Hoad (Eds.), *Words.* Cambridge: D. S. Brewer.

Sinclair, J. (1991). *Corpus, concordance, collocation.* Oxford: Oxford University Press.

Sinclair, J. (1996). The search for units of meaning. *Textus 9*, 75–106.

Sinclair, J. (1998). The computer, the corpus, and the theory of language. In

G. Azzaro and M. Ulrych (Eds.), *Transiti linguistici e culturali* (vol. 2). Proceedings of the Eighteenth AIA Congress, "Anglistica e . . . : metodi e persorsi comparatistici nelle lingue, culture e letterature di origine euoppa." Trieste: EUT.

Sinclair, J. M. (1972). *A course in spoken English: Grammar.* London: Oxford University Press.

Skehan, P. (1989). *Individual differences in second-language learning.* London: Edward Arnold.

Söderman, T. (1993). Word associations of foreign language learners and native speakers – A shift in response type and its relevance for a theory of lexical development. In H. Ringbom (Ed.), *Near-native proficiency in English.* Åbo: Åbo Akademi.

Sökmen, A. (1992). *Common threads.* Englewood Cliffs, NJ: Prentice Hall Regents.

Sökmen, A. (1997). Current trends in teaching second language vocabulary. In N. Schmitt & M. McCarthy (Eds.), *Vocabulary: Description, acquisition, and pedagogy* (pp. 237–257). Cambridge: Cambridge University Press.

Sonaiya, R. (1991). Vocabulary acquisition as a process of continuous lexical disambiguation. *IRAL 29*(4), 273–284.

Spolsky, B. (1995). *Measured words.* Oxford: Oxford University Press.

Stahl, S. A. (1983). Differential word knowledge and reading comprehension. *Journal of Reading Behavior 15*(4), 33–50.

Stahl, S. A., & Murray, B. A. (1994). Defining phonological awareness and its relationship to early reading. *Journal of Educational Psychology 86*(2), 221–234.

Stoffer, I. (1995). University foreign language students' choice of vocabulary learning strategies as related to individual difference variables. Unpublished Ph.D. dissertation, University of Alabama.

Stoller, F. (1986). Reading lab: Developing low-level reading skills. In F. Dubin, D. E. Eskey, & W. Grabe, (Eds.), *Teaching second language reading for academic purposes* (pp. 51–76). Reading, MA: Addison-Wesley.

Stubbs, M. (1980). *Language and Literacy.* London: Routledge and Kegan Paul.

Stubbs, M. (1995). Collocations and semantic profiles: On the cause of the trouble with quantitative studies. *Functions of Language 2*(1), 1–33.

Suárez, A., & Meara, P. (1989). The effects of irregular orthography on the processing of words in a foreign language. *Reading in a Foreign Language 6*(1), 349–356.

Summers, D. (1988). The role of dictionaries in language learning. In R. Carter & M. McCarthy (Eds.), *Vocabulary and language teaching* (pp. 111–125). Harlow, England: Longman.

Swan, M. (1997). The influence of the mother tongue on second language vocabulary acquisition and use. In N. Schmitt & M. McCarthy (Eds.),

Vocabulary: Description, acquisition, and pedagogy (pp. 156–180). Cambridge: Cambridge University Press.

Swinney, D. (1979). Lexical access during sentence comprehension: (Re)consideration of context effects. *Journal of Verbal Learning and Verbal Behavior 18,* 645–659.

Takala, S. (1984). *Evaluation of students' knowledge of English vocabulary in Finnish comprehensive school* (Rep. No. 350). Jyväskylä, Finland: Institute of Educational Research.

Thomas, M. H., & Dieter, J. N. (1987). The positive effects of writing practice on integration of foreign words in memory. *Journal of Educational Psychology 79*(3), 249–253.

Thorndike, E. L., & Lorge, I. (1944). *The teacher's word book of 30,000 words.* New York: Teachers College, Columbia University.

Tinkham, T. (1993). The effect of semantic clustering on the learning of second language vocabulary. *System 21*(3), 371–380.

TOEFL. (1998a). *TOEFL 1998–99 Information Bulletin for Computer-Based Testing.* Princeton, NJ: Educational Testing Service.

TOEFL. (1998b). *TOEFL Sampler.* Princeton, NJ: Educational Testing Service.

Trappes-Lomax, H. (1997). *Oxford learner's wordfinder dictionary.* Oxford: Oxford University Press.

Tribble, C., & Jones, G. (1990). *Concordances in the classroom.* Harlow, England: Longman.

Tyler, A., & Nagy, W. (1989). The acquisition of English derivational morphology. *Journal of Memory and Language 28,* 649–667.

Upward, C. (1988). *English spelling and educational progress.* CLIE Working Papers 11.

Ure, J. (1971). Lexical density and register differentiation. In G. E. Perren & J. L. M. Trim (Eds.), *Applications of linguistics: Selected papers of the Second International Congress of Applied Linguistics, Cambridge, 1969* (pp. 443–452). Cambridge: Cambridge University Press.

van Ginkel, C. I., & van der Linden, E. H. (1996). Word associations in foreign language learning and foreign language loss. In K. Sajavaara & C. Fairweather (Eds.), *Approaches to second language acquisition.* Jyväskyä.

Venezky, R. L. (1970). *The structure of English orthography.* The Hague: Mouton.

Vives Boix, G. (1995). The development of a measure of lexical organization: The association vocabulary test. Unpublished dissertation, University of Wales, Swansea.

Wallace, G., & Larsen, S. C. (1978). *Educational assessment of learning problems.* Boston: Allyn and Bacon.

Wallace, M. J. (1982). *Teaching vocabulary.* Oxford: Heinemann.

Waring, R. (1997). The negative effects of learning words in semantic sets: A replication. *System 25*(2), 261–274.

Waring, R. (1998). Receptive and productive foreign language vocabulary size II. Unpublished manuscript. Available at *http://www1.harenet.ne.jp/~waring/vocabindex.html*

Warren, H. (1994). *Oxford learner's dictionary of English idioms.* Oxford: Oxford University Press.

Webster's third new international dictionary. (1963). Springfield, MA: G. & C. Merriam Co.

Weltens, B., & Grendel, M. (1993). Attrition of vocabulary knowledge. In R. Schreuder & B. Weltens (Eds.), *The bilingual lexicon* (pp. 135–136). Amsterdam: John Benjamins.

Weltens, B., Van Els, T. J. M., & Schils, E. (1989). The long-term retention of French by Dutch students. *Studies in Second Language Acquisition 11*(2), 205–216.

West, M. (1953). *A general service list of English words.* London: Longman, Green.

Wong-Fillmore, L. (1976). The second time around: Cognitive and social strategies in second language acquisition. Unpublished doctoral dissertation, Stanford University.

Woodrow, H., & Lowell, F. (1916). Children's association frequency tables. *Psychology Monographs 22*(5), No. 97.

Yorio, C. (1980). Conventionalized language forms and the development of communicative competence. *TESOL Quarterly 14,* 433–442.

Zettersten, A. (1978). *A word-frequency list based on American English reportage.* Copenhagen: Universitetsforlaget i København.

Zimmerman, C. B. (1997). Historical trends in second language vocabulary instruction. In J. Coady & T. Huckin (Eds.), *Second language vocabulary acquisition* (pp. 5–19). Cambridge: Cambridge University Press.

Index